W9-DGL-817

For Democracy's Sake

For Democracy's Sake

Foundations and Democracy Assistance in Central Europe

Kevin F. F. Quigley

Published by
The Woodrow Wilson
Center Press

Distributed by
The Johns Hopkins
University Press

Woodrow Wilson Center Special Studies

The Woodrow Wilson Center Press
Editorial Offices
370 L'Enfant Promenade, S.W.
Suite 704
Washington, D.C. 20024-2518 U.S.A.
telephone 202-287-3000, ext. 218

Distributed by
The Johns Hopkins University Press
2715 N. Charles Street
Baltimore, Maryland 21218
order department telephone 1-800-537-5487

Printed in the United States of America

☉ Printed on acid-free paper.

9 8 7 6 5 4 3 2 1

Library of Congress Cataloging-in-Publication Data

Quigley, Kevin F. F.
    For democracy's sake : foundations and democracy assistance in
Central Europe / Kevin F. F. Quigley.
        p.   cm. — (Woodrow Wilson Center special studies)
    Includes bibliographical references and index.
    ISBN 0-943875-80-3 (cloth : alk. paper). — ISBN 0-943875-81-1 (pbk. : alk.
paper)
    1. Economic assistance—Europe, Central. 2. Non-governmental
organizations—Europe, Central. 3. Economic assistance—Europe,
Central—Statistics. 4. Democracy—Europe, Central—International
cooperation. 5. Free enterprise—Europe, Central—International
cooperation. 6. Technical assistance—Europe, Central. I. Title.
II. Series.
HC244.Q35   1997
338.91'0943—dc21   97-1541
                                                                        CIP

The Woodrow Wilson International Center for Scholars

The Center is the living memorial of the United States of America to the nation's twenty-eighth president, Woodrow Wilson. Congress established the Woodrow Wilson Center in 1968 as an international institute for advanced study, "symbolizing and strengthening the fruitful relationship between the world of learning and the world of public affairs." The Center opened in 1970 under its own board of trustees.

Woodrow Wilson Center Special Studies

The work of the Center's Fellows, Guest Scholars, and staff— and presentations and discussions at the Center's conferences, seminars, and colloquia—often deserve timely circulation as contributions to public understanding of issues of national and international importance. The Woodrow Wilson Center Special Studies series is intended to make such materials available by the Woodrow Wilson Center Press to interested scholars, practitioners, and other readers. In all its activities, the Woodrow Wilson Center is a nonprofit, nonpartisan organization, supported financially by annual appropriations from the U.S. Congress and by the contributions of foundations, corporations, and individuals. Conclusions or opinions expressed in Center publications and programs are those of the authors and speakers and do not necessarily reflect the views of the Center staff, Fellows, trustees, advisory groups, or any individuals or organizations that provide financial support to the Center.

Contents

Figures and Tables

Abbreviations and Acronyms

Academia	Academia Istropolitana
Adenauer	Konrad Adenauer Stiftung
AID	Agency for International Development
Autonómia	Autonómia Alapítvány
Bank	World Bank
Batory	Stefan Batory Foundation
Boll	Heinrich Böll Stiftung
Bosch	Bosch Stiftung
Bradley	Lynde and Harry Bradley Foundation, Inc.
CAF	Charities Aid Foundation
Carnegie	Carnegie Corporation of New York
CASE	Center for Social Economic Research
CDF	Cooperating Dutch Foundations
CASLIN	Czech and Slovak Library Information Network
CED	Center for Economic Development
CEP	Civic Education Project
CEU	Central European University
CERGE	Center for Economic Research and Graduate Education
CHARTA 77	Charta 77 Foundation
CIPE	Center for International Private Enterprise
CKH	Charity Know How
Collegium	Collegium Budapest
COMECON	Council for Mutual Economic Assistance
CSCE	Conference on Security and Cooperation in Europe

CSDF	Civil Society Development Foundation
CSDP	Civil Society Development Program
DAC	Democracy after Communism Foundation
DemNet	Democracy Network Program
EBRD	European Bank for Reconstruction and Development
Ebert	Friedrich Ebert Stiftung
ECF	European Cultural Foundation
ECU	European currency unit
EF	Eurasia Foundation
EPCE	Environmental Partnership for Central Europe
EU	European Union
EUROMA	European Union's Regional Roma Programme
FCS	Foundation for Civil Society
FDS	For Democracy's Sake
FOCUS	Center for Social and Market Analysis
Ford	Ford Foundation
Four F	Four Foundations
FSLD	Foundation in Support of Local Democracy
FTUI	Free Trade Union Institute
Fund	International Media Fund
G-24	Group of twenty-four industrialized countries
GMF	German Marshall Fund of the United States
Gremium	Gremium of the Third Sector
HESP	Higher Education Support Program
Humboldt	Alexander von Humboldt Stiftung
HZDS	Movement for Democratic Slovakia
ICN	International Center for Foundations and Other Not-for-Profit Organizations
IEWS	Institute for EastWest Studies
IMC	International Management Center
IMF	International Monetary Fund
IPS	Institute for Policy Studies
IWM	Institute for Human Sciences (Institut für die Wissenschaften von Menschan)
IYF	International Youth Foundation
Jones	W. Allen Jones Foundation

KLON	Nongovernmental Organizations Data Base
KOR	Workers' Defense Committee
MacArthur	John D. and Catherine T. MacArthur Foundation
MBA	Masters of Business Administration
Mellon	Andrew W. Mellon Foundation
MONA	Foundation of Women of Hungary
Mott	Charles Stewart Mott Foundation
Mszp	Hungarian Socialist Party
NATO	North Atlantic Treaty Organization
Naumann	Friedrich Naumann Stiftung
NED	National Endowment for Democracy
NDI	National Democratic Institute
NFF	National Forum Foundation
NGO	Nongovernmental organization
NIASPACEE	National Institutes, Academies, and Schools of Public Administration in Central and Eastern Europe
NIS	Newly Independent States of the Former Soviet Union
NITCF	Nonprofit Information and Training Center Foundation
ODA	Civic Democratic Alliance
ODS	Civic Democratic Party
OECD	Organization for Economic Cooperation and Development
Olin	John M. Olin Foundation
OSCE	Organization for Security and Cooperation in Europe
OSF	Open Society Fund
OSI	Open Society Institute
Partners	Partners for Democratic Change
PCT	Pew Charitable Trusts
Phare	Poland and Hungary Assistance for Restructuring of the Economy
PPP	Parliamentary Practices Project
RBF	Rockefeller Brothers Fund
SAIA—SCTS	Slovak Academic Information Agency—Service Center for the Third Sector

Sasakawa	Sasakawa Peace Foundation
SEED	Support for Eastern European Democracy Act
Seidel	Hanns Seidel Stiftung
SFH	Soros Foundation Hungary
Smith Richardson	Smith Richardson Foundation, Inc.
SOCO	Social Costs of Economic Transitions
STV	Slovak Television
Stiftenverband	Stifterverband für die Deutsche Wissenschaft
SzDSz	Alliance for Free Democrats
TVP	Public Television (Poland)
UN	United Nations
Volkswagen	Volkswagen Stiftung
Westminster	Westminster Foundation
WSF	Foundation for Water Supply to Rural Areas

Acknowledgments

*D*emocracy is one of the most alluring and elusive of things. It is an ideal that inspires, but its reality all too often frustrates. Fundamentally, democracy is about people with different backgrounds, interests, and capabilities working toward some common purpose. In a small way, this book and the process by which it was produced holds a mirror to the democratic experience.

This book was motivated by an interest in understanding Central Europeans' attempts to build democracy during these momentous recent years and in examining what role outsiders have played in that process. It was produced as the result of the engagement of a large number of individuals with differing interests and experiences but with a common goal: examining recent democracy building experiences to learn lessons necessary to improve these and comparable efforts in the future.

This would not have been possible without the generous support of the Pew Charitable Trusts, the Ford Foundation, and the Rockefeller Brothers Fund. Although their activities were scrutinized here, these foundations never sought to influence this book in any way. In fact, they encouraged close scrutiny. For their openness to this examination and their unstinting support, I am extremely grateful to Rebecca Rimel from the Pew Charitable Trusts; Susan Berresford, Shepard Forman, Joseph Schull, and Mahnez Isphani from the Ford Foundation; and Colin Campbell and Bill Moody from the Rockefeller Brothers Fund.

The sine qua non of this book was the engagement of Central Europeans, who were most knowledgeable about and affected by efforts to build democracy in their countries. These individuals, who were involved in the project's advisory committee or as participants in the workshops that helped shape this book, are identified in Appendices 1 and 2. Besides these, there were more than two hundred individuals who agreed to be interviewed for this book. Although there are too many names to list here, these individuals gave generously of their time and wisdom, and the book is better for it. Many of them are quoted and identified subsequently.

I am also grateful to a number of colleagues who read earlier drafts and provided many helpful suggestions. Among these are Rudolph Andorka, Paul Balaran, Andras Biró, Thomas Carothers, Eric Chenoweth, Catharin Dalpino, David Daniel, Pavol Demeš, Jim Denton, Zdeněk Drábek, Shepard Forman, Deborah Harding, Robert Hutchings, Joe Julian, Antoni Kaminski, Stanley Katz, Eric Kemp, John Lampe, Irena Lasota, Miklós Marschall, Juraj Mesík, Petr Pajas, Richard Quandt, Walt Raymond, Joanna Regulska, Anthony Richter, Anna Rozicka, Eugene Staples, John Sullivan, Michael Vachon, Kristof Varga, Ladislav Venyš, and anonymous readers.

Every book needs a home. It would be hard to construct a more hospitable home than the Woodrow Wilson Center. From the moment I mentioned the idea for this book, Sam Wells, the center's deputy director, and Rob Litwak, director of International Studies, were supportive. John Lampe, director of East European Studies, was an active and welcome participant in every step of the project.

Throughout the project that shares the same name as this book, I was lucky to have excellent support. Nancy Popson served as an invaluable research assistant, managing everything from organizing workshops 4,000 miles away and authoring case studies to keeping track of expenses in fourteen different currencies. The project also benefited from the involvement of three interns, Peter Kocsis, Michael Strübin and Jennifer Topping, who contributed insights and enthusiasm derived from their own knowledge of and experiences in Central Europe.

This book is based on data that has not been collected before from organizations that are not always as transparent and accessible as they encourage others to be. In fact, in numerous instances my initial inquiries for information regarding foundation activities were met by rejection letters stating that my research did not fall within their funding guidelines! More precious than funding for this book, however, was the information provided by these foundations and other organizations involved in democracy assistance efforts.

In this regard, this book was greatly aided by: Maggie Alexander, International Youth Foundation; Miriam Aukerman, Ford Foundation; Friedrich Bauersachs, Friedrich Naumann Stiftung; Kennette Benedict, John D. and Catherine T. MacArthur Foundation; Lorne Craner, International Republican Institute; Barbara Crosby, World Bank; Nadia Diuk, National Endowment for Democracy; Aurelius Fernandez, International Media Fund; Dan Fogel, Katz School of Business, University of Pittsburgh; Hillel Fradkin, Lynde and Harry Bradley Foundation, Inc.; Michael J. Gary, Howard Gilman Foundation; Carl Gershman, National Endowment for Democracy; Marianne Ginsburg, German Marshall Fund of the United States; Paul Mischa Gregory, PlanEcon; Otto Hafner, Volkswagen Stiftung; Deborah Harding, Open Society Institute; Priscilla Hayner, Joyce Mertz-Gilmore Foundation; Irmgard Hunt, German Marshall Fund of the United States; Nadia M. Hickel, DoenStichting; Armin Höller, Hanns Seidel Stiftung; Janet Ice, United States Agency for International Development; Michael Joyce, Lynde and Harry Bradley Foundation, Inc.; Helga Junkers, Volkswagen Stiftung; Timothy J. Kenny, Freedom Forum; Rudolph Kerscher, Fritz Thyssen Stiftung; Katalin E. Koncz, Open Society Institute; Richard S. Lanier, Trust for Mutual Understanding; Julia Lönnecke, Robert Bosch Stiftung; Jeanette A. Mansour, Charles Stewart Mott Foundation; Deborah Marrow, Charles Getty Grant Program; Lise Mathol, European Cultural Foundation; William Moody, Rockefeller Brothers Fund; Clare Morris, Westminster Foundation; Iveta Mozsnyakova, Sasakawa Peace Foundation; Aryeh Neier, Open Society Institute; Cornelius Ochmann, Bertelsmann Stiftung; John Penny, Phare Democracy Programme; James Piereson, John M. Olin Foundation; Rodger Potocki, National Endowment for Democracy; Richard Quandt, Andrew W. Mellon Foundation; Heide Radlanski, Alexander von Humboldt Stiftung; Franz-Josef Reuter, Konrad Adenauer Stiftung; John Richardson, European Foundation Centre; Paulette Rosselet, Trust for Mutual Understanding; Raphaëlle Sadler, Charity Know How; Joseph Schull, Ford Foundation; Anne-Marie Seydoux, Foundation de France; Aleksander Smolar, Stefan Batory Foundation; Paul Samogyi, Free Trade Union Institute; Heinz-Rudi Spiegel, Stifterverband für die Deutsche Wissenschaft; Mark Steinmeyer, Smith Richardson Foundation, Inc.; Rüdiger Stephan, European Cultural Foundation; Ernst Stetter, Friedrich Ebert Stiftung; Nancy Stockford, John Merck Fund; Rupert Graf Strachwitz, Maecenata; John Sullivan, Center for International Private Enterprise; Patricia Thomas, Nuffield Foundation; Stefan Toepler, Johns Hopkins Institute for Policy Studies; Sylvie Tysboula, Foundation de France; Elise van Oss, Open Society Institute; Claire Walters, Charity Know How; Ken Wollack, National Democratic Institute; and Annetta Zubeková, Civil Society Development Foundation—Slovakia.

Last, but by no means least, I want to acknowledge gratefully the support and encouragement of Susan Flaherty, who endured my all-too-frequent absences and became all-too-familiar with what is discussed here.

For Democracy's Sake

1

Introduction:
A New World

*A*fter the fall of the Berlin Wall, developing democracy and free markets were the clarion calls sounding from Central Europe. Many heard these calls and responded in a variety of ways. The assistance representing this response was not as large as expected, although many expectations were overblown. Nor were all the exuberant promises fulfilled. Nevertheless, the international community responded with considerable fanfare and significant resources. From 1989 to 1994, the international community made commitments to Central Europe, namely to Czechoslovakia (after 1993 the Czech Republic and Slovakia), Hungary, and Poland, of 34.3 billion European currency units (ECUs) or approximately $44.3 billion.[1] These commitments overstate the actual assistance flows, since many were loans, some of which were never disbursed, rather than grants. Nevertheless, this represents a significant response.

A surprisingly large number of organizations participated in this response. As might be predicted, the international financial institutions, such as the International Monetary Fund (IMF) and the World Bank (Bank), developed large programs. So did the governments of the industrialized democracies. Perhaps most remarkably, there was an unprecedented response from more than sixty European and North American foundations, most of which had not previously been active internationally (Appendix, table 1). This response was stimulated, in part, by Central Europeans themselves. Given that under communism the state controlled all spheres of social and political life, as part of a strategy of building democracy Central Europeans articulated a need to rebuild civil society—the sphere that mediates between state and citizen.[2] Besides the obvious fact that foundations controlled desperately needed financial resources, their extensive experience in working with and being part of civil society resulted in them being deemed suitable partners by many Central Europeans. These foundations included organizations that use funds from their own resources and those that receive government funds but act autonomously, such as the German political foundations[3] or the National Endowment for Democracy (NED) and its related organizations.[4] Unless otherwise noted, when using the term *foundation* this study will mean foreign foundations from Western Europe, North America, or Japan.

Much of this response to the momentous events of 1989–1990 in Central Europe, particularly from international financial institutions such as the IMF and the Bank, focused on developing free markets through encouraging stabilization, liberalization, and privatization. The programs of the large industrialized countries, especially Germany and the United States, concentrated on market-oriented reform efforts. Besides programs designed to strengthen markets, there were also those to assist democracy. In the United States the authorizing legislation for these programs was the Support for Eastern European Democracy (SEED) Act. Many in the international community perceived a link between these two types of programs. In fact, many presumed that democracy could not be built unless based on a thriving market economy.[5] Many of the programs of the international community reflected this perception.

Interest in assisting democracy in Central Europe was stimulated in particular by lingering security concerns, a sense of common purpose, and a perception that democracies make good markets and are less likely to go to war.[6] Although promoting democracy is not completely novel, it has never been a primary concern of the international community. By the late 1980s, however, as the cold war was winding down, interest in promoting democracy was growing. For example, in the United States both the Bush and Clinton administrations identified promoting democracy as a critical dimension of their foreign policy, even if their commitments did not match their rhetoric.[7]

This interest in promoting democracy is expressed not only by the United States, but also by other industrialized democracies, such as Denmark, Germany, Great Britain, the Netherlands, Norway, and Sweden. That these industrialized democracies are involved in efforts to promote democracy is not especially surprising. What is remarkable, however, is that countries such as Barbados, Chile, Costa Rica, India, Portugal, and South Africa are becoming involved in similar efforts.[8] Equally noteworthy is the fact that multilateral organizations—including the United Nations (UN), the Organization for Security and Cooperation in Europe (OSCE), the Council of Europe, and even the Bank—are also beginning to engage in democracy assistance efforts even if they sometimes describe these efforts as "encouraging good governance" or "protecting human rights."[9]

FIGURE 1 Foundation Assistance to Central Europe, 1989–1994

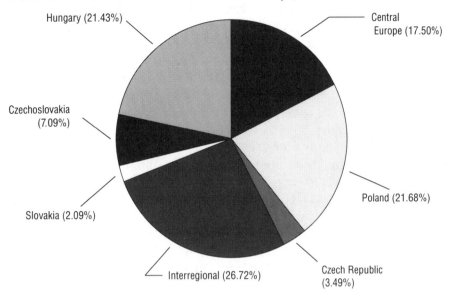

Recently, foundations have played an important part in democracy assistance efforts. In fact, foundations provided more resources for democracy assistance programs in Central Europe than did the U.S. Agency for International Development (AID). Although these numbers are difficult to assess, given the considerable overlap among program categories and the lack of a uniform definition of *democracy assistance,* foundations seem to have provided more than $450 million to Central Europe from 1989 to 1994. This contrasts favorably with AID's $339 million over a roughly comparable period.[10]

Foundation involvement with democracy assistance in Central Europe seems somewhat serendipitous. Although only a few of the foundations that became involved—such as the Ford Foundation (Ford) and Rockefeller Brothers Fund (RBF)—had prior experience in the region, most of those that responded felt compelled to react to what they saw as a historical moment. In responding, foundations generally did not have a clearly articulated strategy. Rather, they tended to react opportunistically to circumstances. Consequently, their strategies evolved over time. Many foundations, similar to public donors, initially focused on supporting economic reform. Only later did they shift their attentions toward working with nongovernmental organizations (NGOs) and civil society as a means to strengthen democracy.[11]

In some regards, foundations' programs may be important not only because of what they invest in, but also because of whom they invest with and how they invest. As one foundation leader suggested, foundations invest in democrats not democracy.[12] Foundations also tend to focus attention on sectors essential to democratization, namely, education, environment, human rights, and support for the NGO sector. Foundations generally assume that NGOs help citizens in newly democratic societies develop the ways and means to encourage their governments to be more responsive to their concerns.

Although the overall sums provided by foundations are not especially large relative to the total resources of the international community, they may have a significance beyond their size because they tend to be disbursed more quickly than public funds, involve less politicized decision making, and do not rely on the state as partners.[13] Also, the funds given by foundations, as opposed to funds from most of the international community, are easier to assess, since they are generally given as grants, rather than as a mix of loans, grants, and debt relief. Foundation assistance does, however, have some limitations similar to other kinds of assistance because much of foundation funding is disbursed through intermediaries.

Although there is a growing interest in democracy assistance programs within the international community, basic questions remain regarding the most effective strategies and techniques. Perhaps the major unanswered question is how to make these programs sustainable. As one project director asked, how do you "make Western funds indigenous?"[14] Critical consideration regarding these democracy assistance programs has now begun, but there are still many questions that need to be asked, let alone answered. This initial critical attention has also tended to focus on the role of public funders, especially the international financial institutions and the large bilateral assistance programs, such as AID.[15] As yet there has been little attention paid, to funders, such as foundations, that are NGOs. This study is an attempt to remedy that deficiency.

As the recent experience in Central Europe attests, foundations have played an important, albeit modest, role in assisting democratic development there. Given the near certainty of declining resources for foreign assistance, especially in the United States, it is highly likely that the role played by foundations and other NGOs may expand. In addition, foundations may have strengths unmatched by other donors in the international community for certain types of democracy assistance efforts, such as working with civil society.

Phases of Assistance

One difficulty in assessing democracy assistance programs in Central Europe is the fact that they have changed significantly. Over the past six years, there has been considerable evolution in the kinds of projects supported, as well as the perceptions of Central Europeans, whose responses have come in three phases so far: (1) unfettered enthusiasm, (2) skeptical enthusiasm, and (3) growing disenchantment.[16]

During the unfettered enthusiasm phase, which lasted roughly from 1989 to 1991, there was considerable ardor for things "Western," including foreign assistance provided by multilateral institutions, bilateral programs, and foundations. Although much of the assistance during this phase was positive, some was entirely inappropriate and showed scant awareness of local circumstances. For example, one foundation executive recalled with dismay a Pulitzer Prize–winning journalist lecturing Central Europeans that governments invariably lie and therefore cannot be trusted. This lecturer seemed to be unaware that after living under governments based on lies for more than forty years there was little chance that Central Europeans would trust their governments.[17] There was also a wave of technical advisors who made flying visits mainly to capital cities to offer advice on how to build a market democracy. In Warsaw Western advisors became known derisively as the Marriott Brigade, implying that they stayed only at the most expensive hotels and were completely insulated from the realities of Polish life. There also was a plethora of conferences and workshops on topics related to democracy and civil society that Central Europeans viewed as somewhat useful. During this phase, foundations, with the possible exception of the Soros foundations, tended to rely heavily on Western partners as intermediaries.

During the skeptical enthusiasm phase, which began perhaps in 1991 and lasted through 1993 or so, there was still some enthusiasm for Western assistance, but many Central Europeans were becoming increasingly skeptical about its utility. This skepticism was fed through a growing awareness that the preponderance of the funds provided by public funders and foundations stuck with the Western partners and that technical advisers who were uninformed about the local political context could provide little useful information to busy decision makers overwhelmed with the problems of governance. In addition, conferences and workshops that had been seen as a useful way to expose individuals from Central Europe to their Western counterparts came increasingly to be perceived as tiresome, expensive, and relatively useless.

The third phase, which began around 1993 and continues to the present, is characterized by a growing disenchantment with Western assistance. There is also a sense that, despite significant progress related to economic reforms, democracy is fragile and its prospects uncertain. Opinion polls, such as those conducted in December 1994 by the Center for Social and Market Analysis (FOCUS) in Slovakia and its colleagues in the Czech Republic, suggest that in both countries nearly 70 percent of the individuals polled responded at least somewhat affirmatively to the question, "democracy in our country is fragile."[18]

Although it is unrealistic to expect that democracy assistance could have influenced these attitudes significantly, there is a growing sense that the amount of assistance was too meager, came too late, affected too small a percentage of the population, and was given with scant awareness of local circumstances. As one former official positioned to observe a wide range of assistance programs from a vantage point in Czech President Havel's office stated, "The psychologist should not tell his patient what is wrong, as the patient knows better than anyone else what his problems are."[19] This official argued that countries must define their own problems; they cannot let others do this for them. Many would disagree with this view—especially in the first phase some of the elected leaders of the newly democratic governments did not know where to begin—but clearly there is at least a gram of truth here.

By the third phase, however, both Central Europeans and their foundation partners had a much clearer sense of what was required. Although a number of foundations have announced plans to phase out their activities in Central Europe,[20] those that remain appear to have become increasingly adept at the work. There is growing evidence that foundations are reallocating portions of their activities away from capital city elites and are increasing engagement with grassroots groups that are trying to affect governments' prior monopoly on information and action. Foundations also appear to be making more concerted efforts at institution building, that is, they are focusing their attention on developing durable institutions that may survive the eventual withdrawal of their financial support.

These recent shifts have had important democratizing effects, since they are widening the circle of participants in the policy-making process, introducing and strengthening previously mute voices in the debate on national priorities and policies. They are also contributing to the development of a broader and more pluralistic institutional landscape, an important feature of democratic society.

The relative success that some foundations are having, especially with strengthening civil society, is now being emulated by a number of public funders.[21] In shifting the foci of their grant making away from the formal institutions of democracy and the loci away from capital cities, foundations are helping provide some needed momentum to decentralization, which is critical to long-term prospects for democratic development in Central Europe and is in stark contrast to the highly centralized governments in Central Europe prior to 1990.

Foundations are also placing increasing attention on the challenges of sustainability, keeping activities going after the foundations' resources are withdrawn. As one individual involved in democracy assistance argued, "Sustainability must be the measure of success."[22] Foundations' focus on sustainability is not just limited to financial concerns, but, equally importantly, to leadership, decision making, and internal administrative issues.[23]

Purpose

To begin to examine the effectiveness of foundation-funded democracy assistance programs, this study will consider the role played by foundations in Central Europe over a five-year period, 1989–1994. Although occasionally this study will discuss developments after this period, it will generally confine itself to 1989–1994, since the data for that period is most complete. Now seems to be an especially appropriate moment to examine what these programs have accomplished and whether lessons can be learned that might improve programs in Central Europe or apply to other contexts. There is a growing urgency to this task. As noted above, dissatisfaction with democracy mounts in Central Europe, and support for this region is dwindling.

This study will concentrate its attention on Central Europe for a number of reasons. These countries have received the preponderance of support from international, national, and foundation programs, and this level of response from the international community may not be repeated. These Central European countries are also considered well along in marketization and democratization, even though they started from diverse places, have not all progressed at the same rate, and now appear to be traveling on slightly different paths. Thus, they provide an unprecedented opportunity for demonstrating the results of democracy assistance efforts. A related reason is that the very lack of cohesion among Central European countries provides an opportunity for interesting comparisons. Examining closely the experiences of foundations in Central Europe may also cast some light on what has become the conventional wisdom: that strengthening NGOs and civil society is comparable to strengthening democracy. Perhaps most importantly, the experiences of the Central European countries in grappling with the dual transition away from centrally planned, authoritarian systems toward more market-oriented, democratic systems is reflected in many other countries in transition. Thus, lessons learned from a close examination of these four Central European countries may apply elsewhere.

Concepts and Techniques

One of the difficulties embedded in democracy assistance is the lack of a shared understanding about what constitutes democracy. Despite initial widespread enthusiasm for the developments of 1989–1990 in Central Europe, events since then have served to remind us that a democratic form of government does not ensure democracy. Thus, for the purposes of this study, democracy will be defined as broad participation in political

FIGURE 2 **Foundation Assistance to Central Europe by Type, 1989–1994**

U.S. dollars (in millions)

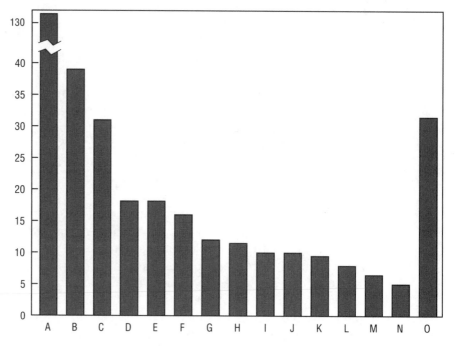

A – Higher education; **B** – Economic reform and education; **C** – Nongovernmental organizations; **D** – Democratic institutions, law, elections, and local government; **E** – Free press; **F** – Libraries; **G** – Conflict and security; **H** – Environment; **I** – Safety net; **J** – Human rights; **K** – Public discourse; **L** – Arts and culture; **M** – Civic education; **N** – Lower education; **O** – Other.

processes, regular competition for top levels of political office, and extensive protection of political and civil rights.[24] Foundations tended to focus much of their attention on extending and enhancing citizen participation. Foundations also tended to recognize that democracy requires a complex web of formal and informal institutions and processes that take time and effort to construct. It must be undergirded by a supportive political culture and set of values, and be accepted by the broad citizenry as well as the elites, while protecting basic political and civil rights.

Given this broad, functional understanding of democracy, it is clear that a wide variety of programs could be considered "democracy assistance." Examples would include activities that target the formal institutions of government, such as assistance to the parliament and the judiciary, as well as assistance to other institutions considered critical to the functioning of a democracy, such as political parties, trade unions, independent media, and civil society (figure 2). Programs can also seek to secure democratic processes through monitoring elections, changing civilian-military relations, or encouraging competition over policy. Other activities can address perhaps the most difficult challenge, that is, affecting values essential to democratic citizenship through supporting civic education and public participation. Such programs may target particular societal concerns, such as the environment, community development, and other issues around which citizens can organize themselves, and through those experiences, develop skills important to democratization. Many foundation programs involve a mix of all of these (figure 2).

Another problematic issue is whether these programs *promote* or *assist* democracy. These terms are sometimes used interchangeably, yet there is a subtle distinction between them. *Promoting democracy* suggests that the impetus for further democratic development is external. *Assisting democracy* recognizes that the principal responsibility for developing democracy rests with the Czechs, Hungarians, Poles, and Slovaks and that democracy assistance programs play only a marginal role in that process. Thus, this study will use the phrase *democracy assistance* to describe programs designed to support Central Europeans in their own efforts to develop more democratic societies.

The term *foundation* requires some further explanation, too. For purposes of convenience, this study will speak generally about foundations, although there are significant differences among the approximately sixty foundations studied here. Besides the sources of their funding, these differences include, but are not limited to, strategy, structure, and approach. For example, NGOs like the Soros group of foundations articulated early on a vision of open societies built upon local structures. Others, such as Ford, emphasized human rights and legal reform, initially administered from New York. Due to the limitations imposed by their charters, the Andrew W. Mellon Foundation (Mellon), the Carnegie Corporation of New York (Carnegie), and the Pew Charitable Trusts (PCT) worked exclusively with U.S.–registered organizations. These distinctive structures and approaches will be discussed more fully in the context of specific projects.

This study uses the phrase *public funders* to apply to official assistance programs, such as those of AID, as well as international financial institutions, including the IMF, the Bank, and the European Bank for Reconstruction and Development (EBRD). In contrast, this study will use the term *private* or *NGO funders* to describe democracy assistance programs supported by foundations including the Friedrich Ebert Stiftung (Ebert), National Endowment for Democracy (NED), and the Soros foundations. As discussed, there is considerable diversity among the approaches and activities of these foundations. Most of them, however, tended to emphasize the NGO sector.

Besides terminology, some explanation is also required of issues related to techniques used in working with the institutions and processes of democracies. Foundations primarily supported training, technical assistance, research, and institution building directly or through intermedi-

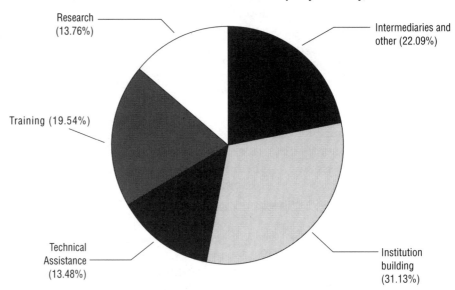

FIGURE 3 Foundation Assistance to Central Europe by Modality, 1989–1994

Research (13.76%)

Intermediaries and other (22.09%)

Training (19.54%)

Technical Assistance (13.48%)

Institution building (31.13%)

aries (figure 3). Types of projects ranged from training journalists, providing technical assistance to institutions central to the transition (such as privatization ministries or central banks), and supporting research on the social costs of transition to building independent policy research institutes or think tanks. Thus, there was and is substantial diversity among the very types and modes of projects considered democracy assistance. In some ways, this diversity may contribute to a pluralizing effect that helps accelerate democratization. In any event, it is important to recognize that this broad label aptly applies to many activities.

Approach

In reviewing the role played by foundations, this study recognizes that there are a multitude of factors that influence a country's ability to develop democracy. Among others, these factors include levels of education, access to information, ability to travel, continuing economic growth, social and political stability, strong leadership, and a conducive political culture.[25] Furthermore, if democracy, as this study suggests, involves a complex web of formal and informal institutions and processes undergirded by a supportive set of values, then it is important to comment on the different strands making up democracy in each of the Central European countries. These different strands include parliaments, the media, the judiciary, and NGOs, among others. They will be discussed in a general way at the start of chapters 2 through 5. Given the variety of these factors, there is considerable risk of overstating the importance of democracy assistance (regardless of who is providing it). Mindful of this risk, this study's principal focus is the extent to which foundations can spur democratic development, particularly in the NGO sector.

To examine the role played by foundations, this study draws on data from approximately sixty foundations in Europe and North America that have not previously been collected. These data provide new information on the total resources provided by foundations to Central Europe, the numbers of foundations involved in the region and in each country, the range of their activities, their different objectives, and their various operating styles. Further data related to the role played by foundations in Central Europe can be found in the Appendix tables.

In addition to using these data, this study will profile one prominent foundation-supported project in each of the four Central European countries, as well as one regional project and one Soros-related foundation. These profiles are meant to spotlight some of the major areas to which foundations have made relatively large investments, namely: education, the environment, human rights, local government, and the NGO sector.[26] As figure 2 suggests, some areas, such as economic reform and the development of a free press, received a greater share of foundation resources than others, but since those areas also received substantial funding from other sources, they are not discussed in depth here. These project descriptions are here to provide some texture for the discussion of the role played by foundations in assisting Central Europeans to develop more democratic societies. They are not meant to be comprehensive evaluations of any of these projects but instead are put forward to help identify patterns of activities and to develop conclusions regarding foundations' performance in assisting democracy.

As distinct from some other efforts, this study assumes that Central Europeans' views on these matters are essential. Thus, it is based on over two hundred interviews with Central Europeans and others involved in or knowledgeable about democracy assistance efforts. In addition, this study relies on a series of workshops at which Central Europeans played an important role in examining efforts to strengthen democracy in their region.[27] It also draws on the author's experience as a foundation executive administering democracy assistance programs in Central Europe from 1989 to 1995.

Recognizing the wide range of democracy assistance programs, as well as the inherent complexity associated with the process of building democracy (to which Ralf Dahrendorf and others have alluded),[28] this study, following these project descriptions, considers three levels of effects: how these programs influence participating individuals, how they alter institutions, and how they affect issues or society at large.

Although this framework has some limitations, it will undergird this study's views of what projects have worked best. A major limitation is that the task of assisting democracy cannot be easily quantified or readily converted into measurable objectives. This does not, however, undercut the importance of establishing clear objectives for democracy assistance programs and assiduously assessing their progress towards achieving these objectives. All too often foundations promised more than they could achieve with their resources. In part, this contributed to exaggerated expectations, as well as difficulty in precisely gauging what the foundations accomplished.

The following four chapters examine the roles played by foundations in each of the Central European countries. After a brief discussion of the state of economic and political reform in these countries, there is a discussion regarding the extent of external involvement, in particular, by multilateral, bilateral, and foundation programs. Then each of these chapters profiles an institution in a sector important to the democratization process that has received major foundation investment. This is followed by a discussion of other important foundation-supported projects to convey a picture of the range of foundations' activities and their varied styles and approaches. These illustrative projects also provide an opportunity to discuss the results achieved and the lessons learned.

Chapter 6 discusses foundation-sponsored regional projects that supplement country-specific work. Chapter 7 is devoted to the individual who has played the leading role in democracy assistance in Central Europe, George Soros. The eighth and final chapter will present conclusions and offer recommendations more generally regarding democracy assistance programs.

2

Czech Republic: Standing Apart

Of the four Central European countries, the Czech Republic seems to have traveled the smoothest path in developing more democratic institutions. Foundations' assistance to democracy programs there is set in this context. The relative ease of democratic development in the Czech Republic is noteworthy given that it was the most collectivized and closed of the Central European countries. One legacy of the 1968 Soviet invasion that crushed the short-lived Prague Spring was that Czechs had less access to Western information and fewer opportunities to travel than their neighbors. Given the more repressive nature of the Czech regime, the opposition was not especially widespread or well organized. Nevertheless, the Czech events in November 1989 that so moved the world, the so-called Velvet Revolution, took place at a breathtaking pace, eclipsing the dissidents' wildest dreams. In literally a matter of days, Civic Forum—a national umbrella organization aligned with Public against Violence in Slovakia—orchestrated the Communist government's turning over power to democratically oriented forces.[1]

Events just a little more than three years later, when Czechoslovakia peacefully separated into the Czech Republic and Slovakia, reinforced the image that even the most difficult tasks, such as dividing a country, are done smoothly and easily in Prague. This separation, referred to as the Velvet Divorce, stands in stark contrast to the bloody separation of the former Yugoslavia.

The Czech Republic's ability to stabilize its economy, to attract significant foreign investment, and to develop rapidly a relatively liberal economy where the majority of economic output is the result of private initiative suggests that its path toward a market system has been soft and smooth as velvet. The Czech Republic can boast significant economic accomplishments, although surface appearances mask more complex underlying circumstances.

The Czech economy has been growing impressively (table 1). As Prime Minister Václav Klaus stated, "I believe that the Czech Republic has already crossed the Rubicon dividing the old and new regime. It is an important achievement; we may become the proof that the transformation from communism to a free society can be realized."[2] Unemployment and inflation are low and steady, and compare favorably with all of Eastern and Central, as well as Western, Europe. This low unemployment has, however, come at some cost—mainly in unsustainable subsidies to large enterprises. Despite a highly successful voucher privatization program that transferred ownership of the preponderance of small- and medium-sized firms from the state to private concerns, many of the largest firms (those with the greatest number of employees) have not been privatized. These large state enterprises continue to receive significant subsidies.

Despite the ardent free market rhetoric of Prime Minister Václav Klaus, who argued that "the reforms must be bold, courageous, determined, and therefore, painful . . .",[3] the Czech Republic eschewed a "shock therapy" approach.[4] Instead, it followed a carefully moderated strategy that has produced significant, if incomplete, economic reform without the socially unacceptable costs of high unemployment. The Czech Republic's economic success is evidenced by the fact that it was the first country in Central or Eastern Europe to join the club of industrialized democracies, the Organization for Economic Cooperation and Development (OECD), which it did on 19 December 1995.

The Czech Republic's economic achievements are a major factor in the country's noteworthy political stability. Unlike the other Central European countries, there has been continuity of leadership in the presidency and the Parliament throughout the reform period. This continuity and stability is, in part, the basis for the country's significant political progress following the dizzying days of November 1989.

The Czech Republic's new constitution took effect on 1 January 1993. It pledges to build a free and democratic society based on respect for human rights and the principles of civil society. With the possible exception of minority rights for the Roma—sometimes known as the gyp-

TABLE 1 Czech Republic, Major Economic Indicators, 1989–1994

	1989	1990	1991	1992	1993	1994
Per capita GDP (in 1990 U.S. dollars)	9,371	9,498	8,190	7,657	7,577	7,774
Growth rate of GDP (in percents)	4.5	−1.2	−14.2	−6.4	−0.9	2.6
Average change in consumer prices (in percents)	1.3	9.7	56.6	11.1	20.8	10.0
Unemployment rate (in percents)	n/a	0.8	4.1	2.6	3.5	3.2

Source: PlanEcon, *PlanEcon Review and Outlook for Eastern Europe*, December 1995

sies—it generally has done well in this regard. In addition, the constitution established a parliamentary form of government, which has been led by a coalition between the Civic Democratic Party (ODS) and the Civic Democratic Alliance (ODA). Under the constitution, the president is elected by the Parliament for a five-year term.

The new constitution aims to establish a rule of law similar to that in Western Europe. Consequently, a distinction is drawn between public law (penal code, administrative regulations on matters such as finance, tax, and the environment) and private law (civil and commercial codes). The Czechs, consistent with their aspirations to become fully integrated into Europe, have signed the Council of Europe convention and its various protocols, as well as numerous European conventions on refugees and terrorism.

The new constitution also provides the legal basis for an independent judiciary. Judges are appointed by the president and serve for life, with the exception of members of the Constitutional Court, who serve ten-year terms. Since the adoption of the new constitution, a parliamentary form of government has been successfully introduced. Three stages of national and local elections have been held, the most recent in June 1996. These resulted in the election of a relatively stable coalition government, while stands in stark contrast to its neighbors in its remarkable degree of popular support. Although the Klaus government lost its absolute majority in the June 1996 election, this did not indicate a significant shift to the left among the electorate.[5] In fact, among the Central European countries, the Czech Republic stands apart as the only country where, aside from the initial transition period, a former Communist has not been elected to lead the government.[6] Support for Communist groups remains relatively modest. Czech elections produced a parliament through proportional representation for the lower house and direct election for the upper house. The Parliament's activities are marked by a high degree of transparency. Unlike the past, its proceedings are televised and open to the public, and laws are also now published.

The Czech Republic has also made considerable progress in another area essential to democracy and key to eventual membership in NATO, that is, the civilian control of the military. Under the constitution, the president is the supreme commander, and the Defense Ministry is led by a civilian. The Parliament has both legal and de facto control over budgetary and policy matters affecting the defense sector. Important for a fledgling democracy, the constitution also precludes political activity by the armed forces. In the Czech Republic, as in most of the other Central European countries, significant progress has also been made in reforming the police force. Although the police do not serve perfectly a civic role, they no longer serve primarily to maintain totalitarian leaders in power.[7]

Perhaps one of the most important political changes in the Czech

Republic has been the development of an independent NGO sector. Since 1988, the number of independent civic associations, many of them supported by foreign foundations, has grown more than tenfold. The number of registered civic associations increased from approximately 2,000 to more than 29,000 by 1995, including the development of approximately 2,500 local foundations.[8] Some, such as the Committee of Good Will (a.k.a. the Olga Havel Foundation) and the Civic Forum Foundation, have relatively significant resources.

Although growth in the Czech Republic's NGO sector has been impressive, it has been inhibited by the lack of a clear legislative framework, including the lack of tax incentives, and the absence of a culture of giving that could generate the needed local support. Recognizing this need, the NGO sector received special tax treatment between 1989 and 1994. However, the 1994 tax law withdrew this treatment due to abuses. In part, this resulted from the views of Prime Minister Klaus, who denounced tax deductions for voluntary activities on the grounds that such deductions are undemocratic and place the interests of the donor ahead of the general interests of the public.[9] Now the Finance Ministry has the authority to provide preferential tax treatment for NGOs by regulation on a case-by-case basis. Although this arrangement is not ideal, since it removes some certainty and bureaucratic discretion does not lend itself to democratic decision making, it does provide the possibility for advantageous tax treatment for financial supporters of NGOs. Unfortunately for the NGO sector, passage of revised legislation providing for preferential treatment was stalled by preelection politicking during the spring of 1996.[10]

The media is another area where the Czech Republic has made significant progress since 1989. Reflecting, in part, the views of a president who argued the importance of speaking truth to power, press laws were reformed.[11] As a consequence, the Czech press is considerably freer and more independent than is the press in neighboring Slovakia. For example, a long-standing law against defaming public officials was repealed in 1994 (although defaming the president remains prohibited), and previous penalties for irresponsible journalism were eliminated. Although the electronic press is essentially state supported, a number of local radio stations and two of the four national television channels are now privately owned. One foreign-owned national broadcast television station, TV Nova, now claims a 68 percent market share in the country.[12] Even with government or party support, the Czech media tends to be editorially independent. However, TV Nova has not been immune to pressure from the government's broadcast board. Fearing that the station represented a commercial monopoly on the airwaves, the broadcast board allegedly supported an attempted hostile takeover of TV Nova early in 1996. At this time, however, it seems that the greatest threat to free media is not government interference. Rather, it is a lack of financial resources and growing competition from international, electronic media.

Regarding freedom of information more generally, the Czech Republic has changed dramatically since 1989. As of 1995, 99 percent of all Czech families owned televisions, of which 28 percent had access to cable stations.[13] According to the Bank, the number of phone lines has increased more than ten times, growing from 176 per 1,000 in 1992 to over 1,900 per 1,000 in 1995.[14] The Czech Republic also now enjoys full access to the Internet and has twenty-six gopher servers in ten different cities.[15]

External Involvement

The Czech Republic has perhaps received more media attention from the international community than any other country in Central Europe. This is due, in large part, to its highly visible leadership: President Václav Havel and Prime Minister Václav Klaus. These men, sometimes referred to as the "two Václavs," are known as the country's leading intellectual and head cheerleader for economic reform, respectively. Together, they have given the Czech Republic a high profile in the West. As one official quipped, "It gives the Czech Republic Mr. *New York Review of Books* and Mr. *Wall Street Journal.*"[16]

As part of Czechoslovakia (that is, through the end of 1992), the Czech Republic received relatively less foreign assistance for the economic and political transition than either Hungary or Poland, although the sum it did receive was still significant relative to amounts received by Eastern European countries. Of total funds committed to Central Europe, the Czech Republic received 16.4 percent of that from international financial institutions, 20.7 percent of that from the European Union (EU), and some 9.7 percent of that from independent foundations.[17]

The great preponderance of AID assistance to Czechoslovakia and subsequently to the Czech Republic was directed at economic restructuring—80 percent of the $125 million obligated during fiscal years 1990–1994. Programs aimed at strengthening democratic institutions received the smallest percentage of the three areas where AID was active, representing $5.1 million or 4.1 percent. However, some of the resources used to support NGOs in AID's third program area—improving the quality of life (e.g., support for environmental and social services organizations)—may also have had a democratizing effect by extending venues for citizen participation.[18]

As the Czech Republic, the country has received considerable attention from Western Europe and North America, but this has generally been in commercial form. For example, the Czech Republic has experienced a boom in tourism that has brought a significant influx of hard currency. It had more than sixteen million visitors in 1995, with tourism grossing $2.6 billion, or roughly $260 per capita.[19] In addition, there has been substantial direct foreign investment in the Czech Republic. Both tourism and foreign investment have tended to be directed towards relatively few pockets, especially those in and around Prague. There is growing evidence of uneven patterns of development, with Prague rapidly outpacing the rest of the country.

In large part due to its leadership, the Czech Republic has received significantly less assistance, relatively speaking, than the other Central European countries. At least since 1994, Prime Minister Klaus has argued that his country had already successfully completed the economic transition. He said that ". . . we have already reached the level of several European countries that were lucky enough to have bypassed forty years of communism."[20] Thus, the Czech Republic no longer required foreign assistance, and ". . . (A) prickly resistance to outside advice [became] one of the planks of Prime Minister Klaus's domestic political platform."[21] Klaus suggested that it would be inappropriate for a country that was interested in joining the EU and other pan-European organizations to continue receiving foreign assistance.

Another reason that the Czech Republic received relatively less foreign assistance is that many officials in the Czech government, perhaps more quickly than their neighbors, lost patience with the operating styles and modes of many Western funders, which relied heavily on training and technical assistance. By the second phase of assistance, officials in Prague began to complain about the limited utility of foreign technical advisers, who were more interested in "advising than in cooperating."[22] These officials suggested that they had better things to do than to educate foreign advisers who knew little about circumstances in the Czech Republic.[23] Consequently, Prime Minister Klaus pushed aggressively to discontinue foreign assistance programs in the Czech Republic, especially after the Velvet Divorce. Reflecting its economic success, the Czech Republic repaid its more than $1.4 billion in obligations to the IMF by the end of 1994, well ahead of schedule. As a consequence, AID plans to terminate all programs in the Czech Republic by 1997, "graduating" the Czech Republic considerably earlier than the other Central European countries.

Klaus's attitudes about foreign assistance had an impact, essentially diverting resources to other places. Most foundations became active in Czechoslovakia late in 1989 or early in 1990 but by 1992 began to shift their attention elsewhere. After 1993, a number of foundations made concerted efforts to work in Slovakia, although some continued to support organizations, such as the Jan Hus Educational Foundation, that were operating joint programs in the Czech Republic and Slovakia.

Overall, however, foundations devoted relatively less attention to the

Czech Republic than they did to the other Central European countries. Their support was, nevertheless, instrumental in the NGO, educational, and environmental sectors. This support was also critical for a few key independent institutions, some of which are discussed below.

Education

Foreign foundations played an important role in the Czech Republic's educational sector, especially during the first phase of assistance. For example, Mellon and PCT, in response to a request from its cofounders, provided start-up grants to the Center for Economic Research and Graduate Education (CERGE), affiliated with Charles University in Prague. When these grants were made in 1990, they represented one of the largest grants in the region made by a foundation. Mellon provided a $900,000, three-year operating grant, and PCT provided $300,000 to support Western faculty over three years.[24] These foundation grants were subsequently followed by AID and other foundation support, providing an example of public-private cofinancing, although this was not explicitly coordinated.

CERGE was cofounded by Josef Zielenec, the current foreign minister, and Jan Svejnar, then a professor of economics at the University of Pittsburgh. Relatively unusual for the region, CERGE seeks to merge teaching and research, which under the Communist system had been conducted separately by the universities and the academies of sciences, respectively. From an institutional point of view, CERGE is an interesting hybrid, a new institution coupled with a long-established institution. It involves a partnership between prominent Czech and émigré economists, as well as between Western and Central European academic institutions.

Recognizing that economic education and policy research needed to be entirely restructured, Zielenec and Svejnar hoped to establish the region's first doctoral program in economics based on a Western curriculum and world-class standards and taught in English. They also hoped to develop simultaneously a research capacity that could eventually rival that of the IMF and the Bank. Recognizing the difficulty of working strictly within an established institution, CERGE's founders sought and won a high degree of autonomy from the educational authorities, while still being linked both to Charles University and the Czech Academy of Sciences. They were able to win this autonomy because CERGE's programs did not directly compete with those of Charles University or the Academy of Sciences and because the foreign funding they secured provided CERGE with significant prestige.

Foundation staff were enthusiastic about Zielenec and Svejnar's vision for CERGE. Supporting reform of economic education and enhancing the quality of economic research relevant to the transition were central to the guidelines of both Mellon and PCT, although these did change over time. Foundation support to CERGE is particularly noteworthy in that its relatively long-term and flexible nature enabled CERGE to attract other resources. Zielenec and Svejnar were adept at leveraging these initial foundation resources into support from AID and other international institutions, such as the EU. In addition, the Soros foundations provided travel support and stipends for students from outside Czechoslovakia. CERGE's success with foreign funding, coupled with its unique combination of research and teaching, enabled it to obtain additional support from the Czech government.

After a somewhat rocky relationship with the Central European University's (CEU) campus in Prague with which it initially shared premises on Táboritská Street, CERGE relocated in 1993 to more centrally located premises at a building of the Academy of Sciences, close to Wenceslas Square. These premises included facilities suitable to policy seminars for high-level participants from the Czech government, as well as for the international financial community in Prague. This ability to establish close links with the country's financial leaders is another factor contributing to CERGE's success.

CERGE's experiences with foundations were also noteworthy in that the basic concept was developed by Czechs working with an émigré affiliated with an institution (the University of Pittsburgh) that had strong links with Central Europe. Although the concept originated in Prague, the role of Jan Svejnar cannot be underestimated. Jan is a well-respected economist and a former student of Richard Quandt at Princeton University. Quandt administered Mellon's Central European program. Although Svejnar's relationship and reputation were not sufficient to account for CERGE's success, they did provide it with a good head start.

In addition, CERGE's founders were also unusual in developing a seven-year plan to become self-sustaining.[25] Although this goal turned out to be overly optimistic, the clarity of CERGE's initial vision and its recognition of the long road ahead must be considered contributory factors in its success.

Equally important to CERGE's success was the locally designed and managed structure it developed. Although Mellon and PCT provided resources through the University of Pittsburgh, from its inception CERGE was clearly designed to be in and of the region. The role of the foundations was a modest and reactive one, merely responding positively to plans developed in Prague.

Although CERGE had many positive attributes, such as strong local leadership with a clear vision, being a locally developed project, and finding local cofinancing, these were not sufficient to enable it to avoid institutional growing pains completely. In spite of a series of administrative and leadership challenges, including developing local faculty and the clarifying of CERGE's relationship with Charles University, the Academy of Sciences, and CEU, these positive factors mitigated some of the effects of CERGE's growing pains. These positive factors helped CERGE survive where some institutions faced with similar challenges would have collapsed. Thus, CERGE provides an example of how foundations played a reactive role in supporting a newly developed institution that has now achieved considerable success.

Featured Projects

The NGO sector itself is one of the areas where foundations have had a discernible effect in the Czech Republic. The Information Center for Foundations and Other Not-for-Profit Organizations (ICN) is an example of an independent institution seeking to support the development of the NGO sector established essentially with support from foreign foundations.[26] ICN's mission involves providing information about legal, financial, and management issues for NGOs, providing training for NGO leaders, and facilitating cooperation between Czech and international NGOs. Parallel organizations seeking to strengthen the NGO sector exist in the other Central European countries. Examples include the Nongovernmental Organizations Data Base (KLON) in Poland, the Slovak Academic Information Agency—Service Center for the Third Sector (SAIA—SCTS) in Slovakia, and the Nonprofit Information and Training Center Foundation (NITCF) in Hungary.

ICN is an indirect outgrowth of the Four F (Four Foundations) international office. Four F attempted to promote communication and cooperation between organizations existing under the previous regime to serve ordinary people and four newly established foundations (The Olga Havel Foundation, the Civic Forum Foundation, the Charta 77 Foundation, and the Board for Humanitarian Cooperation). Four F initially received support from the Charities Aid Foundation (CAF) until its functions were taken over by ICN.

ICN grew out of a conference of major Czech and Slovak NGOs held in Stupava in October 1991. Conference participants identified the lack of information, training, and other services as impediments to the development of NGOs. Following this conference, a working group was established that registered ICN in the Slovak Republic in February 1992 and in the Czech Republic in October 1992.

The Czech working group was led by Jana Ryšlinková, a former member of the federal Parliament. Ryšlinková worked with an American volunteer, Rachel Stein, to establish ICN's office in Prague after securing operating support from CAF and RBF. ICN also received initial program support from the Charles Stewart Mott Foundation (Mott) to sponsor a national conference for NGOs. With additional funding from the Sasakawa Peace Foundation (Sasakawa), ICN began a database, a library, and training programs. These activities helped attract funding from the European Cultural Foundation (ECF) and the Civil Society Development Foundation (CSDF)—a program funded by EU's Phare (Poland and Hungary Assistance for Restructuring of the Economy), which provides grants to local NGOs.[27] Foundation staff members responded well to the leadership of Ryšlinková, many of whom she had met during a twelve-week Eisenhower Exchange Fellowship in the United States just prior to ICN's establishment.

Although successful, ICN, like many other NGOs in rapidly changing societies, has experienced a considerable number of institutional challenges, in areas of personnel, administration, governance, and finance. In part, this resulted from the fact that ICN was a brand new organization in a brand new area of activity. It also resulted from the fact that ICN was loosely adopting a model for information and service organizations developed in countries with robust and well-established NGO sectors. Over time, governance issues came to the fore, as the board sought to develop its own role since the institution had been initially dominated by its founding director and the board's role was relatively undefined. Furthermore, ICN was created in the midst of an extremely uncertain legal and financial environment for NGOs. ICN was entirely dependent upon foreign foundations, some of which withdrew their support by the third phase of assistance because of the Czech Republic's economic success and the assumption that foundation support was no longer required. ICN also experienced considerable difficulty in attracting local support. In this regard, foundation support directed early on at stimulating local support may have been extremely useful.

In retrospect, it is clear that foundation assistance was decisive in the establishment of ICN. Perhaps derivative of their views of the importance of the NGO sector and experiences with comparable institutions in their own countries, foundation staff were highly supportive of developing NGO information and training centers. Some foundation staff tended, perhaps over optimistically, to see these NGO service centers as essential instruments for the establishment of a vibrant civil society. They are perhaps necessary, but they are no means sufficient for developing civil society.

Besides ICN, the Czech NGO sector has benefited from the establishment of a number of other organizations, such as CSDF. CSDF, initially formed in 1993, was funded by a 2.6 million ECU (approximately $3.9 million) grant from Phare. It provides necessary information and services for the development of the NGO sector. Unlike ICN, CSDF is also a grant-making organization that provides financial resources to other NGOs. CSDF offers grants to support information activities, training activities, and projects of individual NGOs. Since its establishment, CSDF has been involved in providing important resources to the fledgling Czech NGO sector. Equally important, it places Czechs in a decision-making role regarding the allocation of these resources.

The Foundation for Civil Society (FCS, originally called the Charter 77 Foundation—New York) is an example of another important institution that was set up with support from foundations, primarily the Soros foundations. Established in 1990 by Wendy Luers, the wife of a former American ambassador to Czechoslovakia, FCS was initially designed as an umbrella organization channeling resources into Czechoslovakia. FCS's founder suggested that its principal currency was its contacts, as well as its links to power structures in the United States and Czechoslovakia. These attributes have made FCS successful in attracting support from a wide range of public and private funders, including some fourteen foundations.[28] Luers attributes FCS's success to focusing on a single country and not overselling itself.[29] Its flexibility and its ability to get the job done, doing whatever is required, has also contributed.

Over time, FCS has built up an array of effective programs, including its Expert Adviser program, a number of educational and cultural fellowship programs, and a highly influential series of conferences as part of its Project on Justice in Times of Transition. This project draws on the experiences of other societies for developing techniques to encourage reconciliation after the collapse of an oppressive regime.

FCS's excellent contacts, multilingual staff, solid programming, and locations in Bratislava, New York, and Prague were recognized in its selection by AID to administer the Democracy Network (DemNet) Program in the Czech Republic and Slovakia. As part of DemNet, FCS administers a $1.5 million small grants program in the Czech Republic and a $3 million program in Slovakia.

Yet despite its considerable success in fund-raising and programming, FCS's long-term prospects are uncertain. It relies almost exclusively on foreign funders. Despite its solid connections on the ground, it is still primarily an American organization. Most of its board members are U.S. citizens.[30] Although FCS has attracted support from an impressive number of public and private funders and has a highly energetic and well-respected local staff, whether it will survive now that much foreign funding is being phased out is in doubt. The question of long-term sustainability confronting FCS is a dilemma facing virtually all of the newly independent organizations in the Czech Republic.

Similar to FCS, the Institute for EastWest Studies (IEWS, formerly the Institute for East-West Security Studies) is another intermediary organization that many foundations initially relied on because of its extensive experience in the region. Established by John Mroz in 1981 at the height of the cold war, IEWS was one of the relatively few organizations active in Central and Eastern Europe prior to the changes in 1989. In 1990, IEWS established a European Studies Center just outside of Prague. To do so it received a $3.0 million grant from the John D. and Catherine

T. MacArthur Foundation (MacArthur), one of the largest grants in Central Europe provided by a private foundation other than the Soros foundations. Following the changes in Central Europe, IEWS sought to shift its focus away from security matters towards economic, financial, and social issues. With the help of Ford and RBF, among others, it expanded its indigenous staff and over the next few years established centers in each of the Central European countries. IEWS also sponsored efforts to examine assistance to the transition that provide a benchmark for this and other similar work.[31]

Of late, IEWS has encountered significant financial difficulty as foundations have increasingly sought to indigenize their support and provide correspondingly decreasing amounts to intermediaries such as IEWS. By the second and third phases of assistance, intermediaries whose strengths resided in their extensive networks and convening power were perceived as less central to foundations' strategies. Consequently, IEWS sought to develop local organizations that could compete for EU and corporate funding. This has been a considerable challenge for IEWS, as well as for other intermediaries. IEWS's regional work will be discussed in greater detail in chapter 6.

Besides IEWS, a number of other research and advocacy institutes active in the Czech Republic have received considerable support from foundations. One of these is the Civic Institute, which is primarily funded by the Lynde and Harry Bradley Foundation, Inc. (Bradley), the John M. Olin Foundation (Olin), and the Smith Richardson Foundation, Inc. (Smith Richardson). The Civic Institute is a strong advocate for political and economic freedom, as well as for limited government. Among other things, it publishes translations of major works of political theory. It also organizes lectures and seminars on important public policy issues, and thus, plays a role in extending public debate. It is governed by an international board but administered by Czech citizens. The Civic Institute is roughly analogous to an independent research institution or think tank, so it was a relatively easy partner for foundations, which have had extensive experience with like institutions. The institute's philosophical orientation was also a strong selling point for its funders, although this did preclude some foundation support.

The Czech Helsinki Committee is another advocacy group that has received extensive support from foundations. The committee was established in 1988 by thirty dissidents to monitor the implementation of the Conference on Security and Cooperation in Europe (CSCE) and other human rights agreements. Following the Velvet Divorce, the committee split into two national groups: the Czech Helsinki Committee and the Slovak Helsinki Committee. The Czech committee provides legal assistance (educational seminars for judges, lawyers, and policy officials) and legislative monitoring, and it has created a human rights information and documentation center that is open to the public. The committee was perceived as an important foundation partner prior to the Velvet Revolution and in the first phase of assistance but less so later.

Foundations have also been active in education and journalism in the Czech Republic. For example, under the auspices of the Charter 77—New York Foundation, the Independent Journalists Initiative was created. Led by James Greenfield of the *New York Times*, the Initiative established the Center for Independent Journalism in Prague in 1991. The center, affiliated with Charles University, has conference rooms, editing equipment that can be used for training and counseling journalists, and a library replete with journals. As with numerous other projects in the Czech Republic, there is some sense that this center was too slow in being established and therefore has been of limited utility. The center was most needed in 1990 and 1991, but by the time it became fully operational in 1992 the most pressing need had passed.[32]

Perhaps one of the most important foundation-sponsored projects in the Czech Republic is the Czech and Slovak Library Information Network (CASLIN). This consortium, involving the National Library in Prague, the National Slovak Library in Martin, the Brno State Library, and the Bratislava University, was initiated by a proactive grant from Mellon. It links four of the most important research institutions in the Czech Republic and Slovakia, which adopted identical hardware and software for their automation efforts. Quite remarkably, this project has continued even after the Velvet Divorce. CASLIN is supervised by Professor Andrew Lass of Mount Holyoke College. Since he is neither Czech nor Slovak, this removed some tension. Lass has played an instrumental role in obtaining matching government funds and generating national awareness of the importance of preserving and enhancing research libraries.[33]

CASLIN contains a number of exemplary characteristics from a grant-making perspective. Mellon responded to a clear need for an institution that would have a broad social impact and to which others paid little attention. Mellon was able to replicate successfully its experiences in other contexts and did eventually attract other resources. Perhaps, most importantly, this project has had the unintended consequence of encouraging institutions to cooperate that had been inclined to compete or ignore each other.[34]

Foundations have also been active in establishing business education programs. For example, RBF helped establish the first independent Western-style business management training center in the Czech Republic. The Bradley foundation also supported a U.S. Business School in Prague. These projects were important in the first phase of foundation involvement in Central Europe, but their importance has diminished as other public and corporate funders expressed interest in supporting business education and training.

The German foundations, with the possible exception of the political foundations (such as the Konrad Adenauer [Adenauer] and Ebert Stiftungen), are not especially active in the Czech Republic. The party foundations have organized seminars on political campaigning, building democratic societies, strengthening party skills, and expanding media skills. They have also organized training workshops for union workers facing insolvency. The Humboldt Stiftung (Humboldt), which relies primarily on support from the German government, is one German foundation that has been quite active in the Czech Republic. Between 1989–1992, Humboldt awarded 328 fellowships valued at approximately $4.3 million and provided $665,621 for equipment to a variety of institutions of higher education in Czechoslovakia. In 1993–1994, it provided 48 fellowships valued at approximately $900,000 and $103,052 for equipment.[35]

Results

As suggested earlier, the results of projects intended to foster democracy can be assessed in three related ways: in terms of their effect on individuals, their effect on institutions, and their effect on society at large. Recognizing the inherent difficulty and time required to affect democracy-oriented change in societies in transition, many foundations, implicitly if not explicitly, initially adopt a strategy of investing in talented individuals with vision. Over time, these individuals are expected to develop new institutions that will help the society address its problems more successfully.[36]

The approximately twenty-five foundations that have provided some $47 million to support hundreds of projects in the Czech Republic have made an impact on the lives of tens of thousands, if not hundreds of thousands, of Czechs. The most pronounced effects were probably produced by foundation-supported training programs, which exposed Czechs to new ideas and approaches and strengthened their links to a variety of individuals with common interests in Europe and North America. The Czechs involved in such programs now have much greater access to information, which enables them to exercise their rights as citizens. Given modern telecommunications and ease of travel, some of these effects would eventually have been produced anyway. Still, foundation-supported training programs seem to have been useful. Although this may seem obvious, the most helpful of these programs were those targeting young people and individuals who, by virtue of their current positions or career prospects, were well situated to contribute to the reform efforts but who otherwise would have had few opportunities to participate in training programs.

Foundation assistance has also been modestly helpful, establishing or bolstering independent institutions despite occasional problems, such as CERGE, ICN, and others discussed here. Especially important is the role of CSDF and FCS in providing small grants to strengthen NGOs. While recognizing that even with foundation support all of these institutions face a number of serious challenges to their mature institutional development, it is possible to say that without foundations many of these institutions would not exist in their current form or at all. Because they exist, the Czech Republic is considerably more pluralistic than it was. The circle of participants in the policy-making process has widened considerably, and a range of views is expressed on a variety of important public policies, in stark contrast to the monochrome and monopolistic Communist period.

The press or media is another area that has benefited, albeit modestly, from foundation involvement. Foundation-supported programs such as the Independent Journalism Center have provided Czech journalists exposure to the techniques and approaches of the Western media. However, these effects have not been produced simply by foundations. The media, have also been affected by market forces, as private investors continue to purchase media outlets throughout Central Europe. Thus, it would be easy to overstate the role of foundations vis-à-vis the free media.

In the Czech Republic, perhaps more than in other Central European countries, foundations relied on intermediaries, including FCS and IEWS. With their local staffs and extensive contacts in the Czech Republic, these intermediaries quickly established presences on the ground and began effective programming. The involvement of intermediaries clearly resulted in the Czech Republic's receiving increased foundation attention and, consequently, greater foundation resources than they otherwise might have. However, the intermediaries tended to have considerably higher overhead than local institutions. They may also have retarded the development of comparable, self-reliant local institutions and thus limited the local ownership by stakeholders that is essential to long-term sustainability.

On the broadest and most challenging level, there is considerably less evidence that any foundation has had a significant societal impact. That is not altogether surprising, since foundations' resources—time, money, and personnel—are relatively modest. Nonetheless, Czechs involved with foundations suggest that not only have they benefited directly from foundation involvement, but they have also learned some important lessons about pluralism from the large numbers of foundations involved in their country.[37]

Despite supporting individuals and institutions in certain important sectors, perhaps some of the most important contributions of foundations were more intangible. Czechs have mentioned that the single most valuable contribution was the simple fact that foundations were engaged at a time when they were needed.[38] Foundations provided their Czech partners with a sense that they had indeed returned to Europe, that they were once again part of the global community. Of course, this sentiment is difficult to quantify and may not be especially satisfying to those who want an exact accounting of what foundation resources have produced. Nevertheless, the fact that virtually every Czech interviewed for this study or who participated in the study's workshops alluded to the intangible benefits of this foreign assistance provides considerable weight to this claim.

3

Hungary: The Long Road

I n an effort to describe what has happened since Hungary's first democratically elected government took office in 1990, it is tempting to rely on the classic French aphorism, "the more things change, the more they stay the same."[1] This expression, similar to most generalizations, both captures and misses something important. It is suggestive of the situation in Hungary, but it does not fully capture the reality of the complex, time-consuming, and not always straightforward movement toward a more market-oriented democratic society. The adage does capture, however, a pervasive sentiment that, given robust expectations for dramatic change, the pace and scope of change in Hungary has been slow and meager and that the country has been on a seemingly long road toward reform.[2]

Among the Central European countries, expectations for reform were perhaps highest for Hungary, since it had the lengthiest experience with economic reform. As early as 1968, Hungary had begun modest reform, allowing for increased enterprise autonomy. Between 1988 and 1991 comprehensive economic reform was introduced to liberalize most prices and foreign trade, as well as to reform the banking and tax systems. As of 7 November 1995, the Hungarian forint was made convertible, the last of the Central European countries to introduce current account convertibility. Small-scale privatization was implemented in 1992–1993, and most large-scale enterprises were transferred to the private sector by 1995. Estimates suggest that by 1995 the private sector was responsible for nearly 60 percent of GDP.[3]

Despite these reform measures, however, the Hungarian economy was not performing especially well, although Hungarians had among the highest living standards in the region (table 2). From 1989 to 1994, inflation averaged over 24 percent, and unemployment increased to double digits, while real wages declined slightly. Overwhelmed by the largest per capita foreign debt in the region, the economy experienced a series of internal and external macroeconomic imbalances. This led to a deterioration in Hungary's once favorable international image. As a legacy of its earlier reforms, at the end of the 1980s and early in the 1990s Hungary received the largest share of foreign direct investment in Central Europe. But by the mid-1990s, given continuing economic stagnation, Hungary's share of the total Central European direct foreign investment declined as its economic performance was rivaled by that of its Central European neighbors.[4]

Despite its modest economic performance, Hungary has been the most politically stable country in Eastern Europe. Since 1990, Hungary has been a parliamentary democracy governed by coalitions. It has held two rounds of national and local elections, the first in 1990 and the second in 1994. Unique among the Central European countries, Hungary is the only nation in which the initial coalition government served its entire four-year term. The first coalition government, led by the Hungarian Democratic Forum under Prime Minister Jozsef Antall, was replaced by a coalition of the Hungarian Socialist Party (Mszp) and the Alliance for Free Democrats (SzDSz) under Prime Minister Gyula Horn. Since 1990, Hungary's president has been Arpád Göncz of SzDSz, who was elected to two consecutive five-year terms.

The country operates under its 1949 constitution, although a number of important provisions were deleted, including those stipulating the leading role of the Hungarian Socialist Workers Party and mandating employment. What is significant about these changes is not so much their extent, but that Hungary has recently developed the necessary institutional framework, including a viable Constitutional Court, to enforce provisions in the constitution. Most of the provisions regarding citizens' rights date from the Communist era, although they were simply hollow promises then. In 1990 Hungary joined the Council of Europe and agreed to implement the European Convention. This resulted in reform of its domestic legislation to bring it into compliance with council standards. This review was supported by foundations, such as Ford.[5] In that same year, Hungary signed the U.N. Human Rights Convention guaranteeing political and minority rights. Along similar lines, in 1993

TABLE 2 Hungary, Major Economic Indicators, 1989–1994

	1989	1990	1991	1992	1993	1994
Per capita GDP (in 1990 U.S. dollars)	6,539	6,190	5,460	5,310	5,280	5,400
Growth rate of GDP (in percents)	0.7	−3.5	−11.9	−3.0	−0.8	2.0
Average change in consumer prices (in percents)	17.0	28.9	35.0	23.0	22.5	18.8
Unemployment rate	0.4	1.9	7.8	13.2	12.1	10.4

Source: PlanEcon, *PlanEcon Review and Outlook for Eastern Europe*, June 1995

the Parliament passed a further bill on minority rights, making the protection of ethnic minorities a basic freedom. There are ongoing plans to draft a new constitution.

Hungary has had a multiparty political system since 1989. There are currently some two hundred registered political parties, but membership in these parties is extremely modest, perhaps involving no more than 5 percent of the country's ten million people. This is not meant to suggest either that membership correlates with support or that party membership is likely to increase. Hungarians are involved in politics and vote for various parties even if they do not formally join them. As a legacy of the past, party membership continues to have negative connotations for many Hungarians.[6]

Of these political parties, only six were able to surmount the 5 percent threshold necessary to take seats in the Parliament. Unlike the Communist period, the legislature operates transparently, and its sessions are openly broadcast on television and radio to the public. Early reforms, such as the 1991 law Local Administration of Self-Governing Bodies, sought to decentralize government, but local governments remain financially weak and unable to carry out their duties effectively.

Over the past few years, Hungary's judiciary has been considerably reformed. Judges are generally perceived to be fair and impartial and are precluded from membership in political parties. The judiciary is now distinct from other branches of government and has unprecedented financial independence from the Ministry of Justice. Judges are appointed by the president in response to proposals from the Ministry of Justice and with the approval of a judicial council. Judges are independent; they can only be removed by a disciplinary council, and they have immunity from prosecution.

Regarding civilian-military relations, there has been considerable change during the 1990s. The Defense Ministry, headed by a civilian since 1990, is responsible to both the president and the Parliament. Parliament is now empowered to make war, declare a state of emergency, and authorize use of armed forces either at home or abroad. Some experts believe that Hungary has made important progress on civilian-military issues over the past few years. One reason is the country's desire to join the EU and NATO. Another reason is the presence of large numbers of NATO troops using bases in Hungary as a staging area for the Bosnia deployment. The presence of these NATO troops, which are subject to civilian rule, appears to have had a positive influence on the Hungarian military.

Outside of the formal institutions and processes of government, there has been considerable improvement in Hungary's political circumstances. For example, from 1989 to 1993 the numbers of registered independent foundations and associations increased more than 400 percent, growing from 8,886 to 35,915. Although some of this growth can be attributed to attempts to evade taxes (the nonprofit sector receives some preferential tax treatment), in large part it has occurred because foundations were recognized in a 1987 law, freedom of association was allowed as of 1990, and government policy has been generally supportive. Growth in the NGO sector is also the result of the fact that Hungary has a very strong tradition of supporting nonprofit organizations.[7]

In regard to freedom of the press, a new media law took effect early in 1996, after two-and-a-half years of wrangling.[8] The media war that occurred from June 1992 until December 1995 blocked the allocation of new frequencies and licensing grants. The new law provides for basic media freedoms and are generally seen as sound, if overly complicated.[9] The broadcast media law allows for privatization of some broadcast frequencies and the creation of public foundations to be overseen by a board elected by the Parliament for the public television and radio stations and satellite television station, Duna. Presidents of television and radio stations are chosen based on competitive application rather than appointment, and after 1997 the budgets of the public broadcasting stations are to be immune from the annual budget process. The media law contains provisions pertaining to liability under criminal law for writers and editors engaged in unfounded libel or defamation as well as incitement to hatred. In a pattern similar to that in much of Central (and in fact Western) Europe, the print media have been largely privatized and have considerable independence. The national television and radio, on the other hand, are still state owned, although there are twenty-six private local television stations, thirty-one private radio stations, and hundreds of cable stations. Legally, the state-owned electronic media have editorial independence, but they have not, in fact, been entirely independent. This is evidenced by the government's dismissal of the chief executives of both national television and radio in 1994 and the cancellation of political programs in late 1993. Consequently, the Freedom House rating of the state of press freedom in Hungary slipped from "free" to "partly free" in 1993 and 1994.

Since 1988, Hungarians have been free to travel abroad, and restrictions on internal movement, put in place after 1956 but generally not enforced, were officially relaxed in 1989. Over the past few years, Hungarians' access to international media outlets, as well as access to the Internet, has increased dramatically. Hungary now has fifty-one World Wide Web servers in thirteen different cities, along with twenty-one gopher servers in nine cities.

As a consequence of the economic, political, legal, and social changes discussed above, simply characterizing Hungary as a place where not much has changed obscures the fact that important changes have occurred. Despite these changes, there is, among advocates of reform, a sense of disappointment that these changes have not gone far enough or fast enough and that the road to reform has been much longer than anyone anticipated.[10]

External Involvement

Hungary has received relatively more external funding than the other Central European countries. Of total funds committed to Central Europe, Hungary received nearly a third, or 30.5 percent, of all the funds from international financial institutions, 20.8 percent of funds from the EU, and some 19.9 percent of funds from foundations. The EBRD has been an especially important donor. During the period 1990 to 1993, the EBRD made $722 million of its $1,769 million commitments in Hungary, representing nearly 41 percent of its total commitments.[11] Recognizing that Hungary's population of roughly ten million represents less than 16 percent of Central Europe's population of sixty-five million, these commitment levels suggest extensive external involvement and support.

The large majority of AID assistance to Hungary was directed toward economic restructuring, involving some 80 percent of the $192 million obligated during the five-year period covering fiscal years 1990–1994. Similar to the pattern in other Central European countries, projects to strengthen democratic institutions received the smallest percentage of the three areas where AID was active, representing $10.3 million or 5.4 percent. Some of the resources used to support NGOs in AID's third program area—improving the quality of life—through projects to improve housing and health care and to strengthen the social safety net, for example—may, however, have a democratizing effect.[12]

Especially in the early 1990s, Hungary received considerable private, commercial attention from Western Europe and North America. It was the largest target for direct foreign investment in the region. In addition, Hungary, given its picturesque capital on the Danube, experienced a boom in tourism that has brought with it a significant inflow of hard currency.

Foundations, especially Soros, have been quite active in Hungary. Following the 1984 opening of the Soros Foundation Hungary (SFH), the first independent foundation to begin operating in the region, some twenty-five other foundations have become engaged in Hungary. Largely as a result of Soros support, which represents 50.4 percent of foundation support in the region, Hungary received 19.9 percent of all the foundation resources for Central Europe. In fact, despite Poland's population being almost four times larger than Hungary's, Hungary received comparable amounts of foundation assistance.

Human Rights

Foundations have supported the protection of human rights in Hungary in a variety of ways. Before the political changes of 1989–1990, foundations tended to support Western organizations engaged in monitoring human rights, such as Amnesty International and Human Rights Watch. Following the political liberalization that took place during the first phase of assistance, foundations shifted strategies toward working more closely with indigenous organizations. One example of such an indigenous human rights project (broadly defined) is Hungary's Autonómia Alapítvány (Autonómia) which has developed one of the most important partnerships between foundations and a newly established independent institution. It is especially noteworthy because of the large role played by foundations in its establishment, as well as the fact that Autonómia's core mission of protecting minority rights is not broadly supported.

Autonómia was founded in 1990 by András Biró, a Hungarian national who spent three decades abroad as a journalist and U.N. consultant.[13] Autonómia's original mission was to support Hungarian civil initiatives in three fields: (1) environmentally sustainable development, (2) civil society generally, and (3) poverty and ethnic minorities, with special attention to the Roma community. These three fields were chosen because they seemed to be those most damaged by the Communist regime and because these areas drew the greatest potential support, especially from overseas foundations. Autonómia subsequently narrowed its mission to focus primarily on projects aimed at alleviating the poverty of and discrimination against the Roma in Hungarian society.[14] This focus is significant in that it shows a devotion to a group toward which the Hungarian government and population are apathetic, if not hostile.

The Roma make up the largest Hungarian minority, with about 500,000 people, or 5 percent of the population.[15] Although the Roma have been in Hungary since the sixteenth century and 75 percent of them identify Hungarian as their native language, discrimination against them is widespread. The Roma's circumstances were exacerbated by the fall of the Communist system in 1989, when they were left without marketable skills. Since then, they have been plagued by high unemployment: in 1995 the unemployment rate for the non-Roma population was 15 percent, while that of the Roma was 48 percent.[16] Despite greater educational opportunities under communism, the Roma still remain largely undereducated, and their housing situation has deteriorated. Furthermore, discrimination has been on the rise, with incidents of racism and hazing directed against members of the Roma community increasing.[17] Despite this discrimination, the Roma have established close to two hundred independent ethnic organizations throughout Hungary since 1989.[18] However, the organizations and the community at large remain without significant resources, including the fact that successful Roma tend to sever their links with the community.[19] It was this dire situation that led Biró and his staff at Autonómia to focus on programs to alleviate the Roma's situation.

Autonómia provides grants and interest-free loans to grassroots Roma organizations. Since its resources are limited, Autonómia's board defined geographic priority areas. These include three border regions with large Roma populations and high rates of unemployment. In the first five years, Autonómia financed some two hundred projects, totaling approximately $500,000. Of these, 80 percent were agricultural endeavors and 20 percent, industrial.[20]

In the early stages, Autonómia provided interest-free loans to Roma organizations. However, due to deficient monitoring, the rate of repayment was low, and Autonómia was forced to rethink its strategy. Currently, Autonómia offers assistance for two types of projects: survival and development. Survival projects are initiated in communities where there are no material or human resources upon which to build an entrepreneurial project. They take the form of grants and loans aimed at providing for the survival of the individual or family. Development projects, on the other hand, are loans given to unemployed Roma who have work experience, housing resources, and some practice in household farming. The aim of these projects is to help the Roma use their skills in the interest of their community. Autonómia's preference is for development projects; as such, the survival projects serve as a bridge until the organization or community has matured sufficiently to support community-oriented development.

Autonómia's internal evaluation suggests that the loans granted to development projects have been more successful than those given in Autonómia's early years for two reasons. First, the projects are better prepared in that only organizations possessing the resources for a development project are candidates. Secondly, Autonómia has put into place an extensive monitoring program. Monitors are chosen from the Roma community and are trained by Autonómia to pay particular attention to economic feasibility and the development of democratic values and practices. The monitors build mutual trust with groups submitting proposal, and throughout the planning stages of a project encourage the members of the Roma organization to make strategic decisions themselves.[21] Despite this monitoring system, repayment rates remained low: in 1994 only $22,138—2.5 percent of the 1994 budget—was repaid. However, by emphasizing the preparation for as well as the monitoring of loan projects, the repayment rate increased to nearly 50 percent by 1995.[22]

Autonómia has recently expanded the range of its projects. In June of 1994, Autonómia introduced a new project aimed specifically at training entrepreneurs. An eighteen-month program funded by Mellon, the Roma Entrepreneurs Training Project, offers intensive training for Roma leaders to become for-profit and nonprofit organization managers. As of the end of 1995, 30 percent of the program's former students had established their own ventures.[23]

In 1994, Autonómia also began a legal defense trust. The trust supplies legal defense in the face of ethnic discrimination. If imitation is the sincerest form of flattery, the fact that another Roma organization has created its own legal defense fund suggests that Autonómia has pioneered a useful program for the Roma community. In addition, in an example of how private funds can be leveraged to attract public funds, Autonómia—given its successful experiences working with the Roma— was asked to administer the Regional Roma Programme (EUROMA) financed by the EU. The EUROMA program provides training, legal advice, and communication services to Roma self-help organizations in Bulgaria, Hungary, Romania, and Slovakia. Autonómia has also been contracted to provide technical assistance to the Phare Democracy Programme's microproject scheme.

Autonómia has thus been able to highlight its comparative advantages, focusing on the plight of the Roma in Hungarian, and now in Eastern European, society. This decision to focus its activities has enabled Autonómia to work where it is most able and to expand its programs geographically. The EU's confidence that Autonómia can effectively extend its programs into other Eastern European countries is the best reflection of Autonómia's success.

Another symbol of its achievements is the fact that Autonómia and its director, András Biró, were awarded the 1995 Right Livelihood Award (sometimes called the alternative Nobel Prize). This is not to say that Autonómia has not had difficulties or that the road ahead is clear of all obstacles. However, Autonómia has flourished and remained independent, and, despite the lack of attention given to the Roma by the Hungarian population, has even begun to attract local funding. This includes in 1995 the establishment of a national foundation for the Roma chaired by Biró with an annual budget of $1 million. The reasons behind Autonómia's success are fourfold: (1) it had at its helm a charismatic and devoted leader with a clear vision, (2) its structures and staff are indigenous, (3) its mode of program implementation reinforces its mission, and (4) it has been able to attract institutional and long-term support from Western and now local donors.[24]

Biró has been a vital factor in the development of Autonómia. His background and contacts were its main assets at the time of its establishment. Biró's Hungarian citizenship enabled him to appeal to the community, forging relationships with local authorities that would eventually turn into local funding. His thirty years of experience abroad gave

Autonómia the necessary networks to attract significant donations from Western organizations. In addition, Bíró had a clear vision of the type of organization he wished to establish and set definite, obtainable goals. His energy and devotion have been a consistent source of inspiration for Autonómia. Although in the fall of 1995 Bíró retired from his position as executive director, he remains closely connected with Autonómia as a consultant.[25]

Part of Bíró's vision was to create an independent foundation with an indigenous board and staff. This vision coincided well with foundations interested in strengthening independent institutions as part of the essential fabric of civil society.[26] Only two of Autonómia's eight board members are non-Hungarians; one of these is Willem H. Welling from the Netherlands, who was placed on the board at the urging of a foundation.

Autonómia's staff is comprised entirely of Hungarians. In mid-1994, the staff consisted of the executive director, three program officers, a project assistant specifically for the Mellon's Roma Entrepreneurial Training Project, a part-time accountant, and a lawyer on retainer. One of these staff members is a Roma. The indigenous nature of the staff and board provides Autonómia with an inside track with local authorities and community leaders. The staff also brings a deeper understanding of the community and the groups with which they work than could any number of foreign "experts." The board and staff also provide a firm foundation for Autonómia's sustainability: it has put down roots that will hold fast with or without the sponsorship of Western donors.

Another reason for Autonómia's success is that its activities are adapted to the local situation. A case in point is the monitoring system created for Autonómia's development projects. The mechanism was based on the specific situation in the Roma communities that was hindering loan repayment. More importantly, Autonómia's programs are structured to ensure that the means of grant or loan making serve the goals of the foundation. Since empowerment of the Roma community is of utmost importance, Autonómia creates relationships with community leaders based on equality. All development projects are loans and thus are contractual in nature; even survival projects are "charity" only as a step toward the creation of a base for development projects. Autonómia also ensures that there is extensive local participation and that the grantee is not a passive recipient. The project must be initiated, the problems identified, and the solutions implemented by the Roma organizations themselves. In this way Autonómia is alleviating poverty and discrimination in a manner that empowers the community and thus undermines the feudal hierarchy still present in many villages.

Another aspect of the use of loans rather than grants is that Autonómia can recycle some portion of its investment into future activities. This is a small but important step toward financial sustainability. Although loan repayments will not sustain the organization, the recycling of resources suggests to potential funders that Autonómia has the financial savvy necessary in a prospective partner and to be sustainable.

Despite its attempts to recycle resources, Autonómia must obtain other sources of funding. To date it has developed a remarkably broad funding base. By 1994, their supporters included the German Marshall Fund of the United States (GMF), RBF, Ford, Mott, Sasakawa, SFH, the Freudenberg Stiftung, the Open Society Institute (OSI), and the Dutch Embassy.[27]

Unlike many other struggling organizations in Central Europe, Autonómia has been able to wrest long-term grants and donations for administrative costs from Western donors. From its inception, Autonómia has received core cost financing that supports its basic operations from its donors, enabling it to conduct its programs without significant restrictions. In 1994, several Western donors agreed to support the organization for the next two to three years. Funders also agreed to a onetime donation that would be used to create a reserve fund.[28] Autonómia has also been unique in its ability to find local donors. After four years of disappointing fund-raising, including partnerships that failed due to the restrictions that would have been placed on the organization, local sources have stepped forward with donations. In 1995, SFH granted Autonómia $37,000 and the National Employment Fund, a governmental body, contributed $82,000.[29] Much of this fund-raising success has to be attributed to the confidence that foundations and other funders have in Biró.

In the face of apathy in Hungarian power structures and society toward the Roma, Autonómia's accomplishments in attracting local and Western funding and in remaining stable and viable are impressive. In addition, the fact that Autonómia is run in an open and democratic fashion and consciously seeks to engage and empower the people it serves is also noteworthy. Thus, it is an example of how an organization's operations can reinforce its basic goal—strengthening the Roma community.

Featured Projects

In addition to Autonómia, a number of other independent organizations have been active on human rights and other legal issues in Hungary. Among these are the Democracy after Communism Foundation (DAC) and the Foundation of Women of Hungary (MONA). Founded by the Laszlo Rajk College at the Budapest University of Economic Sciences, the Istvan Bibo College of Law at the Eötvös Lorand University in Budapest, and the Federation of Young Democrats, DAC is involved in a variety of educational initiatives on law, politics, and economics. DAC has a strong regional focus and has been supported by the SFH, GMF, Ford, and others. With support from the Westminster Foundation, MONA organized a number of meetings between women's groups and parliamentarians, local government officials, and leaders of the business and academic worlds to enhance awareness about women's issues in Hungary.

Besides work in human rights, foundations have been active in Hungary's education sector in each of the first three phases of assistance. There are a number of important educational projects initiated with foundation support. After CEU, which represents the largest single foundation investment in Central Europe and will be considered in chapter 7, one of the most important projects is the Collegium Budapest (Collegium). The Collegium was created by a consortium of European public and private funders and Hungarian institutions of higher education. It seeks to bridge the East-West divide through scholarly exchange and has attracted an outstanding group of scholars.[30] The European foundations supporting the Collegium include FritzThyssen Stiftung, Volkswagen, Daimler Benz Fonds, Stifterverband für die Deutsche Wissenschaft, Boehringer Ingelheim Fonds, Zuger Fonds, Landis and Gyr, Stiftelsen Riksbankens, Jubileumsfond, and Doen Stichting (the Netherlands Lottery).

In addition, the Collegium receives public funds from governments in Germany, France, Switzerland, Austria, and the Netherlands. Directed by an international board of trustees, the Collegium has its own Hungarian foundation that will be completely autonomous after a short period of joint administration with the Ernst Reuter Foundation. Each year the Collegium selects up to twenty scholars who conduct research organized around certain focal themes drawn from the humanities, the social sciences, and the natural sciences. The Collegium's supporters hope that it will develop into an institute of advanced studies comparable in stature to those in Berlin, Princeton, and Stanford, upon which it is loosely modeled.[31]

One of the more interesting foundation-sponsored projects in Hungary is the National Széchényi Library Consortium, involving some ten university, college, and municipal libraries. This consortium improved operations by introducing better computers, printers, and copying equipment (with support from Mellon) to enhance their patrons' access to information. Recognizing that citizens require access to information to exercise their civic responsibilities, this project has had important democratizing effects.[32] It also has been successfully replicated and appears sustainable, two important measures of success.

Business education is another field that received substantial support, especially during the first phase of assistance to Hungary. Foundations, especially those from the United States, perceived a need for business education in the economic transition.[33] Recognizing that the United States has a comparative advantage in business education, a number of U.S. foundations were instrumental in the establishment of the International Management Center (IMC) in Budapest, which also received AID support.

IMC, the first Western-style business school in Central Europe, was a joint venture between various commercial entities and private foundations. Key partners in this venture were the Hungarian Chamber of Commerce, the Hungarian Credit Bank, Szensore Consulting Commerce, the San Paolo Bank, and the Milan Chamber of Commerce. Private support has been provided by SFH, RBF, Ford, and Mellon. To fulfill its objective of enhancing business management in Hungary, IMC offers a variety of courses for different populations, ranging from young to midlevel to senior managers.

Investments in business education by foundations seemed justified during the first phase of assistance. However, within a relatively short period the large international financial institutions and bilateral assistance programs, especially from the United States and Germany, began to provide significant resources to business education. In addition, as large multinational corporations, such as General Electric, made major investments in Hungary, their own business training programs became increasingly important. Thus, during the second and third phases of assistance foundations were justified in shifting their resources away from business education towards other more pressing needs.

In Hungary, foundations have also supported with increasing salience during the third phase of assistance a variety of civic educational activities. For example, the Westminster Foundation provided funds for voter education before the May 1994 elections, and NED provided funds to develop curricular material on democracy for secondary school use. As part of this curriculum development effort, NED also supported training teachers in these new curricular materials.

Similar to the other Central European countries, foundations have supported the development of the NGO sector in Hungary from the first phase of assistance. For example, Mott and RBF helped establish NITCF in Budapest. NITCF is part of a cooperative network of information-gathering and training centers, like ICN in the Czech Republic (discussed in the previous chapter). NITCF gathers data on the NGO sector, provides management advice, and offers training, as well as advocating stronger legislative support for the sector. In addition, to help counteract some of the negative images associated with the sector NITCF is working to develop a code of ethics. NITCF has had some success in achieving these goals and promoting the development of a more vigorous NGO sector; however, it cannot be said that it has had a determinative role in these developments.

Results

In Hungary, as elsewhere in Central Europe, foundations have supported a variety of training and exchange programs. For the most part, these programs have provided participants with new skills and, perhaps more importantly, linked them up with individuals involved with comparable issues. Programs that targeted the younger generation, such as the National Forum Foundation's internship program and the Hoover Institution's Diplomat Training Program, appear to have been successful.[34] Although both of these were regional programs, in the first phase of assistance they targeted Hungary and the other Central European countries.

On the institutional level, there is a fair amount of evidence that foundations have had some impact. For example, foundation support has been critical to the establishment of a number of independent educational and nonprofit organizations, such as Autonómia, DAC, IMC, and NITCF. Although these are small institutions whose resources cannot compete with those of a still highly centralized state, these independent institutions, along with others, have a role in opening Hungarian society. They help contribute to an important and necessary process of pluralization. Without foundation support, these organizations would not have developed as quickly, if at all.

Without the initial support of foundations, it is unlikely that either the IMC or the Collegium would have been established. Although it is possible to argue that investment in business education is a relatively low priority—especially given the prospect for funding from the private sector—foundation support for business education appeared to be an appropriate early contribution to economic reform. However, as economic reform gained momentum, foundations' priorities rightly shifted toward other areas.

Similarly, the Collegium could be criticized as an enterprise that merely benefits elites at a high cost per participant without having any discernible impact on society. Nevertheless, if the Collegium realizes its ambition of being a major intellectual center linking East and West, it could help lead Hungary back to a greater role in Europe. Thus, the Collegium would be a suitable investment. The support the Collegium has received from a diverse range of Western European funders suggests that there is considerable interest in building an intellectual bridge between East and West and that it is likely to be sustainable.

Besides education, foundations have played an important role in the area of civil rights (broadly defined). In support for the Roma and women's issues in Hungary, foundations have had some impact. It is not an overstatement to say that without the support provided by foundations the concerns of the Roma and Hungarian women would not be addressed to the degree they are now.[35] This is not to suggest that Hungarian society is adequately addressing women's or Roma issues, but what attention these issues are receiving can be attributed to organizations that have, in the main part, been assisted by foundations.

Foundations have also played a relatively large direct and indirect role in the development of Hungary's NGO sector. Although this sector has grown dramatically, it must still be considered fledgling, since so few constituent institutions are self-sustaining at this time. Directly, the foundations have supported training opportunities for many of the leaders of the sector, such as Miklós Marschall, who is now the leader of Civicus: World Alliance for Citizen Participation. Foundations have also been instrumental in the establishment of organizations designed to advance the sector's interests, including NITCF. Indirectly, virtually all foundation support has been for independent institutions, which taken together, helps strengthen the NGO sector. Although this is an area where public funders—such as Phare and AID—are becoming increasingly engaged, foundations, given their backgrounds and experiences, have made a discernible contribution.

On the societal level, foundations have yet to have much impact in Hungary other than through encouraging individuals who have raised important issues, such as concerns about women and the Roma, and helping to strengthen independent institutions. They may, however, have helped reinforce the sentiment that Hungary belongs firmly in Europe.

There is one other result that is worth mentioning and that has implications beyond Hungary. Since Hungary began traveling the path toward reform long before its Central European neighbors, it was an arena where foundations could and did obtain valuable experience before becoming active elsewhere. This was especially true for George Soros, but it was also true to a lesser extent for a number of the other foundations, such as Mellon and PCT. The experiences George Soros gained after establishing the SFH in 1984 helped him develop a much sharper vision for the possibilities associated with foundation activities in societies in transition. In addition, the experience of the SFH provided a number of useful insights regarding structures, sectors, and the relationship with the state that would be applied to virtually every other country in the region. Given the prominence of Soros's role throughout the region after 1989, the importance of SFH's experience and the lessons learned in Hungary cannot be underestimated. This role is examined in more detail in chapter 7.

4

Poland:
First among Equals

*B*iologists tell us that all the cells in our bodies are changed approximately every seven years. Politically, Poland has experienced comparable changes in its body politic. Less than seven years after the Workers' Defense Committee (KOR) was established on behalf of a modest number of beleaguered workers and intellectuals, it grew into Solidarity, a world renowned mass movement that so threatened the government that martial law was imposed. Then, slightly more than seven years after the imposition of martial law, Solidarity leaders engaged in the Roundtable Talks with the man responsible for martial law and negotiated terms for the first relatively free elections in the Soviet bloc—elections that would result in a Catholic as prime minister and, shortly afterwards, a shipyard electrician (the leader of Solidarity) as president. Even more remarkable is that less than seven years after the epoch-making Roundtable Talks, Poland would have former Communists serving as both prime minister and president, the latter having defeated Lech Walesa, the Solidarity hero from Gdańsk.

The dizzying speed of these changes suggest some of the complexities associated with both the process of democratization in Poland and the forces influencing that process.[1] Despite this complexity, Poland has made significant and objectively assessable progress on the road toward market democracy. These accomplishments include considerable progress in economic reform (table 3). The Polish economy is credited with being the healthiest in Central Europe and one of the fastest growing in Europe, with annual GNP growth over 6 percent in 1995. Inflation, while still high, is declining, as is unemployment. The Deutsche Bank has compared Poland favorably with the rapidly growing "Asian tiger" economies such as Korea, Taiwan, and Singapore.[2]

On the political side, although the government has changed every year since 1990, there has been a fair amount of continuity in policy since the first post-Communist government under Prime Minister Tadeusz Mazowiecki. Poland has experienced at least two rounds of democratic elections at the national and local levels. Although many people are disappointed with the results of these elections, few contest that these elections have been free and fair.

Unlike its three Central European neighbors, Poland opted for a presidential parliamentary system. The country operates under the so-called small constitution, a constitutional law regarding the relations between legislative and executive branches that left many remnants of the 1952 Stalinist constitution intact.[3] Lacking a new constitution (the seventh draft is underway and its prospects for acceptance are uncertain), there is considerable ambiguity about the precise division of responsibilities between the president and the Parliament.[4] Unfortunately, this constitutional ambiguity has created some instability at the heart of Polish government in ways that have not always been supportive of democratic development.

On a more positive note, Poland is considerably more pluralistic than it was in 1989, although given the strong role of the church and Solidarity, Poland was the most pluralistic country in Central Europe before then. There is growing evidence of a multiparty democracy, with an estimated two hundred fifty parties involving approximately four hundred thousand members. Although not all of these parties have representatives in Parliament or contribute to effective governance, this large number of parties suggests considerable diversity in views. Perhaps the most singular development in this regard is the rapid increase in the number of NGOs. There are now more than twenty thousand registered NGOs, more than triple the number in 1991. Within this number there are a large variety of business and farmers' associations, free trade unions, civic associations, and social organizations.[5] Also noteworthy is the fact that both the church and Solidarity have dramatically less influence than they had before 1989.

In other important ways Poland has made less-than-hoped-for progress on the road to democracy. Although the Defense Ministry is led by

TABLE 3 Poland, Major Economic Indicators, 1989–1994

	1989	1990	1991	1992	1993	1994
Per capita GDP (in 1990 U.S. dollars)	4,821	4,376	4,060	4,150	4,300	4,500
Growth rate of GDP (in percents)	0.2	−11.6	−7.0	2.6	3.8	5.0
Average change in consumer prices (in percents)	251.0	586.0	70.3	43.0	35.0	32.0
Unemployment rate	n/a	6.3	11.8	13.6	16.4	16.0

Source: PlanEcon, *PlanEcon Review and Outlook for Eastern Europe,* June 1995

civilians, they do not yet control the military effectively. A succession of defense ministers, appointed by the president under the terms of the small constitution, have generally been unsuccessful in reigning in the army generals who basically ran Poland during the 1980s.[6]

The judiciary is another area where change has been slower than expected. Legal and penal code reform were introduced in 1990. Under these reforms, the prosecutor general's office was abolished, and a system of misdemeanor and appeals courts was placed under the jurisdiction of the Justice Ministry. Although the relationships between and among these levels of the judiciary are still somewhat murky, judges, many of whom remain from the Communist era, tend to act independently. However, following the election of President Aleksander Kwasniewski in November 1995 there were troubling reports that two prosecutors were fired for overzealous investigations into the finances and educational history of the president-elect.[7]

As is true with the other Central European countries, the media are dramatically more independent now than they were in 1989. The emerging pattern, however, is much more typical of Europe than of the United States. The print media are mainly privatized, with many newspapers owned, at least in part, by foreigners. The electronic media, except on the local level, tend to be state owned.[8] The public television station (TVP) was made into a shareholder company in 1993, but the Treasury is the only shareholder, giving the minister of finance power to dismiss the board if displeased with the fiscal-year audit. TVP is regulated by the politicized National Broadcast Council created in December 1992. Until June of 1995, when the Parliament revoked his power to appoint the chair of the council, Walesa had used that power to alter the balance on the council. The structure of the National Broadcast Council now generally makes it difficult for the president to exert political pressure; the majority of the council's members must now be won over.

Although freedom of the press is somewhat limited by laws against programs that offend morals or religion or disclose state secrets, annual surveys on the state of press freedom declare that the Polish media have been independent and free since 1990 when the State Censorship Office was closed.[9] However, the resignation in March 1996 of the president in response to the replacement of the director of TVP by a political appointee bodes ill for future independence of the television media. Alternatives to TVP do exist, however, with two million Poles having access to cable television and almost one million to satellite television.[10]

On the personal level, changes have been very dramatic. Travel, both nationally and internationally, is not restricted. Long lines for basic commodities were eliminated virtually overnight with the implementation on 1 January 1990 of the Balcerowicz reforms to liberalize the Polish economy. Unlike past practice, citizenship is rarely revoked. In anticipation of joining the EU, Poland abolished visa requirements in 1992 for citizens of any European country, allowing for freer movement into and out of Poland. Besides greater freedom to travel, Poles now enjoy unfettered access to information. Access to international information networks and sources, such as the Internet and Western news reports, has expanded dramatically. Although difficult to quantify precisely, the fact that Poles can travel freely and have easy access to information has important consequences for the democratization process in Poland.

As the foregoing suggests, Poland's record regarding the formal institutions and processes of democracy is mixed and not unlike those of its neighbors. Progress has been made, but it has not always been linear. There have been setbacks, such as persistent and destabilizing bickering between the president and the Parliament, as well as the church's excessive intrusion into Poland's political life.

The record regarding the development of democratic processes, however, is quite good, especially related to the most obvious process—elections. There have been successive rounds of free and fair elections airing intensely competitive divergent views on Poland's best path toward the future. There is also considerable evidence of competition among ideas and groups outside of the electoral process. Such competition is essential for democratic development and a change from the more monopolistic patterns of the past.[11]

The record regarding the development of democratic values, however, is more difficult to discern and must necessarily be impressionistic. Democracies are characterized by their respect for political and civil rights, even if there are few examples that live up to this standard perfectly. After some anti-Semitic incidents in the early 1990s, Poland seems to have become increasingly tolerant. That is not to say that anti-Semitism or other forms of intolerance have been eliminated, but intolerance does seem at least to be submerged if not actually diminished.

Poles, again much like their neighbors, have had considerable difficulty in shaking off some of the more pernicious legacies of the past. Under Communism, distrust of those outside the family and a close circle of friends was endemic.[12] While the patterns of Polish citizens' economic, social, and civic engagements are clearly expanding in important new ways, there is still little evidence that Poles have developed the kind of trust in each other and in their institutions that is increasingly considered essential to democratic development.[13]

External Involvement

Poland has been the principal Central European beneficiary of Western attention. After Solidarity dramatically wrested authority from the Communist government in 1989, Poland received nearly half of all the commitments provided by the Group of Twenty-Four Industrialized Countries (G-24) between January 1990 and December 1993.[14] A significant portion of this assistance involved debt relief, so its effects are not easily discernible. As suggested earlier, it is important to distinguish between commitments and actual disbursements and to recognize the form of assistance—whether it be as grants, loans, or debt relief. Although much of these commitments involved debt relief and loans, they were nevertheless substantial and reflected serious Western attention to Poland.

Western attention resulted for a variety of geographic, demographic, historical, and economic reasons. Among these are the fact that Poland is the largest of the Central European countries. Its 1994 population of 38.4 million is roughly one-and-a-half times the population of the other three Central European countries combined. Another reason is that Poland is the crossroads of Europe. Much of Poland's history has been written because of its geography. The country has been vulnerable to the voracious ambitions of great empires to the West, East, and South— the German, Russian, and Hapsburg empires, respectively. In addition, as table 3 (p. 44) makes clear, Poland had a significantly lower GDP than the other Central European countries, and thus there was a more compelling need.

Poland has also benefited from the fact that it is widely credited with being at the vanguard of change in Central Europe, both in terms of Solidarity's role in the transition from communism and in the enthusiasm with which it undertook reform. This enthusiasm is exemplified by the Balcerowicz reforms, which were implemented to considerable applause and worldwide attention. The international community also accepted the importance of the demonstration effect: that is, Poland's succeess in moving to a market democracy could positively influence its neighbors both in Central Europe and farther east.

In addition, Poland, perhaps more than any other Central European country, has strong ties to Western Europe and North America. There are large and influential Polish communities in France, England, and the United States, among other places. Poles often remind American visitors that Chicago is the second largest Polish city in the world. These émigré communities, including many dissidents who were forced to emigrate after the protests and demonstrations in 1968, provide an important bridge to the West. These links have been critical throughout Poland's recent history, especially during the Solidarity years, the era of martial law, and the immediate post-Communist period.

Poland's links abroad and its vanguard role are major explanations for the seemingly disproportionate attention that Poland has received from the international community, especially from international financial institutions and the United States. For example, Poland received 16,871.7 million ECUs, or 49.2 percent, of all commitments from the G-24, 2,826.6 million ECUs, or 59.7 percent, of all commitments from the Bank, and 2,346.8 million ECUs, or 45.2 percent, of all commitments from the IMF.[15] After counting in the commitments made to regional projects from which Poland benefitted no other Central European country has received anything close to the level of commitment Poland has gotten.

In its first five years, Phare provided 4,248.5 million ECUs to fourteen countries in Eastern and Central Europe involved in the transition toward a market democracy. Poland received a significant, but proportionate, percentage of these resources: the EU obligated 1,024 million ECUs, or 24.1 percent, to Poland. Of the other Central European countries, Hungary received 377 million ECUs, the Czech Republic 233 million ECUs, and Slovakia 80 million ECUs.[16]

The U.S. bilateral assistance program, administered through AID, provided a relatively large share of its resources to Poland. From 1990 to 1994, AID obligated $722.3 million, or 40.2 percent, of its SEED resources to Poland.[17] Perhaps this is a reflection of the fact that at the time a well-known Polish-American from Chicago was chairman of the powerful Ways and Means Committee of the House of Representatives, but no other country received a comparable amount of attention from the U.S. government.

Poland also figured prominently in the activities of foundations, although the foundation response appears to have been more balanced than that of the international and bilateral donors. Virtually every foundation active in Central Europe was involved in Poland. It received approximately 20 percent of the foundation resources provided to Central Europe. Given the geography of the region, it is not surprising that the German foundations played a very large role in Poland in terms of financial resources provided. Of the German foundations, Humboldt and the Bosch Stiftung (Bosch), which placed particular importance on education and exchange, played some of the largest roles of any foundation. They provided 18.1 million and 10 million, respectively.[18] Another noteworthy project is the extensive support for Polish students to attend German universities provided by the Haniel Stiftung, also reflecting links between Poland and Germany. In fact, one-third of all the places at the European University Viadrina are reserved for Polish students with Haniel Stiftung support.

Besides these German foundations, Mellon made major commitments in Poland, especially for the development of libraries and higher education, and Ford was instrumental in establishing an important research institution and underwriting an influential summer school on economics and foreign policy. The Soros foundations made one of the most important grants in 1988 for the establishment of an independent Polish foundation, the Stefan Batory Foundation (Batory). This will be discussed in greater detail in chapter 7. In addition, Ebert and the Free Trade Union Institute (FTUI) provided important assistance to fledgling independent trade unions in Poland. In fact, FTUI provided extensive support to Solidarity throughout the 1980s, although it is sometimes criticized for working with specific unions rather than working to developing a supportive framework for trade unions.[19]

Local Government

Local government is another area where foundations have had considerable involvement. The Foundation in Support of Local Democracy (FSLD) is one organization involved with local government that has been deeply engaged with foreign foundations from the first phase of their efforts to assist Poland.[20]

Established in September 1989, FSLD is an independent, nonpartisan, NGO that seeks to provide support to local government. FSLD's particular aim is to promote the ideals of civic self-governance as the basis for democracy. At the time of its establishment, the founders, including Jerzy Regulski, Andrzej Celinski, Aleksander Paszynski, Walerian Panko, and Jerzy Stepien, were former members of the Lech Walesa Civic Committee and comprised an influential segment of the democratic opposition. Many of these individuals held high-level positions in a variety of the post-Communist governments. For example, Jerzy Regulski served twice as plenipotentiairy for Local Government and subsequently as Polish Ambassador to the Council of Europe.

FSLD is governed by the Council of Founders, which provides overall guidance. This council is assisted by the board of management, which oversees FSLD's administration and program direction overall. The council of founders, in turn, is assisted by the council of directors. The latter entity involves directors of the affiliated regional training centers and colleges of local government and public administration. This organizational structure is complicated and somewhat problematic, since there is overlapping jurisdiction without clear lines of authority.

This structure also suggests a problem common to many independent organizations in Poland and other parts of Central Europe. That is, although many of their programs are quite successful, their organizational structure and administrative arrangements are not very sophisticated. One explanation for this lopsided development is that much of the external assistance was devoted to program development, and relatively scant attention was paid to governance and management issues.

Organizationally, FSLD is comprised of sixteen regional training centers (in Białystok, Częstochowa, Gdańsk, Jelenia Góra, Katowice, Kielce, Kraków, Lódź, Lublin, Olsztyn, Opole, Poznań, Rzeszów, Szczecin, Warsaw, and Wrocław) and five colleges of local government and public administration (Białystok, Kielce, Lódź, Olsztyn, and Szczecin). Two of these regional training centers, Lódź and Szczecin, are now accredited by the Ministry of Education and other professional certification. In addition, and rare for an independent Polish organization, FSLD maintains a permanent office overseas, at Rutgers University in New Jersey, headed by Professor Joanna Regulska, daughter of FSLD's founding chairman.

Regulska plays an invaluable bridging role, representing the interests of FSLD to potential and current Western funders as well as providing technical expertise to FSLD on programming and management. Born and brought up in Poland, Regulska is an example of a Polish émigré with strong ties to her homeland who has been helpful in engaging others in Poland. She has done this by being an effective advocate in both the policy-making and funding communities for a grassroots organization with a democratically oriented approach. Regulska's approach contrasts with the top-down grant making that emphasizes economic structural adjustment and was typical of much of the first phase of activity by both public and private funders.

FSLD has generally had positive interactions with foundations. Reflecting this, it has received support from a diverse group of funders. FSLD's results have been greatly facilitated by its clear sense of mission, its board and staff leadership, and its ability to adapt organizational structures to local circumstances.[21]

The father-daughter combination of Regulski-Regulska is one of the main reasons why FSLD has been so successful in obtaining funding from diverse sources—public and private, European and North American. In 1994 alone, FSLD was funded by some six American foundations (or organizations providing funds obtained from American foundations), two German foundations, and the Fondation de France. FSLD also obtained impressive support from a variety of public sources. Its most important source is the EU, which provided some 45 percent of its budget. AID, the Norwegian government, as well as local U.S. and Polish government entities have also supported FSLD. In addition, FSLD has successfully marketed programs on a fee-for-service basis to selected customers. This represents an extremely impressive set of funders and bodes well for the organization's sustainability.

FSLD's principal programs revolve around enhancing the capacity of local government to respond effectively to citizens' concerns. Its essential mission involves training local government officials through its workshops and the technical assistance it provides, and the research, foreign scholarships, and internships it supports. FSLD's outreach is extremely comprehensive in that it has some form of contact with more than 90 percent of all Polish municipalities. By the end of its fifth year, 1995, 113,551 individuals had participated in its programs. Given its breadth of contacts and its basic mission of enhancing self-government, FSLD's activities are central to democratization.

In many ways, FSLD is an exemplary independent institution in post-Communist Central Europe. That is not to suggest that FSLD's experience has been problem free. In fact, given its founding committee's close identification with a particular segment of the democratic opposition, FSLD has at times had a problematic relationship with the state. In addition, the numbers and range of organizations involved in FSLD have created considerable management challenges, since not all of the affiliated institutes and colleges are of comparable quality. This has created some difficulties in FSLD's attempts to obtain certification from the Education Ministry. Developing effective communication and information sharing within FSLD, as well as with the municipalities, has been and continues to be a challenge.

Despite these challenge, FSLD has been exemplary in that it has a clear mission, indigenous leadership, and locally adapted structures with some local financing. In fact, most of the participants in its training programs pay fees. In addition, a number of for-profit organizations have developed to offer comparable training, suggesting that there is considerable demand for such services.[22]

In addition, FSLD has been successful in maintaining a clear sense of its mission and place in Polish society, which has prevented it from being enticed by funders into fields that may detract from its institutional capabilities. (Unfortunately, this is a common pitfall for organizations unduly influenced by foundations.)

FSLD's efforts were also greatly assisted by Regulska, who was instrumental in helping the many private foundations that had not had extensive involvement in Central Europe prior to 1989. The relative ease with which a foundation officer could communicate with Regulska in New Jersey cannot be underestimated as a contributory factor to positive funding decisions. In Poland, as in other countries, these bridging agents were especially important because of the paucity of independent institutions that could readily serve as foundation partners.[23]

Regulska's emphasis on reforming local government as a key strategy in democratization appeared to resonate with foundations that were seeking ways to complement their top-down programming with more local and grassroots activities.[24] Foundation support was augmented by public funds, and FSLD was asked to share its experiences in other parts of the region. These factors, plus the fact that others are emulating its activities, are clear measures of FSLD's success.

Featured Projects

Since more than thirty foundations have been active in Poland, a wide range of projects designed to aid democratization have been established. Perhaps the most important of these are educational, funded primarily by foundations to establish a set of independent institutions to foster the pluralism essential to democracy. These educational projects have received substantial sums throughout all three phases of assistance. For example, from 1989 to 1994 Humboldt provided approximately $16.3 million in support for scholarly exchanges.[25]

Besides the numerous educational exchange programs sponsored by Humboldt, Bosch, and the Soros foundations, one of the most important projects supported in Poland is Mellon's work with libraries. From 1990 through 1994, motivated by a longstanding interest in libraries, Mellon provided $6.5 million to automate the national library and a number of major university libraries, including those at Jagiellonian University, Warsaw University, and university consortia in Kraków, Lublin, Gdańsk, Poznan, Torun, and Wrocław.[26]

These Mellon projects are especially important because one of the quintessential features of democracy is citizen access to information. Under communism information was tightly guarded and centralized. Libraries did not offer easy access to patrons. Enhancing the ability of large numbers of individuals to gain access to information is essential to democratic development.

These library projects are also important because they were not all located in Warsaw but rather were dispersed throughout the country. Thus, as with FSLD projects, they contributed to decentralization, in contrast to the pattern that predominated under the Communist regime. In addition, Mellon was the first funder significantly involved in these types of projects, although its investments eventually attracted support from other foundations, most notably the Volkswagen Stiftung and the Soros foundations.

In this regard, Mellon's work, guided by Professor Richard Quandt, sets a standard for foundations. Mellon identified a critical area where relevant experience could strengthen an essential institution. Furthermore, the foundation paved the way for other funders. Foundations often suggest that identifying a problem, recognizing a comparative advantage, building sustainable institutions, and performing a catalytic role are key characteristics of good grant making. Mellon's work with libraries in Poland and other parts of Central Europe is a rare case in which all of these characteristics coincide.

Besides this project, a number of other important initiatives from foundations have established or bolstered new institutions. One such initiative is the Fondation de France's provision of seed capital to create the Fondation de Pologne in 1990. Founded by Charles de Gaulle and his cultural minister, André Malraux, the Fondation de France serves as a fund-raising and umbrella grant-making community foundation. Its Polish counterpart has a joint French and Polish board and supports work in local development, social action, education, and the arts. In addition, the Fondation de France established the Polish Foundations Centre, which shares premises with the Fondation de Pologne, as an information resource on the emerging Polish NGO sector.[27] Developing a local organization to tap into Polish resources for purposes the local community deems worthy is an important step.

Recognizing that the Communist Party's prior monopoly on much of public life was a common problem throughout Central Europe, a number of foundations have worked to extend and enhance public debate on important policy matters. One strategy involved developing or strengthening independent research institutions or think tanks. Many foundations regard thinks tanks as an important thread in the fabric of democratic society. These think tanks help raise previously muted voices regarding the choices that Polish society faces as well as spark discussions about the consequences of these choices.[28] One example of such foundation activity is Ford's instrumental role in supporting the Gdańsk Institute for Market Economics. This institute, cofounded by Poland's first minister of privatization, Janus Lewandowski—one of President Lech Walesa's original advisors from Gdansk—has influenced economic policy in Poland. It has developed an impressive list of European and North American sponsors, including corporations and foundations.[29] Another important Polish think tank is the Center for Social and Economic Research (CASE), established by former deputy prime minister Leszek Balcerowicz and his wife Ewa, which has also received significant support from foundations.

The German political foundations have also played an important role in extending public debate in Poland. By opening offices in Warsaw, publishing books by Polish authors, and sponsoring seminars on a variety of policy matters, they have enriched public debate. At times, they have provided a rare neutral arena for the venue of this debate.

Another institution that has benefited from involvement with foundations is the Foundation for Water Supply to Rural Areas (WSF). Founded in late 1987 under the aegis of the Catholic Church, WSF's twin objectives are to increase the water supply and to introduce appropriate sewer management methods to private farmers and households in rural communities. This project is one example in which private and public U.S. funders have cooperated well together. Much of WSF's initial support came from a $10 million grant from AID, which was supplemented by support from private foundations, such as Ford. With this external support WSF has financed more than 1,500 water-supply and sewage systems and brought water to more than 120,000 households. The impact of these projects on Polish rural communities goes far beyond access to cleaner water. WSF has also contributed to democratization by using an unprecedented participatory process through which to develop its projects. Through this project-development process rural citizens learn and hone civic skills that are essential to democracy.[30]

In other chapters it has been mentioned that despite their democratizing potential, many foundations, with some notable exceptions, were not especially active in supporting independent media as a means to help educate broad segments of the Central European population regarding democracy. Although the Polish experience is similar to that of its neighbors, there are a few noteworthy exceptions. For example, the International Media Fund (the Fund) established a journalism center in Warsaw to provide university-level and professional training. In addition, the Fund also underwrote the development of new journalism curricula in Kraków and sponsored a series of print and broadcast management workshops.[31] Besides these, PCT helped develop a television series called "Decisions," targeting young people that explored some of the dilemmas and trade-offs associated with a market democracy. Sasakawa developed a similar television series examining structures of market economies. Greater attention to using media to affect a broad segment of society may have been a useful investment for foundations.

Results

Foundations have had a modest impact on the recent democratization process in Poland. Their impact has most strongly affected young people, the capacity of local government, and the fledgling NGO sector. Because of this support there is a much greater plurality of voices within the emerging NGO sector and a much richer diversity of institutions espousing different points of view.

Foundation work in Poland, as in neighboring countries, was also not static. It evolved to meet the changing circumstances. While in the first phase it focused on economic adjustment and promoting institutional pluralism, by the third phase it focused on the development of the NGO sector. It is in this area that the foundations have made their most important contributions.

As noted previously, the results of democratizing projects can be gauged in three related ways: in terms of their effect on individuals, their effects on institutions, and their effect on society at large. The more than thirty foundations that have provided nearly $100 million in support of hundreds of projects in Poland have directly affected the lives of hundreds of thousands of Poles. These projects, with varying degrees of success, have exposed Poles to new ideas and approaches, as well as connecting a variety of individuals with common interests.

The projects that seem to have had the most significant effect, from the vantage point of five years after they began, involved investments in local government and the NGO sector, although investments in a variety of educational programs were also important. The Polish experience with foundations, like that of other Central European countries, seems to confirm that the most successful projects were those headed by local leaders with vision. These local leaders found ways to match foreign with local resources and then adapted programs and structures to respond to their own particular institutional mission.

As mentioned, FSLD has organized programs with more than 113,000 participants during its first five years of operations. What is especially significant about FSLD is that early on, before many other institutions, it realized the essential contribution of local government to democracy. This grassroots orientation contrasted with the top-down approach of many other institutions involved in assisting democracy.

By automating the national libraries and many of Poland's major university libraries, the Mellon, Volkswagen, and Soros foundations enhanced the access of many hundreds of thousands, if not millions, of Poles to information, which is critical for citizens in a democracy. This enhanced access for ordinary citizens, as well as university students and personnel, contrasts starkly with the Communist era when access to library resources was tightly regulated. Even in a country with a population of nearly forty million, programs affecting hundreds of thousands of people have to be considered significant.

Although there is less tangible evidence at this time, numerous foundation-supported educational exchange programs have affected the lives of tens of thousands of Poles. Especially noteworthy is the support for educational programs, sometimes in very modest amounts, provided by Batory. This support enabled thousands of young Poles, who would otherwise have been denied the experience, to acquire an education abroad. Evidence gathered in other contexts suggests that these educational opportunities have an important role in influencing the outlook, understanding, and aspirations of the participants. The effect of these programs will probably not be fully felt or even evaluated for many years to come.[32]

In addition to broader educational programs supported by Batory, most foundations have supported training programs of different sorts targeting specific audiences. For example, Humboldt and Bosch have provided significant resources for Polish scholars to receive advanced training at German Universities.

Although targeted training programs and educational exchange programs tend to affect a small, elite population, most participants suggest that these programs provide them with invaluable learning experiences. Thus, foundation-supported activities positively influenced their participants, even if the number of those participants was relatively small. After considerable initial enthusiasm for these programs (1989–1991), foundations began to shift their support to training programs *in situ*, given the high cost of foreign training and exchange programs.

Considerable evidence also suggests that foundation support has been important in developing or bolstering institutions central to democracy in Poland. For example, FTUI, the National Democratic Institute (NDI), Westminster, and the German party foundations provided important support to political parties in Poland, as well as generally enhancing the election process there.[33] Foundations also played a small, but important, role in providing training or technical assistance to improve the transparency, enhance the responsiveness, or strengthen the effectiveness of certain key institutions, such as the Parliament and the judiciary. Most of these efforts, however, were also supported by public funders such as the EU or AID, so foundations cannot garner all the credit for the positive results.

In the NGO sector, foundations have worked relatively effectively on infrastructural issues, such as providing technical assistance to draft appropriate legal frameworks for this sector, as well as developing infrastructural institutions that gather and share information on the sector's activities. One example is the work of KLON. Although KLON may eventually have developed on its own, it clearly would not have developed as quickly without the crucial and timely support of foundations, such as Ford and RBF.

Although Poland's institutional landscape under communism was richer and more complex than was its Central European neighbors' due to the prominent roles played by Solidarity and the Catholic Church, Poland now has an even richer institutional landscape. Many of the institutions that mediated between the state and society under communism, such as quasi-political associations and trade unions, are loosening their ties with the state and becoming more independent. This is not to say that these institutions are completely autonomous. But this trend towards greater independence is part of the development of a vigorous Polish NGO sector. Given how frequently Polish leaders suggest that foundations have had an important contributory role in these developments, there can be little argument about their importance.[34]

It is in the third area, the effect on society at large, that there is less evidence of foundations' work. Given the complexity of challenges associated with building a market democracy, that is entirely understandable. However, both the rhetoric of the foundations and the expectations of the Poles who were involved with them imply that by now, after more than six years of activity, there should be much greater evidence of societal impact. Not surprisingly, there is not a great deal at which to point on the broadest social level.

One area where there is some indication of the role of foundations is public discourse. Previously, there was little discussion of important policy matters. Foundation support for a variety of new institutions, such as think tanks, trade unions, and civic associations, must be considered a contributory factor to the growing richness in the quality of current discussion. With the help of Mellon and the Soros foundations, Polish citizens now have much greater access to information, which can help them become much more authoritative in articulating their concerns.

There is also ample evidence that a variety of new institutions are espousing different viewpoints on important policy matters and speaking out on a range of environmental, economic, and social matters. These voices are a means of encouraging government to be more responsive to its citizens.

5

Slovakia: Slipping Behind

*A*lthough recently Slovakia has experienced economic growth comparable to that of the Czech Republic, Hungary, and Poland, it has trodden the most problematic path of the four in developing a democratic society. Part of the reason for this has been that Slovakia, unlike the other Central European countries (but similar to the Newly Independent States of the Former Soviet Union [NIS]), has had to build new political institutions and strengthen its national identity simultaneously with undergoing the transition process. Frustration associated with the difficulty of combining state-building with the transition toward a market-oriented economy and a democratic society has resulted in the emergence of a populist political movement—the Movement for Democratic Slovakia (HZDS)—led by Vladimir Meciar.

Slovakia first appeared to slip from the path of democratic reform when Meciar assumed the prime ministership of the Slovak Republic in June 1992. Meciar, with his populistic nationalism, showed little tolerance for democratic practices, and his opponents were portrayed as enemies of Slovakia. Slovakia seemed to stray further from democracy when Meciar assumed the prime ministership of newly independent Slovakia on 1 January 1993 and again in 1994 after his return to office following a brief hiatus.[1] Over the past few years, Mr. Meciar's party and its coalition partners have pushed through a number of highly regressive policies.

The government seems to have worked systematically to eliminate independent voices in Slovak society, whether those voices emanate from the academic, the media, or NGO sector. The Meciar government closed a leading opposition newspaper, antagonized the large Hungarian minority (constituting 10.8

percent of the population), attempted to shut down independent higher educational institutions such as Trnava University, and generally sought to make it more difficult for Slovakia's fledgling NGO sector. It canceled major deals to privatize state enterprises or arranged that cronies of government members were positioned to benefit from these deals. The government called for constitutional changes that would upset the political order by dramatically tipping the balance of power away from the president and the judiciary towards the government. The Meciar government also expressed disdain for decisions of the Constitutional Court. All of these developments resulted in Slovakia receiving two highly critical diplomatic démarches from the EU and one from the United States. Both démarches were deeply resented by the Slovak government. These developments will, however, certainly complicate consideration of Slovakia's application to join the EU, submitted in June 1995.[2]

Slovakia's recent experiences contrast markedly with those of the Czech Republic. As a legacy of the 1968 Soviet invasion that crushed the short-lived attempt to establish "socialism with a human face" in Czechoslovakia, Czechs and Slovaks had less access to Western information and fewer opportunities to travel than their Central European neighbors. Given the repressive nature of the Czechoslovak regime, the opposition in Slovakia—led by Public against Violence and aligned with its better-known Czech counterpart, Civic Forum—was poorly organized and fragmented. During the Velvet Revolution, the world's eyes were more focused on Prague than Bratislava. This fueled a sense that Slovaks were second-class citizens in Czechoslovakia—a sentiment successfully manipulated by Meciar and an important factor in the Velvet Divorce that divided Czechoslovakia into the Czech Republic and Slovakia.

Despite setbacks to democratic development, Slovakia has made considerable economic progress (table 4). Like the other Central European countries, it was hard hit by the breakup of the Soviet trading bloc, Council for Mutual Economic Assistance (COMECON). PlanEcon reports show that the total trade flows between Slovakia and former COMECON countries went down by 11 percent between 1991 and 1992. However, as a full 25 percent of its trade in 1992 was with the Czech Republic, this understates the decline elsewhere.[3] Prior to 1989, the Slovak economy was dominated by three industries: weapons manufac-

TABLE 4 Slovakia, Major Economic Indicators, 1989–1994

	1989	1990	1991	1992	1993	1994
Per capita GDP (in 1990 U.S. dollars)	6,415	6,374	5,682	5,315	5,076	5,254
Growth rate of GDP (in percents)	−1.1	−2.5	−11.2	−6.1	−4.1	3.9
Average change in consumer prices (in percents)	1.4	10.5	56.0	10.3	23.2	10.1
Unemployment rate	n/a	1.5	11.8	10.4	14.4	13.8

Source: PlanEcon, *PlanEcon Review and Outlook for Eastern Europe,* June 1995

turing, production of semiprocessed goods, and lignite mining. Since these industries were not competitive in world markets, the Slovak economy declined precipitously after the introduction of liberalizing measures in 1990.

From 1990 to 1993, Slovakia's GDP dropped by more than 30 percent. During this same period, consumer prices increased by 97 percent, while unemployment soared to 42 percent. By 1994, however, the economy began to stabilize and inflation eased. A growing service sector helped to stimulate positive economic growth. Following small-scale privatization and one round of voucher privatization in 1995, slightly more than 50 percent of GDP was produced by the private sector. A reflection of lingering concerns about political developments in Slovakia, foreign direct investment lagged behind that of the other Central European countries. However, those investments that have been made, such as the opening of a Volkswagen plant and KMart store (which was later sold at a profit to generate revenue for its struggling parent company), are quite successful and have helped boost Slovak exports.[4] Despite some clouds on the horizon, the Slovak economy is one of the most dynamic in Central Europe.[6]

Slovakia's uneven economic reform has been a major factor contributing to the country's relative political insecurity. The Velvet Divorce, although it proceeded much more smoothly than expected, further complicated the difficult process of economic and political liberalization and stabilization. As mentioned above, Meciar took advantage of the unease felt by many Slovaks, especially the rural and the elderly, to push for separation and then to consolidate his control. Meciar, however, has not been completely successful in this endeavor, since he lost a vote of no confidence and was out of power for part of 1994.

Although a parliamentary form of government has been introduced in Slovakia, it appears hollow. The Slovak Parliament adopted a new constitution in September 1992 that on the surface is consistent with basic democratic principles. However, clear legislative enforcement mechanisms are lacking. Slovakia has the veneer of democratic arrangements and procedures, such as the three rounds of elections that have taken place since 1990, but the government's lack of tolerance for and harassment of the opposition belies its rhetorical commitment to democracy. All of this contributes to the citizenry's growing cynicism and apathy about democracy.

In Slovakia an intensely divided government exacerbates the sense of democracy's fragility. In fact, almost three quarters of the population thinks that "democracy in our country is fragile."[6] The prime minister appears in near-constant conflict with the president, Michael Kovac, a former ally who has demonstrated unexpected independence. At the prime minister's urging, the Parliament stripped the president of his power to appoint the director of the state intelligence agency and the chief of the armed forces, functions performed by the president in all the other Central European countries. Despite losing some presidential powers, Slovakia's president continues to resist Meciar's attempts to recentralize power in the prime minister's office. Without this surprisingly independent presidency and the Constitutional Court, which has resisted some of the prime minister's grabs for greater power, it is highly likely that Slovak democracy would be stillborn.

The sense of Slovakia's fragile democracy is heightened by the apparent growth of nationalist sentiment and the consequent growing discord between Slovak politicians and ethnic Hungarians. Two recent laws provide evidence of this discord and have raised considerable concern abroad. The first is the November 1995 passage of the language law, which limits the use of languages other than Slovak in schools, hospitals, the army, and the media. A related law, passed in April 1995, increased the influence of the Education Ministry over district education authorities, thereby making it possible to mandate the teaching of certain core subjects in the Slovak language.[7]

Despite this fragility, perhaps one of the most important recent political changes in Slovakia has been the development of an independent NGO sector. Since 1989, the number of registered independent civic associations—many of them supported by foreign foundations—has grown dramatically, increasing from virtually zero in 1989 to ninety-eight hundred by 1994.[8]

Despite this impressive growth, the NGO sector in Slovakia is under considerable pressure. Although the September 1992 constitution guarantees Slovak citizens freedom of expression, as well as rights of free assembly and association, there is no clear legislative framework supporting the application of these rights to the NGO sector. For example, the Slovak legislature has not yet defined *nongovernmental organization* although it has defined *association, foundation,* and *religious society.* Without appropriate definition NGOs are treated no differently from profit-making enterprises—a serious impediment to their development.

The NGO sector, especially through its involvement with foreign foundations, has come under considerable scrutiny from the government. For example, Ivan Lexa, the current head of the Slovak Information Service, in his annual report to the Parliament on 22 May 1996 stated that "a much more significant influence on life in Slovakia has come from various supranational and international institutions, foundations, foreign interest groups, and their lobbies. The SIS is monitoring their activities and evaluating the goals in which they are engaged here."[9]

Recent growth in the NGO sector is reflected in a series of conferences. In 1991, the first conference of Czech and Slovak NGOs was held in Stupava, Slovakia. Following the dissolution of Czechoslovakia and the creation of the independent Slovak Republic, Slovak NGOs continued to meet annually at what came to be called the Stupava Conference. This conference provides an opportunity for members of the NGO sector to exchange information about the state of the sector and to devise strategies for strengthening it.

In response to a number of attempts to restrict the NGO sector and the legal ambiguity surrounding this sector, representatives from a variety of NGOs established the Gremium of the Third Sector (Gremium). The Gremium is a unique entity in Central Europe. It was established by the Second Stupava Conference of Slovak NGOs in 1994 and is currently made up of seventeen individuals elected by representatives from Slovak NGOs chosen at their annual conference. The Gremium issues formal statements through its elected spokesperson. SAIA-SCTS provides administrative services to the Gremium.

Although it is not formally incorporated, the Gremium has the mission to promote cooperation within the NGO sector and to represent the sector in discussions with government and business. In particular, the Gremium seeks to obtain favorable legal and tax treatment for the NGO sector, as well as to inform effectively the general public about the sector's activities.

The Gremium has also been instrumental in responding to threats from the Meciar government. For example, when the Meciar government began what was perceived as a series of politically motivated audits of the most high-profile NGOs in Slovakia, the Gremium responded. It also spearheaded the Third Sector S.O.S. Campaign, which resisted highly restrictive legislation that would make it difficult for foundations, other than government-related foundations, to operate in Slovakia. This Gremium-led campaign mobilized the NGO sector in Slovakia and abroad. From January to June 1996, nearly 5,000 articles on civil society issues were published in the major newspapers and magazines in Slovakia. Of these, nearly 500 were directly related to the campaign. Critiques of the law were issued by domestic and foreign NGOs, international agencies, and representatives of foreign governments.[10] The law, after being returned to the Slovak Parliament for reconsideration, was approved 20 June 1996 without any changes. However, as a result of the campaign, the Slovak public was much better informed about the NGO sector and its contributions to Slovak society.[11]

The media is another area where Slovakia has evidenced problems in democratic development. Under the 1992 constitution, freedom of the press is guaranteed. However, this freedom has not been respected. The government has intimidated various journalists and sought to close papers affiliated with the opposition.

On a more positive note, there have been some changes in media ownership. As of 1995, there were two private national radio stations and numerous private cable stations. The television monopoly has also been broken up into one private station that broadcasts statewide and three regional stations.[12] However, there is still little alternative to Slovak

Television (STV), which is politically biased toward the Meciar government. With the appointment of Jozef Darmo as the head of STV in December 1994, a number of satirical programs were taken off the air. Furthermore, the news coverage on the state television station often ignores news that deals favorably with Meciar's opponents. In the election coverage of March and April 1995 representatives of the ruling coalition were given 273 minutes of air time on STV, while opposition representatives received only 16. Given this bias, Slovaks are turning in large numbers to the Prague-based station TV Nova, which receives the largest market share of all the stations broadcasting in Slovakia. With 48 percent of viewers subscribing to cable, Slovakians are also increasingly tuning in cable and satellite stations that offer international news and programming.

External Involvement

Slovakia has received less attention from the West than the other three Central European countries not because it only became independent on 1 January 1993, but also because it has the smallest population and the weakest commitment to reform.[13] Reflecting this, Slovakia received only 2.3 percent of total funds committed to Central Europe from international financial institutions, only 1.6 percent of total funds from the EU, and only some 2 percent of total funds from foundations.[14]

The great preponderance of AID assistance to Slovakia was directed at economic restructuring, involving $89 million, or 80 percent, of the $111 million obligated during the five-year period 1990–1994. Strengthening democratic institutions received the smallest percentage of funding, representing $4.1 million, or 4 percent, in the three areas where AID was active.[15]

Although foundations also devoted relatively less attention to the Slovak Republic than they did to the other Central European countries, this began to change after Slovakia became independent and its commitment to democracy began to slip. Since 1993, foundations have provided some $9 million to Slovakia. Foundation support was instrumental in the NGO, educational, and environmental sectors and was critical to a few key independent institutions, some of which are discussed below.

NGO Sector

As mentioned, foundation support has been critical to the development and continued existence of Slovakia's NGO sector. In part reflecting the fact that most foundations did not concentrate attention on Slovakia until after the Velvet Divorce, which occurred well into the third phase of assistance, their efforts tended to focus on NGO development and strengthening civil society. One example of this is the work foundations have done with SAIA-SCTS, one of Slovakia's leading NGOs. SAIA-SCTS, much like its Czech counterpart, ICN, is an independent institution seeking to support the development of the NGO sector and is funded, in significant part, by foreign foundations.

SAIA-SCTS is a nongovernmental, not-for-profit public service agency registered as an association of citizens. It was originally established in 1990 as a special program under the Ministry of Education, Youth, and Sport of the Slovak Republic by Pavol Demeš, then director of foreign relations of the ministry. Demeš was assisted by David Daniel, an American scholar of Slovak history, who served as the organization's director from its founding through 1995. SAIA-SCTS's original goal was to promote "the internationalization, democratization, and modernization of education and research in Slovakia."[16] In 1992, it was officially registered as an NGO. In 1993, it began an NGO training and information project. The rapid growth of the NGO sector in Slovakia and the range of its activities were reflected in the 1994 addition of Service Center for the Third Section to the organization's initial name.[17]

SAIA-SCTS maintains a database on more than sixteen hundred NGOs in Slovakia, trains NGO leaders, provides consultants to NGOs, and publishes the newsletter *Nonprofit* and a directory of Slovak NGOs. In addition, it publishes new or translated material related to the NGO sector and provides administrative support both to the Gremium and the Stupava Conference. Although initially SAIA-SCTS used foreign trainers and materials, since 1994 it has used domestic trainers and prepared materials specifically targeted to the needs of the Slovakian NGO sector.

SAIA-SCTS is a highly decentralized operation with activities in multiple sites. This is extremely important because it breaks with the centralized, capital city–dominant pattern of the past. It maintains offices in six cities—Banska Bystrica, Bratislava, Košice, Nitra, Poprad, and Žilina. SAIA-SCTS's board of directors is comprised exclusively of Slovaks who are active in education, the NGO sector, and business. Its program is directed by a three-member executive committee made up of a president, a director, and a director of academic programs.

SAIA-SCTS, in many ways, represents a common pattern for many new institutions in Central Europe. That is, despite nominal independence, SAIA-SCTS has close, and at times strained, ties to the government. Although SAIA-SCTS is not directly controlled by a ministry, the government initially provided an important percentage of its budget through SAIA-SCTS's administration of projects for the Education Ministry. The cancellation, on short notice, of SAIA-SCTS's major contract with the Education Ministry in the fall of 1995 presented a serious institutional challenge. In NGO sector circles there was considerable speculation over the reason for this cancellation. Many suspected that this contract was cancelled because Pavol Demeš, SAIA-SCTS's founder, currently serves as foreign-policy advisor to the president and thus is a bitter rival to Prime Minister Meciar. The cancellation of this contract may ultimately have the unintended consequence of helping SAIA-SCTS become more independent and self-sustaining.

SAIA-SCTS was able to weather the withdrawal of this major contract because it had developed a variety of other programs, some of which produce independent revenue. In addition, SAIA-SCTS receives support from a variety of foundations, including Ford, RBF, Mott, FCS, Sasakawa, and the Bratislava-based Foundation for the Support of Citizen Activity. SAIA-SCTS's leaders have repeatedly mentioned that foundation support has been critical to their continued existence, without which the Education Ministry's abrupt cancellation may have sounded its death knell.[18]

SAIA-SCTS, much like its counterpart NGO service organizations in the other Central European countries, is perceived as an important partner for many of the foundations active in Slovakia. These foundations view organizations such as SAIA-SCTS, with their information-gathering, advocacy, and training roles, as essential to the development of civil society. Thus, many foundations have made significant investments in SAIA-SCTS. Of course, not all foundations take this approach. Some, such as Mellon and PCT, prefer to invest in institutions that address particular issues rather than organizations that serve the NGO sector broadly. In Slovakia, perhaps because of the hostile environment there, foundation investment in NGO service and training organizations have produced a significant yield, more clearly than they have in the other Central European countries.

Featured Projects

Besides SAIA-SCTS, CSDF has played an important role in strengthening the NGO sector in Slovakia. Set up in July 1993, after the signing of the Financial Memorandum between the EU and the Slovak government, CSDF's mission is to support the development of civil society in Slovakia. In an important contrast to FCS, CSDF has an entirely Slovak board comprised of six leading academic and NGO figures. Although CSDF's funds are derived from the Phare program, the board is completely autonomous. It determines its own priorities and has decision-making authority.

In many ways CSDF's goals mirror those of SAIA-SCTS. These include: improving the legal basis for NGOs, helping new and already existing NGOs obtain information necessary for their work, developing the skills of NGO leaders, supporting cooperation among NGOs domestically and internationally, and enhancing public awareness of the importance of NGOs. To accomplish these goals, CSDF administers three programs in support of information and service, training, and on-going projects. CSDF is especially important to Slovakia's NGO sector because it provides financial resources to other NGOs. In 1994, CSDF funded seventy-two projects, with contributions totaling $370,175, a relatively significant amount.[19]

Besides working with the NGO sector, foreign foundations have also played a modest role in other areas important to the democratization in Slovakia. One of these is education. For example, the Soros foundations, Mellon, and PCT supported the Academia Istropolitana (Academia), a quasi-independent educational institution founded in 1990 to offer postgraduate instruction in public administration. Academia offers a two-year degree program that emphasizes practical problem solving and combines in-class instruction in English with summer internships—training markedly different from that during the Communist era.

Academia was quite successful in attracting external support and developing productive relationships with leading public administration schools in Europe, such as the European Institute of Public Administration and the Ecole Nationale d'Administration. It was successful because, by the end of the second phase of assistance in 1992–1993, foundations and other funders clearly perceived the need for a cohort of government officials to implement the blueprints for reform that had been developed throughout the region. Funders generally either retrained existing government officials or developed the next generation of officials. Given the growing demand for their resources, foundations generally emphasized developing the next generation of government officials because this kind of longer-term approach seemed most consistent with their grant-making strategies.

Academia's success and independence, however, appeared to raise questions within the Meciar government. In fact, after Academia's founding director, Alena Brunovska, vehemently resisted efforts to reduce the Education Ministry's contribution to Academia's budget, she was forced from her position without cause.[20] Clearly, external support was a double-edged sword. It provided significant resources and facilitated relationships with numerous other public administration organizations, yet at the same time it further complicated Academia's relationship with an increasingly adversarial government.

As in the Czech Republic, FCS played an important role in channeling resources to Slovakia, especially following the Velvet Divorce. FCS has been successful in attracting support from a wide range of public and private funders, including some fourteen foundations.[21] Over time, FCS built up an array of effective programs, including an expert adviser program focusing especially on the privatization process, a number of educational and cultural fellowship programs, and a series of conferences on justice and reconciliation. FCS administers AID's $3 million DemNet, which provides small grants to NGOs in Slovakia.

IEWS is another intermediary organization active in Slovakia. A Slovak national who has worked with IEWS since 1989, Vasil Hudák, played a key role in developing IEWS's strategy for Central Europe: promote the Carpathian Euroregion, the first Euroregion in Eastern Europe. This designation makes the area eligible for specific funds and support from the EU. In a remarkable feat that many diplomats would envy, IEWS obtained agreements from the governments of Ukraine, Poland, Slovakia, Hungary, and Romania to seek this designation. The cooperation required to establish a Euroregion is uncharacteristic in post-Communist Central and Eastern Europe. IEWS's work in the Carpathian region is coordinated from its office in Kosice under the leadership of Dalibor Kysela. He is assisted by an advisory board comprised of representatives of the five countries in the region and representatives from foundations in Western Europe and the United States.[22] Perhaps reflecting the difficulty of coordinating a multinational project, this endeavor has not yet achieved its potential.

A number of other research and advocacy institutes active in Slovakia have also received considerable support from foundations. One example is the Slovak Foreign Policy Association, which has been supported by Sasakawa, among others. Another example is the Center for Economic Development (CED), a free market–oriented think tank in Bratislava. Established by Eugen Jurzyca, a participant in a PCT-sponsored economic leaders fellowship program, CED is supported by the Canada Fund, the NED-affiliated Center for International Private Enterprise (CIPE), and Friedrich Naumann Stiftung (Naumann). CED publishes an engaging newsletter, *Slovak Economic Sheet,* which is broadcast over the Internet. CED, similar to other foundation-supported think tanks in the region, has a role in extending public participation and enhancing public debate about issues important to Slovak society. Thus, its mandate fits squarely into the guidelines of a number of foundations active in Central Europe.

The Helsinki Committee is a further example of an advocacy group that has received support from foundations. It focuses on human rights issues. Following the Velvet Divorce, the Czechoslovakia Helsinki Committee split into two national groups: the Czech Helsinki Committee and Slovak Helsinki Committee. As its Czeck counterpart, the Slovak Committee provides legislative monitoring, offers educational seminars for judges, lawyers, and policy officials, and has created a human rights information and documentation center that is open to the public.

In a related effort, ECF has sponsored a series of influential annual symposia on human rights, constitutionalism, and other issues related to the transition. Ford has also supported human rights awareness programs administered by the Milan Şimečka Foundation, which has received supplemental support from NED.

Foundations have been somewhat active in media issues in Slovakia but have been less active in Slovakia than in the other Central European countries. For example, Freedom Forum established the Independent Press Center in Bratislava. This center, conveniently located in downtown Bratislava, has a library replete with journals, conference rooms, and editing equipment that can be used for training and counseling journalists. But given the government's hostile attitude towards an independent media, it has not had much impact on how journalism is practiced in Slovakia.

Among the five German party foundations, Adenauer, Naumann, and Hanns Seidel Stiftung (Seidel), have been most active in Slovakia. Adenauer, for example, has organized seminars on political campaigning, building democratic societies, strengthening parties, and expanding the media. Humboldt has provided significant assistance to Slovakia's academic community. Relying primarily on support from the German government, Humboldt has provided forty-five fellowships valued at approximately $950,897, as well as $183,022 in equipment, between 1993 and 1994.[23]

Results

The approximately twenty foundations that have provided some $9.3 million in support of hundreds of projects in Slovakia have had some impact on the lives of tens of thousands of Slovaks. The most pronounced effects were probably produced by foundation-supported training programs. As a consequence of these training programs, Slovaks have been exposed to new ideas and approaches and have developed links to a variety of individuals in Europe and North America with common interests.

In Slovakia foundations have been helpful simply by being involved. It seems clear that, for a number of reasons, foundations in Slovakia have had an impact greater than the sum of the resources provided. Foundation assistance tended to be relatively swiftly disbursed and involved fewer bureaucratic entanglements than did resources provided by public funders. Also, a number of foundations active in Slovakia, such as FCS, managed to parlay initial investments from international foundations into significant contributions from public funders.

Another benefit is that foundations, which began to increase their attention to Slovakia following the Velvet Divorce, found they could replicate in Slovakia some of the projects most successful in the Czech Republic. For example, the experiences of FCS in Czechoslovakia were quickly transferred to Slovakia, and the CERGE model of a Western-style economics curriculum was replicated in the Applied Economics Program of the Public Administration School at Academia.

Foundations have had their most discernible impact on Slovakia's NGO sector. Their assistance has been instrumental, if not determinative, in the establishment of a number of newly independent institutions, such as SAIA-SCTS. Especially important have been CSDF and FCS (both of which use public funds but act autonomously) in their provision of small grants to strengthen NGOs. Given the pressure being applied by the government, it is quite remarkable that Slovakia's NGOs have developed and are thriving.

With the pressure that has been placed on educational institutions and the media, Slovak NGOs are one of the few remaining circles of freedom in the country and a bulwark against a reversion to the patterns of the past. Whether they will be able to continue to perform this role remains to be seen. However, it is unlikely that they will be able to do so without financial and moral support from international foundations.

The track record of foundations is less apparent in Slovakia than in the other Central European countries, in part, because Slovakia only began to receive attention from foundations and other providers of assistance following independence. Also, given the government's attempts to discredit the NGO sector and its criticism of foundations, Slovak soil has not been terribly fertile for foundation work. For example, following comments made by George Soros at a conference in Davos, Switzerland, the Slovak National Party claimed that his foundations were an enemy of Slovakia and requested that the general prosecutor review their activities with a view toward banning them. At this same time, Roman Hofbauer, an HZDS deputy, accused the Soros foundations and others of anti-Slovak and antigovernment behavior.[24]

Given these generally adverse conditions for the NGO sector, it would be unrealistic to expect foundations to have had a major impact on Slovak society as yet. Nevertheless, the Slovaks interviewed in the course of this research suggested repeatedly that foundation assistance has been important if only for the mere fact of its existence. Foundation involvement helps Slovaks connect to the world outside their borders. These connections provide important moral and financial support, which is helpful in resisting government pressure, as well as making it much more difficult for the government to act in a completely repressive fashion. Certain courses of restrictive actions that were commonly practiced before are now effectively precluded if Slovakia ever wishes to gain membership in the EU. Foundation involvement has helped shape international opinion about Slovakia, which may influence the government's behavior.

Foundations also provided important momentum for the development of new institutions in the NGO sector that were directly responsive to concerns articulated by leaders of Slovak NGOs, such as SAIA-SCTS and the Slovak Helsinki Committee. In a few cases, foundation resources were essential. If not for these resources, such organizations would not have been established or at least would not have developed on such a scale. Perhaps, most importantly, foundation assistance in Slovakia provided the beleaguered NGO sector with a sense that it was not isolated. Organizations in Europe and North America were willing to lend support needed to keep the NGO sector in Slovakia going. Without a viable NGO sector, it seems likely that Slovakia could slip even further behind its Central European neighbors and would become an unlikely candidate for admission to the EU in the foreseeable future.

6

Regional Projects:
Going against the Grain

*B*esides the country-specific projects discussed in the four preceding chapters, foundations have supported a variety of regional and interregional projects. The regional projects focus on the Central European countries, whereas the interregional projects have a much broader scope, taking place across Central Europe, Eastern Europe, and sometimes the former Soviet Union as well. The phrase *regional project* will apply specifically to Central European projects and the components of the interregional projects involving Central Europe.

Regional projects generally involve some of the same areas in which foundations have been active in Central Europe, namely, education, environment, human rights, local government, and support for the NGO sector. Of the approximately $445 million provided by foundations to Central Europe from 1989 to 1994, some $197 million, or 44 percent, involved regional initiatives.[1] Thus, any examination of the role played by foundations in Central Europe must consider these regional projects as well.

Regional projects are significant because they go against the grain. In 1989 and 1990, as many foundations began to explore grant-making possibilities, a common initial reaction was to consider regional projects because funders perceived that the Central European countries had shared similar experiences under communism and because such approaches would be more efficient. But foundation officials interested in regional projects were generally rebuffed by leaders of the newly democratic Central European countries. Having been prodded into regional cooperation through COMECON and the Warsaw Pact, Czechoslovak, Hungarian, and Polish leaders were virtually unanimous in their preferences for country-specific projects; regionalism was to be avoided.

Despite these expressed preferences, over time it became incontrovertible: similarities among the Central European countries offered a compelling rationale for regional projects. Local NGO leaders now seemed to agree. After five years of traveling to Brussels, London, Paris, and Washington, D.C., Central and Eastern European leaders are now just as likely to travel to Budapest, Prague, and Sofia. Thus, these regional projects are helping local NGO leaders "rediscover Central and Eastern Europe."[2]

These regional projects tended to fall into two broad types, both of which will be discussed here. By far the largest type were projects administered regionally, whether they were managed from inside or outside the region. Many training programs, especially fellowship programs, fit into this category. They were regional more out of administrative convenience than from an interest in promoting regional cooperation, although that was sometimes an ancillary objective.

A smaller number of projects were explicitly aimed at promoting regional cooperation through building cross-border ties among like-minded professionals. Examples of these include the Parliamentary Practices Project (PPP), initiated with the help of Ford, and the Global Security Fellows Initiative, established by PCT and administered by Cambridge University. This latter initiative targeted specific areas within the region, such as the so-called Black Triangle, which encompasses an area of Germany, Poland, and the Czech Republic that is severely damaged environmentally. PCT thought that cross-boundary and interdisciplinary ties based on issues such as ethnic conflict and environmental degradation might result in new insights into security in a post–cold war world.

This chapter will discuss a number of regional projects supported by foundations on issues that are important to democratic development, namely economics, education, the environment, and the NGO sector. Although some of these projects are cofinanced by the Soros foundations, this discussion will concentrate on the activities of foundations other than the Soros foundations, which will be discussed in detail in the next chapter.

Environment

The environment is one issue that received considerable attention from foundations. Given the fact that environmental problems are not constrained by boundaries, this is an obvious target for regional projects. It is also an area where foundations have had extensive experience.

The Environmental Partnership for Central Europe (EPCE) is an example of a regional project that was initiated by foreign foundations in the first phase of assistance.[3] Despite robust expectations by environmentalists, environmentally friendly policies were not adopted following the revolutions in Central Europe in 1989. Public attitudes shifted away from environmental concerns toward material and economic improvement. Perceptions about environmental groups also shifted dramatically. Once-respected activists were now perceived as outmoded idealists interfering with economic development.

Environmental groups also faced severe logistical constraints that hampered their effectiveness in communicating their message. The demands of networking and public relations necessitated modern communication equipment, funds for brochures and leaflets, and office space. The environmental movement also needed to offer financial incentives to keep highly qualified environmental professionals, many of whom were being lured into the private sector.

Some philanthropic organizations recognized the demands on this NGO sector and the necessity to help. In late 1989, a number of U.S. and Japanese foundations started to discuss aiding grassroots environmental groups that lacked essential financial and technical resources. These foundations decided to pool their resources to create an effective grants program combined with technical assistance. This represents a virtually unprecedented consortium approach from the needs-identification stage.

The interested foundations determined from the outset to concentrate on the grassroots level and to target their assistance toward the development of NGOs. Implicit in this decision was a commitment to a long-term strategy of broadly based education and training in civic and democratic behavior, as opposed to a short-term strategy of onetime grants. The environment was eventually chosen as the issue to focus on because of the deplorable state of the environment in Central Europe and because of the danger that, in times of sweeping and painful economic change, improvement in the environment would be a low priority. The foundations also perceived that the grassroots environmental movement could challenge the notion of the need for a trade-off between economic development and a healthy environment. Foundations had considerable prior experience with environmental organizations that had been unable to attract significant resources from the international community, the fledgling private sector, or a public sector in flux. They also thought environmental NGOs could help extend citizen participation.

Following an almost two-year design process, during which a Western consultant worked with grassroots groups in each of the Central European countries, the foundations settled on an approach. Given their limited resources and the involvement of others, the foundations agreed to create a regional program—EPCE—administered by the GMF. The foundations provided $840,000 for the first fiscal year (1991–1992), as well as comparable commitments for the next two years. For its first six years, the total contribution to EPCE was $5.4 million, which makes it a relatively well-funded project.[4] (After an extensive review in 1993, the principal funders decided to extend funding for the EPCE by three years, until June 1997.)

The EPCE established administrative structures providing for an efficient grant-making process and, at the same time, reflecting the objectives of the founders to be a "fast, flexible, and nonbureaucratic" funding mechanism.[5] They opened three offices, one each in Czechoslovakia, Hungary, and Poland, with small staffs of three to four that were assisted by a support office in Washington, D.C. A Slovak office in Banska Bystrica was added after the Velvet Divorce in 1993.[6] Each office was headed by a director familiar with the country and fluent in the local language. An effort was made to recruit local citizens in all positions, including the directorships. Each office was independent and could make small grants after a brief consultation with the Washington office. The local offices were assisted by a board of advisors usually consisting of five environmental activists or experts and, occasionally, lawyers and politicians. The board of advisors met regularly, about once every three months, to approve applications.

A number of characteristics are important to the success of EPCE. One of the most important is the fact that, relatively uncharacteristically, a group of foundations working together made a long-term initial commitment of three years. Another crucial factor is that these offices were remarkably independent and attracted a superb staff. The offices had a great deal of latitude in identifying where to deploy their resources and how to develop the necessary relationships within their communities. As a consequence, by almost any standards, EPCE was extraordinarily fast in reviewing proposals and approving grants, generally taking just six to eight weeks.

Another important factor in EPCE's success was the existence of a regional coordinator, located in Wrocław, Poland, and regular meetings of the directors of the country offices. These quarterly meetings allowed the directors to share experiences on a wide range of programming, financial, and legal issues. They were also important to developing country-specific strategic plans.[7] In addition, the U.S. support office helped contribute to EPCE's success. It facilitated communication between U.S. institutions, especially the funders, and the country offices, it worked actively and successfully to widen the financial basis of EPCE, and it acted as a link between the environmental community in the United States and that in Central Europe. For example, it collected information on additional resources available to Central European environmentalists, such as fellowships, stipends, and internships. The Washington office also helped channel American expertise to Central Europe.

Inevitably, this help from the regional coordinator and the Washington office came at considerable cost. They took up funds that could have been made available to the local offices or used in grants to local NGOs. Thus, the regional coordinator's position and the Washington office were phased out at the end of 1996. In this regard, EPCE faced a common trade-off between developing structures that provided needed assistance at the cost of diverting resources that could be used in the field.

In some ways, EPCE is an exemplary project. In the words of the outside reviewer who evaluated the project after its first few years, it was "well designed and well targeted and . . . [was] having an important impact on both environmental reform and democracy building in Central Europe."[8] Although the reviewer may have overstated its impact— there are few clear measures of EPCE or any other program having a clear, demonstrable, causal effect on democracy building—the reviewer characterized EPCE as a model for others to follow. Its pattern of making small grants and its fast, flexible, nonbureaucratic approach to doing so earned the reviewer's approval.

Perhaps the most singular aspect of EPCE is the open, trusting relationship that it has with its local partners. This seems to be mirrored in the relationships the local offices have with grantees. In this way, there is a strong convergence between the project's means and ends. Funders treat the local offices as real partners, in an open, trusting manner. The local offices, in turn, tend to deal with local NGOs in a similar fashion. This convergence, unfortunately, is relatively rare for many assistance programs, but without this convergence between goals and means, these programs are unlikely to be successful.

Despite many positive aspects, EPCE has grappled with the dilemma common to all foundation-supported projects in the region—sustainability. In particular, this means deciding how to develop alternative funding sources and mechanisms to replace the near-certain withdrawal of foundation support. Developing strategies to respond to sustainability was a central issue in the strategic planning exercise that EPCE undertook in late 1994 and 1995. This challenge is extremely difficult, since according to local staff assessments indigenous sources of funding are severely limited. Private charity is still either nonexistent or restricted to more traditional causes like the church.[9] The business community is not yet ready to give money to public causes, and the divide (and sometimes enmity) between environmental groups and business interests remains to be bridged. The willingness of the public sector to devote funds to environmental NGOs varies considerably and is limited by general budget constraints.

Although EPCE and its partners have not yet answered the question of sustainability, they have begun in a serious way to ask the question. They recognize that this is the most important challenge they now face. EPCE local office directors are reminded of how similar the challenges they face are to those forced by neighboring countries. Although their grant making tends to be responsive to local circumstances, the parallel nature of their approaches to common concerns and their ability to share responses to these concerns may be one of the most important benefits of regional projects.

Education and Training

There are numerous important projects that could be discussed here. To suggest the range and scope as well as some associated problems of these projects, this section will simply highlight a cross section of the projects supported by different foundations.

Foundation-supported regional projects in education and training represent a major portion of all regional projects, involving more than 40 percent of all foundation activity.[10] These include projects that are administered in the region, in Western Europe, or in North America. The administrative location is important, since it has a significant bearing on cost and the number of participants. These educational and training projects involve a blending of short-term workshops, midterm fellowships, and scholarships in degree-granting programs.

Examples of short-term workshops sponsored by foundations include PPP designed for representatives of the newly reconstituted parliaments of the region. This project involves a blending of European and North American foundation support, led by Ford and ECF. PPP has a joint European–North American project team led by French parliamentarian Jacques Worms and an American academic, Gerry Lowenberg. Like many other regional projects, this project seeks not only to provide specific technical skills that would be useful to the parliamentarians, but it also hopes to develop a network of reform-minded parliamentarians who could share knowledge and experiences. PPP involves a variety of workshops and seminars that helped shape the experiences of some members of the reconstituted parliaments of Central Europe, such as Hana Suchocka, who served as one of Poland's post-Communist prime ministers. Unfortunately, due to a variety of circumstances—not the least of which is that many of these parliamentarians were defeated in the subsequent election and thus did not participate further—PPP fell far short of its networking goal. Insufficient resources for networking is another factor limiting the success of this, as well as many other similar, projects. Also, especially in the first phases of assistance, regional cooperation was perceived to carry a relatively high opportunity cost in that it would inevitably detract from more pressing issues at home.

Another short-term regional training program is a three-month internship administered by the National Forum Foundation (NFF). NFF offers internships to young leaders from Central Europe in political, communication, and free-market skills. These internships provide an initial week-long orientation, intensive, hands-on experience, and a final week-long debriefing. After six years, NFF has an impressive roster of alumni, many of whom are in senior positions in government, business, and media.

NFF has taken advantage of this network of alumni to recruit new interns, provide placements for technical advisors, and identify new activities. This alumni network was an important reason why NFF was selected as one of two regional grantees for AID's $30 million DemNet program. Despite the good use made of its network—and NFF has made better use than most—this network is not especially well utilized. In NFF's case, as is true with many others, resources devoted to sustaining networks once developed generally fall far short of the rhetorical commitment made by many funders and other interested parties.

Besides short-term training opportunities sponsored by foundations, there are also a number of medium-term regional fellowships. These include fellowships designed to train a new cohort of diplomats, since the premier training previously available at Moscow State University is no longer a palatable option. One such diplomatic training fellowship grew out of conversations in early 1990 between former Secretary of State George Shultz and then Polish Deputy Minister of Foreign Affairs Jerzy Makarczyk.[11] The Diplomat Training Program was initially sponsored by Ford and administered by the Hoover Institution at Stanford University. This program, which initially targeted twelve to fifteen young diplomats from Central Europe, provided an intensive, semester-long international economics seminar that emphasized basic concepts of market economies and the global trading system, and introduced the major international economic institutions. This seminar was supplemented by a series of specialized lectures presented by a distinguished group of economists, including Nobel laureate Milton Friedman. The program also involved site visits to international institutions in New York and U.S. government institutions in Washington. Participants in this fellowship tended to be highly complimentary. Although a number of these fellows left the diplomatic service shortly after completing the program, those who remained appear to have put their fellowships to good use. This fellowship was certainly a good investment during the first phase of assistance, but perhaps became less so later on. Over time the participants in the program shifted from Central Europe to other countries in Eastern Europe and the Newly Independent States. This fellowship program concluded in December 1995.[12]

Another medium-term regional program is Humboldt's research fellowship for scholars in the natural and social sciences. Under this fellowship program, hundreds of Central Europeans annually have an opportunity to conduct research at an institution of higher education in Germany. In addition to stipends for the fellows, Humboldt provides funds for equipment essential to research. It also maintains close ties with the former participants by organizing periodic reunions. Although these fellowships are primarily for academics and tend to be concentrated in the sciences, they are discussed here because they have made a contribution to the opening of societies in Central Europe and rebuilding bridges between Central and Western Europe, especially Germany.

Yet another example of a medium-term fellowship program administered from outside of the region is a program begun at Cambridge University with funding from PCT. This interdisciplinary fellowship program, initially led in the region by Josef Vavroucek, is designed to grapple with nontraditional threats to security, particularly the problems of environmental degradation in the so-called Black Triangle area of the Czech Republic, Germany, and Poland, and problems of ethnicity in the Carpathian region of Ukraine, Slovakia, Romania, Poland, and Hungary. This fellowship program is part of PCT's effort to develop a new, broader conception of security that transcends the narrow, security-based concept of the cold war period.

The regional approach, as well as the broader goal of developing a new concept of security, make this program unique. Yet it shares the problems of numerous other programs: this fellowship targets an elite population, it is extremely expensive per participant, and the achievement of its ambitious goals are extremely difficult to measure. This and similar fellowship programs tend to leave unanswered the question of whether funds supporting them could have been better spent on helping the fledgling institutions of Central Europe make larger strides toward self-sufficiency.

Although the Soros foundations are by far the largest supporter of participants in long-term, degree-granting programs, similar support is also provided by a number of other foundations including Volkswagen. Three American foundations—Ford, PCT, and Mellon—also indirectly support a long-term approach toward strengthening the social sciences in Central Europe. Their joint initiative grew out of the Democracy Seminars begun in the mid-1980s and sponsored by the New School for Social Research in New York at which Central European dissidents gathered with Western academic colleagues to discuss critical issues related to democracy. Growing out of these annual seminars was the idea to have members of the next generation of Central European scholars spend one year at the New School as part of a doctoral program. PCT made a three-year grant of $225,000 for this purpose in April 1992. Mellon also provided approximately $850,000 to the educational institutions represented by the participants in the Democracy Seminars for the period 1990–1995 for spending on libraries and other materials. Participants in these seminars and fellowships have generally found them extremely important career-building experiences.

Given the enormous task associated with restructuring the social sciences in Central Europe, the efforts described here have to be seen as extremely modest. There are two basic ways to gauge the effects of projects like the Democracy Seminars and the Democracy Fellowships: (1) Were funds spent in the way intended, and (2) did they have the desired effect?[13] It is far easier to answer the first question than the second. In most cases, funds were spent as intended. Regarding the second question, the Democracy Seminars and Democracy Fellowships, along with the related activities, were important, timely, and clearly benefited the participants and their institutions. The projects' components were well designed and mutually reinforcing. Their impact on the social science restructuring in the region is so modest, however, that to suggest that these two projects had the impact claimed as the goal of these programs is a clear case of overstatement. Unfortunately, there are too many comparable examples.

If a project were seriously to attempt to restructure the social sciences in the region, one might expect major attention to be paid to developing model curricula in specific disciplines, such as political science and economics. One might also expect support for activities that include training faculty in the use of these new curricula and promoting the necessary support for curricular changes from administrators. Finally, one might expect to see a pilot project implemented that could be replicated if it proved sufficiently successful.

This type of well-conceived, systematic approach designed to effect broad change and matching the available resources with the desired change rarely occurred. It did not occur in the projects sponsored by the New School, nor in numerous other projects with similar grand ambitions. Given these ambitions, which may have been stated merely to win support from funders or to secure support from foundation boards, it is very difficult to answer affirmatively that the project had the desired effect.[14]

Besides educational and training programs that generally occur outside the region, there are numerous efforts to provide training inside the region, especially in economics. For example, Mellon was instrumental in efforts to establish CERGE, still, it also could be discussed here, since it draws its student body from throughout the region.

Foundations also played a role in launching the Masters of Business Administration (MBA) Enterprise Corps. This 1990s version of the Peace Corps sponsored recent MBA graduates for one- or two-year assignments in small businesses and business associations throughout the region. Like many other programs started to support the transition, it initially targeted the Central European countries, but as its experience increased and the opportunities became available, it shifted attention to other countries in Eastern Europe and the NIS.[15] This program provided technical advisors who, because their tenure was relatively long term, developed the language skills and awareness of local circumstances that made them more effective than members of the Marriott Brigade, with their flying visits. Also, perhaps similar to the Peace Corps experience for young volunteers, the MBA Enterprise Corps provided important career-building experiences for its participants.

Besides training in business and economics, foundations have also supported policy research on economic issues related to the transition. One example of such a project was begun in 1993 by the Institute for Human Sciences (Institut für die Wissenschaften von Menschen, or IWM) in Vienna. Founded in the early 1980s by a Polish émigré, Krzysztof Michalski, IWM developed a regional collaborative project with support from foundations. IWM's Social Costs of Economic Transformation in Central Europe (SOCO) project hoped to strengthen policy-oriented research bearing on key social policy issues, such as unemployment. In addition, it attempted to bring Western experience and expertise to bear on helping Central European nations cope with the rising and potentially destabilizing social costs associated with the economic transition. Similar to many other regional projects, SOCO was initiated by a Western foundation, in this case Ford.

Coordinated by a Hungarian project director based in Vienna and overseen by a committee of international experts, SOCO sought to develop in-country, policy-oriented research groups comprised of both researchers and government officials. These teams were charged with analyzing particular policy problems, including the relationship between fiscal and social policy, unemployment and workforce mobility, and decentralization of social policy decision making. These teams, some of which had considerable difficulty working together, produced a variety of policy papers of uneven quality. One of the project's most important legacies is that some of these teams evolved into effective independent institutions, such as the Institute of Public Affairs in Poland and the Slovak Policy Analysis Center (SPACE).

Despite considerable experience within the region, this project developed a number of perhaps predictable problems. The project's financial and human resources were stretched too thin, researchers had difficulty working cooperatively, and the research teams developed unevenly.[16] Despite difficulties caused by working transnationally, however, SOCO was successful in encouraging public discussion of the economic transition and in laying the foundation for future research. SOCO also made an important contribution by highlighting the need for policy makers to be much more attentive to the social dimensions of the economic transition.

As was the case on a country-specific basis, support for the NGO sector has been a major focus of foundations, especially U.S. foundations active in Central Europe. This support has generally taken two forms: training NGO sector leaders and personnel, and fostering regional networking efforts among members of the fledgling NGO sector.

The Charity Know How (CKH), among others, supported a series of training programs to help NGO sector personnel develop expertise in refugee issues affecting the region. CKH also attempted to encourage networking between journalists and the NGO sector throughout Central Europe. Characteristic of CKH's approach, it placed a particular emphasis on linking Central European journalists and NGO leaders with their counterparts in the United Kingdom. Although understanding country-particular interests, some perceive CKH's insistence on links with U.K. organizations as overly self-serving. On the more positive side, if this requirement results in a U.K. NGO making a serious, *long-term* commitment to a Central European NGO with a common mission, the potential for sustainability of that Central European NGO is significantly increased. The dilemma for funders is sorting out those institutions that are motivated by a long-term commitment to the region and those more interested in obtaining resources for their own programming.

Perhaps the most ambitious training efforts for NGO personnel were parallel projects undertaken by two U.S. organizations. The first—the Civil Society Development Program (CSDP)—was launched by two American activists initially supported by the International Youth Foundation to conduct research on the young leaders of Central Europe. These researchers, Dan Siegel and Jenny Yancey, developed virtually unrivaled access to young leaders throughout the region and outside of capital cities. After authoring a landmark monograph supported by RBF,[17] Siegel and Yancey moved to Budapest to train a small team of NGO sector leaders in Hungary and Poland. Their concept was to train others who could then continue training after Siegel and Yancey returned to the United States. After initial funding from foundations, including OSI, RBF, and Mott, Siegel and Yancey obtained funding from the EU Phare Democracy Programme. Somewhat ironically, there was a significantly higher attrition rate among the initial participants in Hungary, where CSDF was headquartered, than in Poland. Consistent with its initial design, in 1996 CSDP established two locally governed and managed NGO training and resource centers. The Polish center has its main office in Warsaw and smaller centers in Gdynia and Krakow. The Hungarian center is located in Budapest. Both the Hungarian and Polish centers receive funding from diverse funders and are developing income and generating activities.

The other regional NGO sector training effort was launched by Lester Salamon from the Institute for Policy Studies (IPS) at Johns Hopkins University. This effort included research, fellowships at Johns Hopkins, and a train-the-trainer approach. Each summer IPS organized a conference on the NGO sector in one of the countries in the region to scout for potential candidates to receive fellowships for academic training and practical experience in the United States after which they would return home to train other NGO leaders. Although this effort was well conceived, IPS experienced difficulties because it was extremely hard to provide consistent and timely follow up without maintaining a presence in the region, especially since IPS administers programs and conducts research globally.

Besides the aforementioned projects, foundations have also tried to support efforts to ameliorate ethnic tensions within Central Europe, an important issue with which the foundations have had previous experience. However, ethnic conflicts are extremely intractable, and devoting resources to addressing these conflicts is often not of importance to the general population. In fact, the citizenry is inclined to perceive devoting resources to issues of ethnicity as a diversion of scarce resources away from more important issues. Opinion polls by FOCUS and other groups indicate that ethnic or minority problems are a low priority for the great majority of Central Europeans.[19]

Recognizing this gap, foundations, such as Mott, have supported the work of Partners for Democratic Change (Partners). This U.S.–based organization has regional affiliates. Partners' goal has been to establish and link together local ethnic conciliation commissions in each of the Central European countries together. These commissions, comprised of members from diverse ethnic, religious, and national backgrounds, receive training in the communication, conciliation, intervention, and mediation skills necessary to mitigate local ethnic disputes. Some of these commissions are clearly more successful than others. Some local Partners commissions, such as those in Slovakia, have developed well-respected training programs that generate revenue and thus have good prospects for sustainability.

Results

Most of the regional education and training programs sponsored by foundations have not yet leveraged significant institutional change in part because just too few people participate in these programs. Also, since there are such a small number of participants, the participants often return to institutions that are not especially hospitable to the changes advocated. Without a "critical" mass of like-minded individuals, enthusiasm for taking on reform-resistant institutions in Central Europe quickly evaporates. Another reason that these regional projects seem to have achieved scant results is that the kind of societal change that the foundations pursue is extremely long term. Thus, it may be too early to discern the full impact of these educational and training programs, especially if building democracy is a generation-long task.

At this point, six or seven years after many of these regional education and training projects began, it is increasingly clear that the programs rooted in the region have the best prospects for achieving long-term change. Programs administered from outside of the region are generally too expensive and involve too few participants to have the desired societal impact.

Besides the administrative location of these projects, the success of these regional projects also depends on the issue involved. Foundations were much more effective when they had some advantage or prior experience with the issue. Foundation work on economic issues, for example, was successful because it occurred during the first phase of assistance before many of the large public institutions, such as the Bank, became vigorously engaged in Central Europe. Foundation work on economic issues and business education was generally less successful in the later phases of assistance, although it was helpful in drawing attention to specific issues, including the social costs of the economic transition.

Given their extensive prior experiences, foundations' contributions to regional education and training in the NGO sector were perhaps among their most important. Despite some difficulties, both CSDP and IPS provided important training opportunities for the new leaders of Central Europe's NGO sector. Both projects were initially supported by foundations, and their successes led to support from public funders, such as AID and the EU. This ability to attract other resources is one of the hallmarks of success.

Foundation-sponsored projects had limited success in fostering regional cooperation. But even this limited success, since little other activity was directed at regional cooperation, helped mend the frayed ties that once bound Central Europe together. Under communism, there were fragile, but important, links among the dissident communities throughout the region. Solidarity's opposition role was an inspiration to dissidents in Czechoslovakia and Hungary. These links, however, seemed to vanish with the fall of the Berlin Wall. Czechs, Hungarians, Poles, and Slovaks alike became less interested in their neighbors. Given dynamic change, understandably their attention was riveted at home. Although Central Europeans appeared to have a passing acquaintance with political and economic developments in their neighboring countries, they were not especially well informed.

This relative lack of attention to their neighbors was poignantly illustrated during the April 1996 "For Democracy's Sake" workshop. At that time, the Slovak Parliament was considering a law to regulate foundations closely. The draft law contained a number of highly repressive provisions, including an exorbitant endowment as a prerequisite for registration. The workshop participants from the United States appeared to be better informed about unfavorable developments affecting Slovakia's NGO sector than were Czech, Hungarian, or Polish participants. This would not have been the case prior to 1990.

It is noteworthy that foundation-supported regional projects, which represent a significant portion of foundation activities in Central Europe, were virtually all initiated from outside. Generally, as numerous examples here demonstrate, projects initiated externally have dimmer prospects than those initiated locally. However, given Central Europeans' recent aversion to regional activities, it is clear that, if there were to be regional activities, they would have to be initiated abroad.

Projects, especially in education and the environment, provided a chance for regional comparison and the sharing of relevant experiences. For the most part they have not yet achieved the desired institutional change. In many cases such change was not achievable, given available resources, so project goals should be considered more as marketing devices than realistic objectives.

In the final analysis, the most important aspect of these regional projects might be that they encouraged Central Europeans to become engaged once again with their neighbors, even if only in a small way. The development of some form of regional cooperation, even merely on the project level, is potentially important to integrating the Central European countries more deeply into European structures, such as NATO and the EU.

At this point, it is clear that Central European aspirations to join the EU and NATO will not be fulfilled for some years. Even more obstacles are likely to lie ahead than those already anticipated. These regional projects may provide the basis for Central European citizens, acting outside government, to forge links that will help them surmount some of these obstacles. In particular, these links may help strengthen the NGO sector throughout the region, which would enable Central Europe to develop an NGO sector more closely resembling that of Western Europe.

7

George Soros:
Leader of the Band

*T*he most prominent supporter of democracy assistance projects in Central Europe is George Soros, the Hungarian-born
financier. Support from the Soros foundations represents approximately 30 percent of the resources provided by all the other
foundations in the region (figure 4). In fact, the Soros foundations
are considerably higher profile and occasionally larger and more
important than those of many official bilateral assistance programs. Leszek Balcerowicz, former deputy prime minister of Poland and the architect of economic reform there, suggested that
Soros had done more than most governments in building democratic institutions in Central Europe.[1]

It is therefore not surprising that at times Soros seems to have
more influence in Central Europe than the U.S. secretary of state.
Given that Soros funds are disbursed quickly and, unlike many
other foundations, involve local people extensively in decision-
making roles, they may be particularly important to democratization. This chapter's explicit focus on Soros and his foundations
is especially apt, since an important part of the story regarding
foundations and democracy assistance in Central Europe is the
story of Soros's support for open societies there.

The Man

Soros was born in Budapest and hid from Nazi persecution
during German occupation. He emigrated to England in 1947
and to the United States in 1956. He is credited with being one
of the most successful investors of the twentieth century. Soros
made his fortune managing the Quantum Fund, an extremely
aggressive mutual fund. Although he may not be the greatest

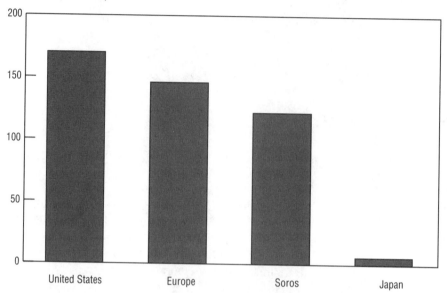

FIGURE 4 **Foundation Assistance to Central Europe by Donor, 1989–1994**

philanthropist of the late twentieth century, he perhaps has the highest profile.[2]

Soros has provided hundreds of millions of dollars to pursue a vision of an open society heavily influenced by his former teacher, the philosopher Karl Popper. According to Popper, citizens require freedom as if it were the oxygen they breathe. Applying Popper's ideas, Soros understands that the meaning of freedom goes beyond a series of rights. To him freedom is essentially the availability of alternatives. In an open society, where ". . . freedom is a fact, the character of society is determined entirely by the decisions of its members."[3] Since citizens in an open society must constantly make decisions regarding available alternatives, such a society will be inherently dynamic. This is diametrically opposed to the situation in closed societies—such as those in Communist countries—where citizens have no alternatives. Soros "believed that the collapse of the Soviet system was a revolutionary event whose outcome would shape the course of history."[4]

Because Soros hopes to "transform closed societies into open ones and to expand the values of existing open societies,"[5] he has focused his efforts on Central and Eastern Europe and the former Soviet Union. Soros recognized the need for the formerly closed societies of Central Europe to develop new patterns and his qualifications to help with this task:

Communism had tried to form a universal closed society. Now that it had failed, it was possible to create a universal open society. The first few moments of creation are always the most important: that is when the pattern is set. I was in a unique position. Not only did I recognize the significance of the moment, I also had the resources to make an impact. There are many people who are willing to sacrifice more than I am for the sake of an open society and there are some people with greater financial resources; but there was nobody else who combined both qualifications. Occupying such a unique position, I felt I had a unique obligation.[6]

Growing out of his personal experiences with charitable organizations as a student in London, Soros suggests that charitable activity often results in dependency or financial abuse. He argues that these two problems can be avoided in just two ways: through anonymous giving or through the development of a foundation bureaucracy. Since foundation bureaucracy is anathema to Soros, who believes that large foundations and other bureaucracies are slow, inefficient, and self-serving, his philanthropic activities began anonymously.[7] Over time, as Soros's foundation grew, it began increasingly to resemble the foundation bureaucracy he once criticized. In fact, by 1994 his foundation had grown to the point where it operated in twenty-four countries and had a staff of more than 1,200, roughly double the size of the foundation Soros had characterized as "bureaucratic."[8]

Although Soros has been criticized for micromanaging the allocation of his foundation's resources, for being quick to change his mind, and for allowing his resources to be monopolized by tight circles of people, he has, probably more than any other single individual, advanced the cause of democracy in Central Europe.[9] As one individual suggested, "Soros played a historic role by opening up spaces of democracy . . . and because of that, despite some problems, he should probably be awarded the Nobel Prize."[10]

Soros has played a distinctive, dramatic, and occasionally disruptive role in Central Europe's transition away from communism and toward democracy. One example is the controversy that erupted in Slovakia following Soros's comments at the World Economic Forum, in September 1995 that Slovakia was lagging behind other Central European countries. Controversy also erupted over Soros's religion (Jewish), profession (money manager), and place of abode (the United States)—signs, in Hungary especially, that an outsider was bearing undue influence.

As with any organization of its size and importance, the Soros foundations have their share of admirers and detractors. Among all the foundations active in Central Europe they are unique because their founder is their principal decision maker and the resources used are his. This fact makes the mere discussion of the foundations complicated. The distinction between the man and the foundations is blurred. In most cases, the man and the foundations can be discussed interchangeably. This is the approach taken here except when a particular Soros operation, such as Poland's Batory, is discussed. In that case the Soros foundation will be identified by the name by which it is known in its country of operation.

The Soros Foundations in Central Europe

Despite Soros's views that there are two basic models of charitable giving—anonymous donation or a bureaucratic approach—he has essentially pursued a third model, an intensely personal, high-profile philanthropy. In 1979, Soros began supporting open societies by providing scholarships to black students in South Africa anonymously. At that time, Soros was also deeply engaged in the Human Rights Watch/Helsinki network that included support for dissidents in Central and Eastern Europe and the former Soviet Union. After supporting scholarships in his native Hungary for some years, he moved to establish SFH in 1984. As the first independent foundation established under communism, SFH assumed a high profile and entered into a complicated relationship with the then-Communist government in Budapest.

After starting SFH, Soros began supporting parallel organizations committed to opening the closed societies of Poland and Czechoslovakia. Batory was established in Poland in 1988, and Charta 77 was established in Czechoslovakia the following year. (Charter 77—New York, later FCS, was discussed in chapter 2 and established in 1990). Just prior to the Velvet Divorce in November 1992, Charta 77 evolved into the OSF—Prague and the OSF—Bratislava.

Following the fall of communism, Soros's efforts in Central Europe shifted from opening closed societies to more self-consciously trying to build the institutions and processes of open societies. The Soros foundations' mission developed as Soros realized that "the breakdown of a closed society does not automatically lead to an open society."[11]

Unlike many of the other foundations operating in Central Europe, the Soros foundations have local offices administered by local staff and governed by local boards of directors. Both Soros's own and other foundation executives think this is the key to the Soros foundations' success.[12] Although the foundations have not escaped criticism for being overly partisan and personalized, they tend to have a relatively broad reach, often managing to get well beyond capital-city elites. For example, in Slovakia the OSF has an office in Presov, as well as in Bratislava. The Soros foundations have pursued a similar strategy in opening regional offices in other countries facing significant obstacles to transition, such as Ukraine and Romania.

That Soros is both the funder and the principal decision maker means his foundations are completely different from others active in Central

Europe. Many of the other foundations are large bureaucracies with long grant-making histories and well-established boards of directors who see themselves as stewards of their foundation's resources. Some others, such as NED and its core agencies and the German political party foundations, act autonomously but use public funds. Thus, other foundations are accountable either to their boards or to their governments, which makes them more cautious than those who are not.

Soros, on the other hand, is accountable to no one. This gives him unparalleled freedom to think and act boldly. He can pursue his interests assiduously, yet change his mind the next day. He can and has invested more than $65 million in a single idea—CEU as a regional institution devoted to pan–Central European culture and education. Soros's freedom may chafe some and be envied by others. His wealth and fame give him virtually unparalleled access to the top leadership in Central Europe and around the world. This freedom can be a powerful stimulus for positive change. If used capriciously or inconsistently, however, it can be extremely detrimental. In any event, Soros, through his foundations, played the starring role in efforts to strengthen democracy in Central Europe. Below we consider one of Soros's country foundations and then a number of the specific activities supported by the Soros foundations.

Stefan Batory Foundation

As mentioned above, George Soros has established local foundations in each of the four Central European countries. Each local foundation has the veneer of a separate identity and follows its own guidelines. Generally, the grants they make focus on education and culture. These foundations are registered by the local authorities and are governed by local laws. Although they rely heavily on Soros for their funding, much of which they regrant to other organizations, they also are encouraged to seek funding from other sources. Because Batory is perhaps the most independent of these foundations, it is discussed here.

Batory was formally registered in Warsaw on 7 May 1988.[13] Soros appointed Batory's Foundation Council, which, along with the board, constitutes Batory's governance mechanism. The council—chaired by Jerzy Turowicz, editor-in-chief of *Tygodnik Powszechny*, one of Poland's leading newspapers—is responsible for oversight of Batory's general affairs and policy making. It also appoints the chair and the members of the board, evaluates the board's performance, and approves the annual budget. Aleksander Smolar, a prominent political dissident who emigrated to France in 1971, serves as chair.

The board of Batory is appointed for a two-year term. Its primary responsibilities are management of Batory's affairs and appointment of the director. Although Batory identifies itself as part of the Soros network of foundations, according to its annual report, "The Stefan Batory Foundation enjoys complete autonomy in taking decisions affecting its activities."[14]

From 1990 to 1995, Batory provided grants of approximately $16.3 million. Batory is especially active in education. It has a strong preference for training young people and for cofinancing projects with other interested funders. It administers scholarship programs abroad, supports professional training, underwrites international academic conferences in Poland, and generally supports curriculum reform efforts. Batory also supports a variety of NGOs and cultural institutions and subsidizes the publication of books and ethnic and cultural journals.

Smolar suggests that Batory's most important work is in NGO formation and local government. He is critical of other foundations' aversion to providing operating support to such organizations, despite their rhetorical commitment to institution building. As a consequence, Batory is one of the few private funders that routinely provides a small number, perhaps eight to ten, of operating grants annually.[15]

Batory occupies an especially important place on Poland's institutional landscape. It has tried, not always successfully, to avoid being perceived as involved in partisan politics. As a participant at the FDS workshop on 5 June 1996 at the Woodrow Wilson Center in Washington, D.C., Irena Lasota argued, "Let us not kid ourselves. Batory operates like a political party. It may be a very nice political party, with which many of us agree, but it is a political party none the less."[16]

This criticism of partisanship is often leveled against successful Central European institutions that work on important public policy issues and is something that Batory staff have strenuously worked to avoid. Batory staff argue that they have worked assiduously to develop "rules and procedures in order to avoid any pressure and arbitrary decisions."[17] In addition, since 1990 Batory has been exemplary in publishing some of the most transparent annual reports of any NGO in the region. These reports provide comprehensive information regarding the sources of funds, as well as how these funds are allocated. Batory staff suggest that even the most cursory examination of their annual reports would make clear that it does not operate in a partisan fashion.

Batory, much like the other Soros country foundations, is relatively open. It makes a point of widely disseminating information on its programs. This information is routinely published in Poland's major papers, such as *Gazeta Wyborcza*, *Polityka*, and *Tygodnik Powszechny*, and in its monthly newsletter, *Bulletin*, which is delivered to radio and television stations and some one thousand other institutions throughout Poland.

Perhaps more than other local Soros foundations, Batory has been able to diversify its funding. The Soros foundations still provide more than 80 percent of Batory's support, but the balance is underwritten by a variety of other organizations, such as the Bank, GMF, IWM, and

Ford, which together contribute 9 percent, and, most impressively, domestic public and corporate sources, which contribute 11 percent.[18] Ford recently awarded a $2.5 million institution-building matching grant to help Batory develop an endowment.[19] This grant gives Batory a significant boost towards sustainability and even greater independence. Despite its demonstrated ability to diversify funding and its stated policy of independence, however, Batory, as well as the other Soros foundations, cannot be thought of as truly independent until the majority of its resources are generated elsewhere or it obtains an endowment.

Although Batory is perhaps more independent and mature than the other Soros country foundations, all the country foundations share many characteristics. In virtually every case, Soros identified a small group of individuals committed to the idea of an open society and endowed them with resources (generally $1 million) to begin to address their problems. The country foundations, although registered as independent organizations in their respective countries and allowed to develop their own grant-making priorities, remain highly dependent on Soros for their financing. In fact, most of these foundations would cease to exist without Soros support, but the same support that enables them to survive, because of the close identification with Soros, generally precludes other funders from playing a very active role. All the Soros country foundations are linked and informally coordinated by OSI offices in New York and, to an increasing extent, in Budapest. The OSI office in Budapest administers the regional programs we will now discuss.

Regional Projects

Perhaps most distinctive of the work of the Soros foundations is their aggressive pursuit of regional projects to supplement the work of the local foundations. Initially, these regional projects were loosely administered, generally from the New York headquarters and sometimes by a local foundation. Since 1993 some of them have been administered primarily by the OSI office in Budapest. These regional projects include efforts to promote educational reform, modernize and enhance access to library resources, provide training for the next cohort or retrain the existing cohort of local government officials, support ethnic minorities (including the Roma), and conduct high-quality policy research on key economic transition issues including privatization. In addition to these substantive issues, the Soros foundations have developed an innovative East East initiative that transfers the know-how and experience from successful projects in countries further along in the transition (such as Poland, Hungary, and the Czech Republic) to others not as far along in this process.

These regional projects are extremely ambitious and are directed at

Central and Eastern Europe and the NIS. Although their scope extends way beyond Central Europe, they will be discussed here simply in the context of the Czech Republic, Hungary, Poland, and Slovakia.

Higher Education Programs

One of the Soros foundations' most important regional initiatives is the promotion of educational reform. Soros's early support for scholarships indicates his recognition of the importance of education to an open society, especially in Central and Eastern Europe and the former Soviet Union, where under Communist rule education was dominated by ideological concerns, and scholars—outside of a number of privileged disciplines, such as engineering and mathematics—were often cut off from contacts with their colleagues abroad. In Central Europe, despite a long and distinguished tradition of higher education, including world-renowned institutions such as Jagellonian and Charles Universities, Communist rule undermined the legacy of open, efficient scholarship. The quality of education suffered, and the strict division between research and teaching facilities resulted in teachers at many Central European universities falling far below world standards.

To rectify the dire situation of education in Central Europe, the Soros foundations established the Higher Education Support Program (HESP) to promote educational reform and to reintegrate scholars and educational institutions in Central Europe into the international academic community. HESP also aims to "restore the region's universities as centers of critical thinking, teaching, and research on public policy issues."[20] To pursue this aim the Soros foundations have a number of programs that support Western scholars in residence at Central European institutions, improve library resources, and underwrite research. HESP also supports a regional program to publish works in local languages. HESP is one of the most imaginative and important projects in the region. Although its ultimate effects will require a long time to discern, Soros is absolutely right that the key to open societies and democracy is education. Thus, this investment will eventually produce important results.

Another of HESP's activities, critical to opening societies, is the effort to enhance electronic communication by providing access to E-mail and other Internet services. One foundation executive described this as an extremely effective means of counteracting the verticality of communism, since electronic communication opens a window on the world that cannot easily be shut. This program is based on a recognition that to strengthen democracy you must spread information.[21]

Another of the more important of these Soros-supported regional educational projects is the Civic Education Project (CEP). CEP supports

Western scholars in teaching and assisting their host institutions in Central Europe with curriculum reform and faculty retraining. The goal is to establish long-term, mutually beneficial relationships between these Western scholars and their host institutions. Although CEP is legally independent, the fact that it receives a majority of its support from Soros and shares office space with OSI in Budapest raises some doubt that it is truly independent.

HESP and CEP have generally been helpful. At a fraction of the cost of many other programs funded by AID and the Bank, they have placed faculty in Central European institutions. The effort to enhance electronic communication has also met with some success, although there have been a number of technical problems to overcome. One criticism about these efforts, however, is that they tend to focus on new institutions and initiatives when existing institutions are starving for resources.[22]

Regional Library Program

Outside of enhancing communication, some of the Soros foundations' most important work furthering democratization may be with libraries. Although this may seem prosaic, democratic experience makes clear that citizens require information to develop the skills necessary to check state power.[23] Under communism, access to information was tightly controlled. In no place was this more evident than in libraries. For example, fewer than two thousand people, out of a population of fifteen million had library cards to the Czechoslovak National Library.[24] Besides limiting access, the libraries of Central Europe tended to be grossly underfunded. Consequently, information about most of their collections was not automated, and rare collections, preserved using antiquated methods, were at risk. Libraries also lacked the hard currency to purchase the journals and new publications necessary to keep abreast of recent developments in most fields.

Recognizing these conditions, the Soros foundations began a major initiative to advance information science in Central Europe, including large-scale automation projects and management and automation training for librarians, support for library school curriculum development, and technical support and training provided by experts such as staff from the U.S. Library of Congress. The automation efforts have progressed well and resulted in innovative consortia linking local, regional, and national libraries and significantly enhancing access to these libraries' collections. The efforts to train librarians to make their collections more accessible have been slightly more problematic, as they require a fundamental reorientation in attitudes and institutional culture.

Institute for Local Government and Public Service

The Soros foundations recognized that as the capacities of the centralized state weakened during the transition, responsibilities for public services would increasingly devolve to regional and local governments unprepared to shoulder these burdens. The Local Government Project seeks to assist in the reform of local government and public service by enhancing the capacity of municipalities to use their resources efficiently, particularly through public administration education. One objective is to encourage local government officials to be responsive to citizens' concerns—a requirement for democratic societies but uncommon under communism. As part of its efforts, this initiative with other foundations established a consortium of regional public administration training institutes called National Institutes, Academies, and Schools of Public Administration in Central and Eastern Europe (NIASPACEE).

NIASPACEE recognized and responded to a clear need. Outside of the FSLD in Poland, there have been few concerted efforts to enhance local government in Central Europe. To date, however, the initiative's record is somewhat mixed. Efforts to train the next cohort of local government officials have been most successful. At times, however, they have been adversely affected by local politics. For example, Academia—which received support from this project and housed the secretariat for the NIASPACEE—was perceived as having a faculty comprised exclusively of opponents to the Meciar government. Consequently, the director was removed against her will by the Slovak government in February 1996. Despite occasional problems, this project is making an important contribution by addressing a need critical to the ultimate success of decentralization, which, in turn, is an important part of democratization.

Soros Roma Foundation

Given Soros's strong interest in human rights, his foundations, much like others, have supported efforts to provide equal treatment under the law to minorities. One prominent example of this is the establishment of the Soros Roma Foundation, which targets the most disadvantaged minority in Central Europe. (As of 1996 this foundation was deactivated. Soros-supported activities related to the Roma are now operated by local country foundations assisted by a program officer at OSI–Budapest.[25])

Although population estimates are uncertain, the Roma represent nearly 10 percent of the population in Hungary, and between 1 and 2 percent of the population of the other Central European countries.

Soros's Roma-related goals are "to empower the Roma through support for education and culture programs, including the training of Roma as teachers, journalists, and human rights advocates, and to promote understanding between the Roma and the majority populations."[26]

Soros's efforts on behalf of the Roma have had some success. They helped focus attention on an important, but unpopular, issue. They also supported the work of Autonómia (discussed in chapter 3), were instrumental in encouraging the EU to establish the EUROMA program, and supported the Hungarian government's initiative in setting up a foundation devoted to improving the quality of Roma life in Hungary. The fact that other funders, public and private, multilateral and national, are emulating these activities is one of the clearest measures of the Soros Roma Foundation's success.

Central European University[27]

The Central European University (CEU) is the jewel in Soros's crown. It is probably the boldest, riskiest, and most important single investment supported by an external donor in the region. CEU provides the intellectual anchor for a number of the Soros foundations' regional projects, such as HESP and the Research Support Program. Books are also published under its imprint.

The idea of a new university arose during a series of seminars in April 1989 at the Dubrovnik Interuniversity Center. Scholars attending the seminars approached Soros with the idea of creating a regional institution that would serve as a center of higher education and educational reform throughout Eastern Europe. By his own account, Soros immediately grasped that, by investing in a new institution, existing institutions would be deprived of needed resources, so he rejected the idea, telling the plan's advocates that he was "interested not in starting institutions but in infusing existing institutions with content."[28]

Soros's view changed with the fall of the Berlin Wall. He then recognized that new institutions were necessary in order to guard the ideas underpinning the recent changes in Central Europe. Thus, in 1990, Soros made a five-year commitment to the creation of a regional educational entity. CEU was envisioned not just as an educational institution, but also as the "centerpiece of the whole foundation network," combining both postgraduate study and grant making to support research and reform in other universities in the region.[29] Creating CEU was a bold step unrivaled by any of the other private or public funders involved in Central Europe.

CEU, founded in 1990–1991, had an ambitious mission. Its seven objectives were: (1) to develop a new curriculum to be used at CEU and other Central and Eastern European universities; (2) to advance standards of teaching, research, and study in the region; (3) to educate the region's new leaders; (4) to encourage cooperation and understanding in the region's populations; (5) to provide advice and assistance for the reform of educational institutions; (6) to assist in developing the institutions of open societies; and (7) to provide new insights into the problems of the post-Communist era.[30]

After some difficulty, CEU was awarded a provisional charter (through 1997) by the State University of New York, acknowledging that CEU's facilities and curricula are consistent with those found in New York's state universities. CEU was recognized as a foreign university in Budapest, Prague, and Warsaw. Initially, the campuses in these cities were not meant to be replicas of any existing university system but rather to harken back to the days of medieval universities, when scholars would roam from city to city. However, this initial concept of the peripatetic scholar turned out to be overly romantic and archaic; since its inception, CEU was perceived to need an administrative structure and facilities similar to a Western university.

The university is governed by an international board of which Soros is the chair, is administered by a rector (through June 1996, Al Stepan), and also maintains a university senate and college councils. All of the departments have advisory boards that guide their activities. Soros has provided libraries on each campus with significant English-language holdings and fully networked searching devices, including CD-ROM capabilities. Students at CEU also have access to financial-, academic-, and career-advising centers. Computer centers are located on the main campus and, since 1996, in the dormitories in Budapest.

Every student from Central Europe that is accepted is given a full scholarship that includes tuition, room, board, and a monthly stipend. Students can also apply for scholarships that allow them to study abroad for a portion of their tenure at CEU. The emphasis at CEU, however, is on training *in the region* the next cohort of leaders and on convincing them to take positions in their own country after graduation. Consequently, students who also receive foreign scholarships are required to finish their programs of study in their own countries. Furthermore, the career centers available on each campus are geared toward arranging internships and jobs that will make the most of the student's new skills within the region. As a result, in the first two years of operation of the CEU economics department, 50.8 percent of graduates went on to a full-time job (as opposed to further education), with 78.5 percent of these jobs located with Western companies in the students' home countries.[31]

CEU offers master's degrees in economics, environmental sciences and policy, history, international relations and European studies, legal studies, medieval studies, political science, and sociology. It has plans to introduce new interdisciplinary programs in Russian and gender studies. Each of these programs has a clear orientation related to the overall mission of CEU. For example, the economics department's goal is to train economists from the region in how to deal with problems arising from the transition from a command to a market economy.[32] All of the courses are conducted in English by faculty both from the region and from the West.

There is little doubt that the investment made in CEU by Soros and his foundations is extremely large—some $65 million between 1990 and 1996.[33] During this same period Hungary's leading university, the University of Economic Sciences, experienced a budget crisis in which the University's enrollment (both day and evening students) increased by 22 percent, while the budget declined in real terms by more than 59 percent.[34]

Although Soros's large investment in CEU seems to have borne fruit, there have been significant problems. For example, the Austrian government decided not to cofund this endeavor, and Slovakia refused to be the site, as first proposed. Also, in May 1996, CEU's Prague board met for the final time to dissolve itself; Soros closed the Prague campus due to controversies with Prime Minister Klaus and the Education Ministry, as well as between faculty at CEU—Prague and other Czech academics.[35]

That CEU has faced a number of challenges is understandable. One of the most obvious is the considerable jealousy other scholars in the region feel for those at CEU, arising from large disparities in salaries and facilities.[36] Salaries at CEU are four to five times larger than at local institutions. CEU's main campus in Budapest, often criticized as excessively opulent, is, along with the Collegium Budapest, perhaps the finest in the region. While many applaud Soros for the bold vision, they are highly critical of its execution. As one individual commented, "Even with a brilliant idea, you can not bulldoze it through."[37]

Despite these problems, CEU appears successful in many regards. Its students are outstanding, and it has begun publishing a series of important books on the region's transition. It has also provided the intellectual underpinnings of many of the Soros foundations' regional activities, such as the Privatization Project and HESP. Ralf Dahrendorf, a leader in the region's educational reform efforts and a member of CEU's board, remarked in 1994, before the closing of the Prague campus, that he was satisfied that CEU had achieved stability and that, "after the initial problems and uncertainties, this is now one of the institutions which have an innovative character."[38]

The fact that the Soros foundations made a major investment in a bold, if risky, venture is one reason why other foundations describe Soros as a "social venture capitalist." Despite foundation rhetoric, this role is played relatively rarely. Still, if it remains successful, CEU will represent a major institution of higher learning that will make a contribution in a variety of fields for many years to come. In that regard, CEU may be the single most important foundation-sponsored project in the region.

Results

As suggested above, Soros and his foundations have perhaps done more than any other individual or institution to promote democracy in Central Europe. Soros has had a clear, if ambitious, philanthropic vision—promoting an open society—and a deep engagement in the region that enabled him to take bold, innovative steps. The fact that he had an explicit vision that provided the theoretical undergirding of his grant making makes Soros unique in the region. Although his vision may have been overly theoretical and may not always have been especially appropriate for Central Europe, Soros has had the financial resources necessary to act on his vision.

In doing so, Soros proceeded in a highly imaginative way. He recognized the centrality of education and the importance of local involvement, which went far beyond the rhetoric of many other funders. Soros's modus operandi—identifying local individuals sympathetic to the idea of an open society and empowering them with the financial resources to grapple with their society's problems—is an innovative approach in foreign assistance efforts. Soros's establishment of local offices staffed almost exclusively by local personnel is also noteworthy. These local offices dramatically extended the reach of his foundations, enhanced their institutional capabilities, and improved the prospects that something important would be left behind. They also were established much more quickly and at a fraction of the cost of placing foreigners in these positions, although there were occasionally start-up difficulties and their local staff were sometimes perceived as partisan.[39]

Besides the mode of operation, the sheer size and scope of the Soros foundations is impressive. It is amazing how many lives Soros has touched. The ten-year report of SFH lists thousands of individuals who have benefited from his philanthropy.[40] Soros has also worked in regions, such as Eastern Slovakia, and with groups, including the Roma, that have received scant attention from other funders, public or private.

Soros has made good use of the fact that he has national foundations in every country in Central Europe and, in some cases, multiple offices in each country. The staff of these offices have become adept at identifying candidates for a variety of regional activities, including CEU and the summer schools in international affairs and economics sponsored by Batory. Without this broad reach, the competitions for these activities would be considerably less open.

His willingness to take risks and act boldly, of course, has caused numerous problems for the Soros foundations. At times Soros's vision blurs when it comes to implementation, and his highly personal style of philanthropy can be problematic. For example, one wonders whether the CEU campus in Prague would have been forced to close if there had been other funders involved with less personally at stake and with personalities that did not clash with those of the prime minister and education minister. Also, because of Soros's high profile, his public statements are perhaps given more attention than they deserve. Thus, relatively mild criticisms of Slovakia by Soros were used as an excuse to harass OSF through a politically motivated audit and to heighten scrutiny of the NGO sector there. Soros's work has also been criticized in his native country because of spurious allegations about his international connections and anti-Semitic slurs against him for his Jewish heritage.

Despite all of the positive attributes of Soros's emphasis on local empowerment, there are weaknesses as well. In numerous instances funds have not been well spent, and examples of false starts—most notably in Moscow, where the process of building a foundation required starting anew numerous times—are rife. This heavy local involvement has also resulted in some lost efficiency in program design and resistance to evaluation efforts across the foundations.

The large sums provided by Soros, such as the $65 million investment in CEU, may also have had a distorting effect. As one Slovak foundation executive suggested, "Sometimes too much is just as bad as not having enough resources."[41] Soros's support has distracted attention and siphoned off resources from existing institutions, many of which are in desperate circumstances. The large sums involved may make it difficult for some of the Soros-sponsored institutions to integrate themselves into their local communities. A critical, and as yet unanswered question, is to what extent are the best practices of these institutions replicated in other institutions? If not widely replicated, CEU and other Soros-sponsored institutions may simply become opulent islands in otherwise empty seas.

The Soros foundations appear to work best when somewhat independent from the man. Perhaps understandably, Soros has difficulty delegating decision-making authority. When he does, however, the foundations work well. For example, although Soros initially bankrolled and is the largest supporter of Batory, its Polish leadership was emphatic about remaining uncompromisingly independent.[42] Batory's independence has been enhanced recently by its ability to attract other foundation support. The fact that Ford recently provided Batory with a $2.5 million grant to help generate an endowment will likely increase its independence and bodes well for its future development.

Another criticism is that the Soros foundations—with possible exception of Batory—are among the most opaque of any active in Central Europe, at least in financial terms.[43] Given that Soros uses multiple funding mechanisms registered in different tax jurisdictions, it is very difficult to determine the precise amounts provided and exactly how these sums were used. It is also difficult to characterize the Soros foundations as independent. Although the national foundations are all legally independent and registered in their respective jurisdictions, they rely heavily on Soros financially.

The publication of the 1994 and 1995 annual reports of the Soros foundations were a leap forward in providing information. Before 1994 there had not been a comprehensive annual publication tracking the foundations' expenditures. This is quite remarkable, since Soros had conducted grant making in the region since 1979 and opened an office in Hungary in 1984. Although the Soros foundations are quite good about publishing newsletters and other materials about programs, this relative lack of financial transparency is not especially conducive to strengthening democratic tendencies. It is very difficult for a foundation to suggest that its grantees be transparent (not to mention financially accountable) when the foundation itself is not. Thus, the Soros foundations have encountered significant difficulty in creating viable evaluation mechanisms.[44] Also, this relative opaqueness makes it easy for the foundations' opponents to distort their activities. Unfortunately, this has happened in Slovakia and Hungary, where opponents have suggested that the foundations are part of a New York–Budapest–Tel Aviv conspiracy.

Some individuals interviewed for this study also suggested that the Soros foundations' track record in Central Europe was better before the fall of the Berlin Wall. Afterwards, criticism mounted that the Soros foundations distributed funds only within a tight circle and that, unless you were a member of that circle, it was impossible to gain support. Another common criticism was that all the grant recipients in Hungary were affiliated with a particular political orientation. While this view might be dismissed as that of disgruntled, unsuccessful grant seekers, this researcher heard it expressed frequently enough and by enough individuals who never sought funding to suggest this was not the case. Despite this criticism, these individuals all acknowledged that Soros helped create genuine "democratic space" in their countries. Soros's own lexicon perhaps expresses it best—he has done better at opening closed societies than at building open societies. To be fair no single institution has performed especially well in building democratic societies in Central Europe, Eastern Europe, or the NIS.

In conclusion, Soros has made a major contribution to strengthening democracy in Central Europe. He has energetically pursued a vision of an open society, and, most importantly, he has backed up his words with significant amounts of his own money. Soros also has been extremely innovative in channeling resources to local organizations. In fact, his emphasis on local grant making structures, where local partners have decision-making authority, is exemplary. The international assistance community should take close note. Although Soros's role has not been played perfectly, it has been certainly been important.

8

Conclusions and Recommendations

*A*s the examples in this study suggest, the sixty or so foundations engaged in Central Europe since 1989 have played a modest role in assisting these countries make progress toward market democracy. The role each of these foundations played is difficult to determine precisely, since many other factors influenced this progress, so many organizations were involved, and foundation programs were not static—these programs evolved considerably during the period of this study, 1989–1994.

Although each of the Central European countries is at a somewhat different place on the road to market democracy, there is ample evidence of considerable progress in all four countries. Throughout the region, economic growth is underway, inflation is generally under control, and unemployment is not as high as feared and certainly better than it is in a number of Western European countries. In each of the four Central European countries, there is now a thriving small-business sector, and the majority of the economy is in private hands.

A less positive development is the large and growing gap between those who are succeeding in the new economy and those who are not. The threads of the once-vaunted social safety net are fraying. Increasingly, pensioners, rural populations, and women are expressing growing dissatisfaction with economic reform and the fact that their standard of living is either falling or failing to keep pace with others'. These growing inequities between the transition's winners and losers are undermining social cohesion.

On the political side, at least two rounds of national and local elections have been conducted in a democratic manner, even if many are disappointed with the results. The reconstituted parliaments of the region are now functioning, if imperfectly, and the judiciary—especially the Constitutional Courts—are becoming increasingly independent. The media, particularly print journalism, is also showing signs of greater independence. In addition, the NGO sector's growth has been steady and impressive despite considerable obstacles, including uncertain legal environments and inadequate financing. Central Europeans now have much greater access to information through electronic networks and international telecommunication systems, as well as through greatly expanded opportunities to travel. These are all positive democratizing assets.

Obviously, there have also been negative political developments, especially related to the growing dissatisfaction with the fruits of democracy. This dissatisfaction results, in part, from overblown expectations. Democracy did not bring general material prosperity or political stability. Instead, it brought change with its attendant uncertainties and competition that resulted inevitably in winners and losers. This dissatisfaction has also been fed by the immaturity of many of the institutions of democracy and the lingering of some antidemocratic practices of the past, such as the tendency towards centralization of information and decision making.

At this time, the Central European countries, with the possible exception of Slovakia, have clearly passed the initial stage of democratic transition. Barring unforeseen turbulence, these countries are well on their way to consolidating democracy: Their democratic institutions will mature, and democracy will become more widely accepted and deeply embedded. As discussed in chapter 5, democratic development in Slovakia is troubled. Its political future is much less certain and resembles that of many of the countries in transition east and south of Central Europe.

Foundations have focused resources on a variety of substantive issues important to the democratization. Foundations focused on particular issues for a variety of reasons, such as their culture, mission, and prior experience. For example, the Soros foundations tended to emphasize education; Ford, human rights; Ebert, independent trade unions; Freedom Forum, media; Mellon, libraries; Mott, NGOs; PCT, economic issues; RBF, environment; and Westminster, political parties. Among the most important issues addressed were economics, education, the environment, human rights, and support for the NGO sector. Despite differences in emphasis and strategy, there was considerable overlap among them. However, over time foundations generally became increasingly explicit that their strategies involved supporting the NGO sector or civil society as the best means available to them to assist democracy. Given their experiences and what they had to offer relative to others in the international community, this was an important and appropriate refinement in their grant-making strategies.

Assessing which among the issues emphasized by foundations was most important would involve the choice of Solomon. It is possible, however, to suggest that some emphases were more important than others at particular moments. For example, just prior to the changes in 1989 and in their immediate aftermath, foundations' support for human rights was critical, since very few other organizations were providing this support. Similarly, assistance to political parties in preparation for the first round of elections in the post-Communist period was equally important, since foundations and their partners had the ability to act quickly. Prior to the extensive involvement of international financial institutions and multinational corporations, assistance to economic reform efforts was useful. As the economies began to revive and the formal institutions of democracy took shape, it became increasingly clear that civil society in Central Europe was underdeveloped. Thus, a greater emphasis on the NGO sector was justified. Foundations generally responded quickly to the dynamic circumstances in Central Europe and were flexible enough to reorient their programming to reflect what they perceived as the region's most pressing needs.

Given the difficulty of clearly determining which emphasis was most important, how foundations operated may be revealing. Thus, much of the following discussion will focus not so much on what foundations did but on how they did it. This discussion is complicated by foundations' using a variety of different grant-making structures and styles. With the possible exception of the Soros foundations, most foundations in the first phase relied heavily on intermediaries. This reliance lessened only after some years when foundations developed a greater capacity to work directly with local institutions either through their own expanded knowledge or through the establishment of offices in the region.

Before then, many foundations also relied heavily on individuals, for many foundations perceive that systemic change begins with individuals. Grant making that emphasizes the individual is reinforced when there is an absence of independent institutions with which foundations can join forces. Given the circumstances in Central Europe in 1989, it is understandable that bridgers, such as András Biró, Joanna Regulska, Jan Svejnar, and Zdeněk Drábek, played an important role.

Accomplishments[1]

Foundations active in Central Europe made one of their most positive contributions simply by being there. This may not seem to be much of a contribution, but it is significant. External involvement sometimes offers a psychological support for resistance to lingering antidemocratic tendencies. For example, foundations and other external organizations helped the NGO sector in Slovakia react to, if not necessarily overcome, repeated pressure from the Meciar government. Foundations also dem-onstrated relevant technical skills and gave Central Europeans the op-portunity to network with their Western counterparts, thereby narrow-ing the wide gap that separated them.

A related contribution was made by the sheer numbers of foundations involved. This study tracked the efforts of approximately sixty different foundations engaged in efforts to strengthen democracy in Central Eu-rope. There are other foundations that fell beyond the scope of this study. Each of these foundations had its own concerns, operating styles, and objectives. In the course of this study, Central Europeans often stated that the very plurality of responses, foundations, issues, and approaches provided a powerful and novel demonstration of the pluralism inherent in democratic societies.

Foundations also contributed by extending the circle, even if only narrowly, of participants in the political and policy-making processes. For the most part, foundations sought partners who were not associated with the previous Communist governments. In doing so, they necessarily helped broaden the numbers and character of participants. Although foundations were criticized for generally confining their activities to cap-ital cities and primarily supporting elites, a number of foundations made concerted efforts to reach beyond these spheres. They sought, with some success, to draw new individuals into the complex process of becoming citizens in a democracy by teaching them to assume greater responsi-bility for their own affairs.

By involving new participants in the policy-making process, founda-tions also helped change the terms of public debate by encouraging renewed attention to environmental issues and to the social costs of transition. Foundations also made a related contribution by supporting the development of new institutions, such as independent policy research institutes (think tanks) and organizations serving the NGO sector. These new institutions were likely to have developed over time, but foundations certainly played a role in providing the momentum.

Conventional wisdom to the contrary, developing or strengthening NGOs should not be construed as identical with building democracy. NGOs are instrumental to democracy, but there are many other factors influencing a society's ability to democratize itself, and the time required for building democracy exceeds the period of this study. Nevertheless, what foundations have done to strengthen NGOs is an important con-tribution that suited foundation experience and interest.

Other advantages of foundations, especially when contrasted with public funders, is the fact that their resources were disbursed relatively quickly (in three to six months, as opposed to one to two years), they adapted easily as circumstances changed, and they operated outside of state-to-state relations. From the perspective of democracy strengthen-ing, all of these characteristics had a positive effect. They also had a direct bearing on building the capacity of citizens to articulate persuasively their concerns to the state.

Shortcomings

Although foundations performed an important role in helping expand the space for democracy in Central Europe, some of their shortcomings—especially in the earliest phases of assistance—are becoming increasingly clear. These shortcomings related to patterns of decision making, the nature of their relationships with their Central European partners, and the creation of unrealistic expectations—the mismatch between stated goals and available resources.

In the first phase of assistance, the work of foundations and public funders was welcomed and viewed rather uncritically. As Central Europeans came to perceive that most foundation resources were devoted to outsiders, they began to view assistance efforts much more critically. This led to a growing "expectation gap," where the robust expectations of both funders and recipients were not realized. Foundations may also have further widened this expectation gap by overpromising. They suggested that their activities would help civil society and democracy develop more quickly than was reasonable. Although they had a role to play, conversations with foundation staff and rather grandiose goals in their annual reports may have led many Central Europeans to believe that the role played by foundations was going to be significantly larger than it was or could be.

Another factor contributing to the sense of disappointment experienced by Central Europeans was that little foundation assistance was truly catalytic. Virtually every foundation suggests that its resources are targeted in ways to attract other resources, but given the fact that all resources are spread thinly, this is more often a wish than reality. Although there are numerous examples of cofinancing by foundations to support certain projects, such as EPCE, and between private and public funders to support key institutions, such as CERGE, there are few examples of pilot programs developed by foundations being taken to a larger scale or replicated with the assistance of other resources.

Perhaps the greatest shortcoming of foundation work in Central Europe is the lack of early and concerted attention to the issue of sustainability, despite the fact that foundations acknowledge its importance. During the first phase of assistance, there were distinct advantages to foot-in-the-door grant-making strategies. This approach allowed foundations to range widely in hopes of identifying suitable partners with whom to work on issues where they had a comparative advantage and prospects for making a contribution. The utility of this strategy vanished quickly. By the second phase, regardless of their particular emphasis, foundations needed to pay more attention to sustainability, which is inconsistent with this exploratory strategy. After all, sustainability simply means that something worthwhile is left behind after foundation attention and resources shift elsewhere.

Foundations' general lack of attention to sustainability is surprising, since many, especially those with prior international grant-making experience, are well aware of its importance. To the extent that foundations and others thought about sustainability they seemed to think of it in narrow financial terms. They were often motivated by concerns of avoiding dependency. Thus, in awarding grants foundation staff were generally quite clear that these were of a limited term and that it was incumbent upon the partner institution to secure other sources of funding. Unfortunately, foundations tended not to be especially helpful in providing much-needed practical assistance in securing such funding. Foundations also rarely provided support that reflected a broader understanding of the administrative, managerial, personnel, and even legal dimensions of sustainability. Absent this, foundation hopes that the independent institutions they supported would attract the resources necessary to survive after the near certain withdrawal of foundation resources were unrealistic.

A related factor limiting foundations' results was a tendency to myopia in their approach to the two principal mechanisms of social organization: the state and the market. They tended to view civil society in a vacuum, not recognizing its organic connections to state and market. Consequently, they generally did not use their resources to leverage the market and state resources that might have strengthened the very institutions and processes central to foundations' concerns. The developing NGO sector may have benefitted from early, concerted efforts by foundations to engage the support of the emerging private sector.

Another shortcoming is that foundations did not marshal their collective resources frequently enough to generate a gestalt whereby their efforts as a whole would be greater than the sum of the parts. Foundations, especially during the first phase of assistance, were quite good at sharing information, especially when they were on opposite sides of the Atlantic. However, these foundations, in part driven by their own mandates and cultures, were less successful at cooperating on program design, implementation, evaluation, or replication. Exceptions, such as EPCE, are all too rare. Although this lack of coordination may not be all bad since Central Europe had been overcoordinated for forty years, this certainly resulted in some missed opportunities.

Foundation work would also have been stronger if there had been more of a convergence between the goal, assisting democracy, and the means chosen. The extent to which foundations relied on Western partners for program design and implementation, not to mention decision

making, probably retarded the goal of Central Europeans assuming responsibility for their own affairs. There were good reasons why, in the
first and second phases, many foundations opted to work with Western
partners initially. But these early decisions had consequences for programming that may have minimized the democratizing effect of their
activities overall. Foundations' efforts to assist democracy in the region
could have benefitted by significant local involvement in all aspects of
their work, from design to implementation to evaluation.

Similarly, foundations' efforts to strengthen democratic tendencies and
encourage democratic values, such as participation, openness, and
accountability, could have been more effective had they more self-
consciously modeled the behaviors they advocated. Too often foundations were perceived as closed circles, opaque and not accountable to
any one. A number of Central Europeans who participated in this study
mentioned that the relationships that foundations had with their partners were mirrored by their partners' relationships with others. This
speaks to the need for foundations to be concerned with the governance
and institutional styles of their local partners and themselves.

Another criticism often mentioned by Central Europeans (and generally directed towards foundations from the United States) is that foundations tended to be biased toward their own versions of democracy.
They sought to create the world in their own image. Thus, American
efforts to strengthen parliaments were often motivated by U.S. concepts
of checks and balances and separation of powers, rather than rooted in
an understanding of parliamentary democracy or European jurisprud-
ence. Similarly, support for strengthening civil society seemed driven by
Tocquevillian notions of a robust NGO sector without consideration that
what works well in the United States may work considerably less well
in Europe. Such notions may not be especially helpful in assisting Central Europeans to join European institutions, such as the EU.

Yet another shortcoming is that some foundations, such as the Soros
foundations, appear partisan and excessively involved in local politics.
To the extent that foundations are perceived to be taking sides in local
politics, their effectiveness is minimized. Of course, there is the perpet-
ual risk that in certain countries, such as Slovakia, any involvement may
be construed as partisan.

In addition, foundations generally did not pay sufficient attention to
evaluation or to learning systematically from their activities. Foundations
rarely involved their local partners in a significant way in the evaluations
that did take place. Systematic learning is key to enhancing the quality
of grant making. If the objective is to encourage local partners to assume
greater responsibility for their own affairs, to become better citizens,
they also need to be partners in the evaluation process. Participating in
evaluating democracy assistance efforts can encourage Central Europe-

ans to be more responsible for program outcomes than they had ever been in the past. This criticism applies not only to foundations operating in Central Europe but to those operating elsewhere as well.

Any such evaluations must, however, be clear about what they can accomplish. The task of assisting democracy cannot easily be quantified or readily converted into measurable objectives. That does not mean that establishing clear objectives is unimportant. On the contrary, it is critical. Without knowing precisely where a project is headed, it is nearly impossible to judge what progress has been made or to suggest alternative routes that may make the achievement of the identified goal easier.

Lessons Learned

There is considerable difficulty in measuring the effectiveness of democracy assistance programs precisely because there is no shared definition of what democracy is, nor is there yet a common agreement about the most effective strategies and techniques for building democracy. In addition, assessments are complicated by the fact that democracy assistance programs in Central Europe changed significantly between 1989 and 1996. Nevertheless, there are a number of factors that contributed to the successes foundations experienced in assisting democracy in Central Europe. Among the most important are significant local involvement; a high convergence between the ends, the means, and the resources available; and an emphasis on sustainability, as well as a focus on issues where foundations had a clear comparative advantage.

As numerous Central Europeans who participated in this study suggested, sustainability is the clearest measure of success. Perhaps the single most important factor in sustainability is providing significant opportunities for local involvement, including real partnerships that develop locally adapted grant-making structures. This local involvement most often begins with a local leader, such as András Biró, Pavol Demeš, Jerzy Regulski, and Jana Ryšlinková, who is experienced and has a clear vision of what the organization should become. While such a leader may not be necessary, he or she is valuable to the organization because of the resources and contacts that he or she can make available.

As the successful projects discussed here suggest, strong, effective leaders by themselves are not enough. Also essential are strong local staffs and boards, and locally adapted modes of operation that support the institution's objectives. Having transparent democratic governance that promotes accountability is important, too. Appropriate local operations and staffs are necessary to build strong, trust-based relationships with both local authorities and leaders in the community. They are also critical to ensuring that the foundation's activities are truly responsive to local needs rather than being a reflection of the foundation's perceptions of what those needs may be. All these steps are helpful for sustainability.

Experience in Central Europe suggests that foundations can assist the achievement of sustainability in a number of practical ways. As mentioned previously, how things are done is often as important as what things are done. Empowering local partners with decision-making authority is essential to any project's long-term success. Engaging them in every stage of the project is also important. In particular, significant local involvement will likely preclude a mismatch between a project's stated goals and the resources available. These insights, derived from experiences in many different contexts, are not unknown in the donor community. However, most assistance efforts in Central Europe did not reflect these insights in their programming.

Recognizing that they are making use of scarce resources—time and money—foundations and other funders interested in assisting democracy can enhance prospects for sustainability by making more concerted efforts to generate alternative means of support. This necessarily requires something more than lip service. Foundations need to make greater efforts to help local partners develop cross-sectoral partnerships, partnerships that draw funding from both private and public sectors while not jeopardizing their autonomy. For example, foundations could devote greater resources to educating the private sector about investing in the NGO sector, as well as underwrite projects that help NGOs raise funds.

Modest changes in foundations' operating styles would also greatly assist efforts to strengthen democracy. For example, providing appropriately conditioned, long-term (three to five year) grants would greatly increase the possibility of creating sustainable institutions, particularly if foundations were inclined to provide core support to a small number of targeted institutions. Grants to cover core administrative costs are the most significant assistance that any donor can give a fledgling institution, especially one operating in rapidly changing circumstances. Institutional funding not only supports the community targeted by the foundation's programs, but also the NGO sector at large. The effects of core cost financing are necessarily long term because a self-sustaining institution will carry out projects for the community long after program-related funding has evaporated.

Future foundations' efforts should also be guided by earlier successes; they should focus on issues where they have a clear comparative advantage. In Central Europe, foundations tended to have the greatest impact on the NGO sector generally and on issues related to education, human rights, and the environment in particular because of extensive prior experience with these issues, even if that experience was not gained in the region. Also, these issues did not receive much attention either from the official assistance programs or from cash-strapped local governments. Thus, foundations were playing to their own considerable strengths.

Conclusions

After more than six years of efforts to assist democracy in Central Europe, there is a much clearer sense of the magnitude and complexity of the task as well as a recognition of how much the task was underestimated. There is also a growing appreciation that democratic form is not the same as democratic content. Although each of the Central European countries is considerably more democratic than it was in 1989, they all have varying distances to go on their respective journeys. These countries may very well end up in destinations quite different from those they set out for or that others had hoped them to find.

The major unanswered questions are how successful are democracy assistance programs and would the resources have been better spent in another region or on other projects? Although success is difficult to measure, this study assessed it on three levels: individual, institutional, and societal. Using this framework, most of the individuals participating in foundation-supported activities tended to regard them as worthwhile. Similarly, although very few, if any, of the institutions that the foundations established or strengthened are clearly self-sustaining at this time, foundations have had a discernible effect on a small number of independent institutions with which they have cooperated closely. The maturation of this small set of institutions, namely NGOs, has helped the countries of Central Europe develop a more pluralistic institutional landscape, an important development in the face of the monopolistic legacy of the past.

It is on the societal level where the effects of foundations are least evident. That is understandable, since all of Central Europe is involved in complex and dynamic changes that will likely take at least two generations to accomplish. Clearly, building a market democracy is a formidable task, beyond the capabilities of any group of funders. Ultimately, this is a task for Central Europeans themselves.

Considering whether change was affected at this third level would not be an issue at this time if not for the fact that so many foundations (and other funders) stated that their goals were to produce these effects. More modest goals would have provided clearer benchmarks for assessing what has been achieved. Clearer goals would have allowed a more precise assessment of the relative merits of different strategies. In the absence of such goals, discussions here and elsewhere gravitate towards what projects did rather than what they accomplished.

Despite the current inability to identify precisely the societal effects foundations have helped produce, this study has provided evidence of effects at the individual and institutional level. More importantly, it has mapped, for perhaps the first time, the unprecedented role played by such a large number of European and North American foundations. Developing a clearer understanding of the potential roles for foundations in overseas assistance efforts is important, given the increasing pressure on publicly funded assistance programs. That pressure will invariably result in foundations and other NGOs playing ever larger roles in foreign assistance. If this assistance is directed towards democratization, especially through strengthening the NGO sector, this study suggests that foundations may have a strong comparative advantage relative to other funders.

The question of whether foundation resources could have been better spent in other regions or at home is difficult to answer objectively. Central Europe is clearly involved in a historic transition with wide-ranging effects. This process is encouraging Central Europe to embrace values prized by the West and to engage in what may be considered a common quest for freedom and prosperity. This recognition of common values and goals is a primary motivation for foundations to be engaged in the region.

Foundations are well aware of the consequences of a Europe divided by an iron curtain. If the transition fails in Central Europe, where there are considerable assets and some prior experience, prospects for the transition in Eastern Europe and the NIS will be dim indeed. A new round of cold war expenditures would inevitably mean that issues of importance to many foundations, such as community development, education, and health, would receive less support due to increased pressure on already dwindling government resources.

This study suggests that lessons learned regarding democracy assistance efforts in Central Europe may well apply in other contexts, especially to the societies of Eastern Europe and the NIS, more recently embarked on the transition to democracy and a market economy. To succeed there foundations will need to target their resources carefully to play to their greatest strengths. They will also need to find more effective ways of empowering the foundations' local partners, who have the ultimate responsibility for building their own versions of democracy.

The author hopes that this study has provided organizations interested in democracy assistance efforts suggestions about how to pursue such endeavors. If the Central European countries provide their citizens ever more participatory, competitive political systems, where civil rights receive greater protection, they will offer a powerful model for others. They will also be the final measure of whether the programs supported by foundations for democracy's sake were sound investments.

1 *Project Advisory Committee Members*

Rudolph Andorka	Rector, University of Economic Sciences, Budapest
Pavol Demeš	Office of the President of the Slovak Republic, Bratislava
Deborah Harding	Vice President for National Foundations, Soros Foundation, New York
Robert L. Hutchings	Director, Division of International Studies, Woodrow Wilson International Center for Scholars, Washington, D.C.
Katalin Koncz	Director, Open Society Institute, Budapest
John R. Lampe	Director, East European Studies, Woodrow Wilson International Center for Scholars, Washington, D.C.
Juraj Mesík	Director, Environmental Partnership for Central Europe, Banska Bystrica
Jana Ryšlinková	Director, Information Center for Foundations and Other Not-for-Profit Organizations, Prague
Vladimir Tismaneanu	Associate Professor of Government and Politics, University of Maryland, College Park
Ladislav Venys	Director, Center for Democracy and Free Enterprise, Prague

Jacek Wojnarowski	Executive Director, Stefan Batory Foundation, Warsaw
Sharon Wolchik	Professor of Political Science and International Affairs, George Washington University, Washington, D.C.

2 *For Democracy's Sake Workshop Participants*

Helen Addison	Institute for Human Sciences, Vienna
Maggie Alexander	International Youth Foundation, Battle Creek
Paul Balaran	Carnegie Endowment for International Peace, Washington, D.C.
Ian Bell	Charities Aid Foundation, London
Robert Benjamin	National Democratic Institute, Washington, D.C.
Carol Berezai	Jan Hus Educational Foundation, Brno
Robert Beschel	World Bank, Washington, D.C.
András Biró	Autonómia Alapítvány, Budapest
Thomas Carothers	Carnegie Endowment for International Peace, Washington, D.C.
Lorne Craner	International Republican Institute, Washington, D.C.
Catharin Dalpino	Department of State, Washington, D.C.
Stephen Del Rosso	Pew Charitable Trusts, Philadelphia
Pavol Demeš	Office of the President of the Slovak Republic, Bratislava
James Denton	National Forum Foundation, Washington, D.C.
Nadia Diuk	National Endowment for Democracy, Washington, D.C.
Zdeněk Drábek	World Trade Organization, Geneva

Graham Finney	Independent Consultant, Philadelphia
Marianne Ginsburg	German Marshall Fund of the United States, Washington, D.C.
Kinga Göncz	Partners for Democratic Change, Budapest
Tereza Grellová	Milan Šimečka Foundation, Bratislava
Robert L. Hutchings	Woodrow Wilson International Center for Scholars, Washington, D.C.
Leon Irish	United Way International, Washington, D.C.
Henrieta Kajabová	Slovak Academic Information Agency, Bratislava
Kotaro Kohata	Sasakawa Peace Foundation, Tokyo
Katarína Koštálová	Slovak Academic Information Agency, Bratislava
János Kovács	Institute for Human Sciences, Vienna
Jacek Kozlowski	Foundation in Support of Local Democracy, Warsaw
John R. Lampe	Woodrow Wilson International Center for Scholars, Washington, D.C.
Irena Lasota	Institute for Democracy in Eastern Europe, Washington, D.C.
Nancy Lubin	JNA Associates, Washington, D.C.
Wendy Luers	Foundation for Civil Society, New York
Miklós Marschall	Civicus, Washington, D.C.
Katarina Mathernova	World Bank, Washington, D.C.
Francis Miko	Congressional Research Service, Washington, D.C.
William Moody	Rockefeller Brothers Fund, New York
Juraj Mesík	Environmental Partnership for Central Europe, Banska Bystrica
Ferenc Miszlivetz	Center for European Studies, Budapest/Szombathely

Krzysztof Ners	Policy Education Centre on Assistance to Transition, Warsaw
Dušan Ondrusek	Partners for Democratic Change, Bratislava
Petr Pajas	Center for Democracy and Free Enterprise, Prague
Nancy Popson	Woodrow Wilson International Center for Scholars, Washington, D.C.
Miroslav Pospíšil	Jan Hus Educational Foundation, Brno
Rodger Potocki	National Endowment for Democracy, Washington, D.C.
Maria Pryshlak	East Central European Scholarship Program, Georgetown University, Washington, D.C.
Vlado Raiman	Slovak Committee of the European Cultural Foundation, Bratislava
Joanna Regulska	Center for Russian, Central, and East European Studies, Rutgers University, New Brunswick
Anthony Richter	Open Society Institute, New York
Mary Ann Riegelman	U.S. Agency for International Development, Washington, D.C.
William Robinson	Congressional Research Service, Washington, D.C.
Anna Rozicka	Stefan Batory Foundation, Warsaw
Jana Ryšlinková	Information Center for Foundations and Other Not-for-Profit Organizations, Prague
Karen Salz	Eurasia Foundation, Washington, D.C.
Joseph Schull	Ford Foundation, New York
Karla Simon	International Center for Not-for-Profit Law, Washington, D.C.
Paul Somogyi	Free Trade Union Institute, Washington, D.C.

John Sullivan	Center for International Private Enterprise, Washington, D.C.
Piotr Szczepański	Foundation for Water Supply to Rural Areas, Warsaw
Vineta Veikmane	Baltic Academic Center, Riga
Samuel F. Wells	Woodrow Wilson International Center for Scholars, Washington, D.C.
Jakub Wygnanski	Nongovernmental Organizations Data Base, Warsaw
Michael Zantovsky	Embassy of the Czech Republic, Washington, D.C.

3 Data on Foundation Assistance

TABLE A.1 Foundation Assistance to Central Europe, 1989–1994
(US dollars, in millions)

Foundation Name	Hungary	Poland	Czecho-slovakia	Czech after 1/1/93	Slovakia after 1/1/93	Region: Central Europe	Interregional	Total
Adenauer (from 1990)	3.56	3.89	1.44	2.16	0.28	0	3.22	14.55
Stefan Batory*	0	9.77	0	0	0	0.12	0.71	10.60
Bertelsmann[a]	0	0	0	0	0	0	3.48	3.48
Boll (from 1993)	0	0	0	0	0	0	1.08	1.08
Bosch (from 1990)[b]	0	9.95	0	0	0	1.93	0	11.88
Bradley	0	0.28	0.43	0.08	0	0.20	2.04	3.03
Calihan (1990–93)	0	0	0	0.02	0	0	0	0.02
Carnegie	0.03	0	0	0	0.30	0	10.68	11.00
CEU Foundation (from 1993)*	1.50	0	0	0	0.01	53.89	3.00	58.40
CKH (1991–93)	0.22	0.24	0.14	0.12	0.04	0.01	0.29	1.06
Charta 77 Foundation (1989–91)	0	0	1.76	0	0	0	0	1.76
Charta 77 - Stockholm (1991)	0	0	0.17	0	0	0	0	0.17
CSDF - Czech (1993–94)	0	0	0	3.05	0	0	0	3.05
CSDF - Slovakia (1994)	0	0	0	0	0.37	0	0	0.37
CDF (from 1991)	2.98	0	1.25	0.83	0.50	0	0	5.56
Doen (from 1990)	0.02	0.34	0	0.04	0	0	0.04	0.45
Ebert	4.30	8.93	4.20	0	0	0	0.56	17.98
ECF	0.03	0.03	0.07	0	0.03	0.03	2.05	2.23
Fondation de France (from 1990)	0	1.86	0	0	0	0	0	1.86
Ford	0.94	4.65	1.16	0.44	0.13	3.46	10.05	20.83
Freedom Forum (1992–93)	0.15	0.22	0	0.01	0	0	0.43	0.81
GMF	0.35	2.32	0.35	0.19	0.24	0.89	0.61	4.95
Getty (from 1994)[c]	0.16	0.49	0	0.26	0.07	0	1.40	2.38
Gilman	0	0	0	0	0	0	0.59	0.59
Humboldt[d]	8.31	18.10	4.92	1.10	1.13	0	0	33.56
Fund (from 1990)	1.78	1.46	0	1.13	0.90	0	1.30	6.57
IYF	0	1.82	0	0	0	0	0.00	1.82
Jones	0	0	0	0.05	0	0	0.55	0.60
MacArthur	0	0.11	2.13	1.30	0.01	0.06	2.37	5.97
Mellon	8.96	11.71	6.44	1.24	1.31	0.20	6.14	36.00
Merck (from 1990)	0	0.04	0.03	0	0	0	0	0.07
Mertz-Gilmore	0	0.04	0	0	0	0.15	0.08	0.26
Mott	0.65	0.93	0.34	0.23	0.20	1.55	4.25	8.16

TABLE A.1 Foundation Assistance to Central Europe, 1989–1994 (*Continued*)
(US dollars, in millions)

Foundation Name	Hungary	Poland	Czecho-slovakia	Czech after 1/1/93	Slovakia after 1/1/93	Region: Central Europe	Interregional	Total
NED[e]	4.00	10.02	2.44	0.42	0.66	0.36	5.42	23.32
Naumann	3.39	2.96	1.84	0	0	0	3.22	11.41
Nuffield (1990–92)[f]	0	0	0	0	0	0	0.35	0.35
Olin	0	0	0	0.01	0	0	0	0.01
OSF Bratislava (from 1994)*	0	0	0	0	2.36	0	0	2.36
OSF Prague (from 1994)*	0	0	0	1.32	0	0	0	1.32
PCT	1.15	3.46	1.60	0.09	0.32	4.84	19.64	31.08
RBF	1.49	1.76	0.47	1.00	0.11	5.22	1.01	11.05
Sasakawa (from 1991)	0.10	0.25	0.13	0.07	0.15	4.35	0	5.05
Smith Richardson	0.05	0	0.07	0	0	0	1.01	1.13
Seidel (from 1992)[g]	0	0	0	0	0	0	8.16	8.16
SFH*	47.49	0	0	0	0	0	0.22	47.71
Stifterverband (from 1990)[h]	0	0	0	0	0	0	1.11	1.11
Thyssen (from 1990)[i]	2.35	0.22	0.04	0.10	0	0.41	0.10	3.23
Trust for Mutual Understanding	0.04	0.09	0.14	0.17	0	0.15	1.24	1.81
Volkswagen	1.11	0.20	0	0	0	0	21.73	23.03
Westminster (from 1992)	0.21	0.28	0.01	0.12	0.17	0.04	0.74	1.57
Total	95.31	96.41	31.55	15.53	9.28	77.86	118.87	444.80

Note: A number of other foundations have been active in the region but are not represented here due to insufficient available data. Among these are: Daimler Benz Fonds, Boehringer Ingelheim Fonds, Zuger Kulturstiftung, Landis & Gyr, Stiftelsen Riksbankens, Jubileumsfond, the Charles Douglas-Home Memorial Trust, the Dulverton Trust, the Esmee Fairbairn Foundation, the Gilchrist Charitable Trust, the Grut Charitable Trust, the Rayne Foundation, the Tom Stoppard Charitable Trust, the Bernard Sunley Foundation, the Korber Stiftung, the Haniel Stiftung, the Alfred Jurzykowski Foundation, and the Wellcome Trust. There are also a number of service companies specializing in managing the donations of anonymous donors active in the region.

a) Figures for the Bertelsmann, Boll, Seidel, and Volkswagen may include programs in Southeastern Europe and the former Soviet Union.

b) Figures listed for the Bosch Foundation and the cooperating Dutch foundations are taken from the Institute for EastWest Studies survey, *Assistance to Transition 1995*.

c) Figures for inter-regional grants by the Getty Grant Program include a total of $900,000 in unspecified grants made between 1990 and 1992 in the region as a whole.

d) Figures for Humboldt are estimated based on the number of foreign scholars and research awards each year and the average amount of stipends or awards.

e) Figures for NED include grants made to their sister organizations, CIPE, FTUI, IRI, and NDI, as well as to other intermediaries.

f) Figures for Nuffield do not include expenditures on fellowships and conferences in 1991, which were unavailable.

g) Figures for Seidel in 1993 are as estimated in the 1992 Annual Report.

h) Figures for the Stifterverband represent undifferentiated spending in the region. Included in this number is an investment in Collegium Budapest of approximately $220,000 between 1992 and 1997.

i) Figures for Thyssen represent its investment in Collegium Budapest only.

* Figures for Soros Foundations in 1994 may include grants made by the Open Society Institute in the respective country.

TABLE A.2 Foundation Assistance to the Czech Republic, 1993–1994
(U.S. dollars, in millions)

Foundation	
Adenauer	2.16
Bradley	0.08
Calihan (1990–93)	0.02
CKH (1993)	0.12
CSDF - Czech	3.05
CDF	0.83
Doen[a]	0.04
Ford	0.44
Freedom Forum (1993)	0.01
GMF	0.19
Getty (from 1994)	0.26
Humboldt[b]	1.10
Fund	1.13
Jones	0.05
MacArthur	1.30
Mellon	1.24
Mott	0.23
NED[c]	0.42
Olin	0.01
OSF Prague (from 1994)*	1.32
PCT	0.09
RBF	1.00
Sasakawa	0.07
Thyssen	0.10
Trust for Mutual Understanding	0.17
Westminster	0.12
Total	15.53

a) Figures listed for the cooperating Dutch foundations are taken from the Institute for EastWest Studies survey, *Assistance to Transition 1995*.

b) Figures for Humboldt are estimated based on the number of foreign scholars and research awards each year and the amount of stipends or awards.

c) Figures for NED include grants made to their sister organizations, CIPE, FTUI, IRI, and NDI, as well as to other intermediaries.

* Figures for Soros Foundations in 1994 may include grants made by the Open Society Institute in the respective country.

TABLE A.3 **Foundation Assistance to Czechoslovakia and Czech and Slovak Regional Grants, 1989–1994**

(U.S. dollars, in millions)

Foundation	
Adenauer (from 1990)	1.44
Bradley	0.43
CKH (1991-93)	0.14
Charta 77 Foundation (1989–91)	1.76
Charta 77 - Stockholm (1991)	0.17
CDF (from 1991)	1.25
Ebert	4.20
ECF	0.07
Ford	1.16
GMF	0.35
Humboldt[a]	4.92
MacArthur	2.13
Mellon	6.44
Merck (from 1990)	0.03
Mott	0.34
NED[b]	2.44
Naumann	1.84
PCT	1.60
RBF	0.47
Sasakawa (from 1991)	0.13
Smith Richardson	0.07
Thyssen (from 1990)	0.04
Trust for Mutual Understanding	0.14
Westminster (from 1992)	0.01
Total	31.55

a) Figures for Humboldt are estimated based on the number of foreign scholars and research awards each year and the amount of stipends or awards.
b) Figures for NED include grants made to their sister organizations, CIPE, FTUI, IRI, and NDI, as well as to other intermediaries.

TABLE A.4 Foundation Assistance to Hungary, 1989–1994
(U.S. dollars, in millions)

Foundation	
Adenauer (from 1990)	3.56
Carnegie	0.03
CEU Foundation (from 1993)	1.50
CKH (1991–93)	0.22
CDF (from 1991)	2.98
Doen (from 1990)[a]	0.02
Ebert	4.30
ECF	0.03
Ford	0.94
Freedom Forum (1992-93)	0.15
GMF	0.35
Getty (from 1994)	0.16
Humboldt[b]	0.00
Fund (from 1990)	8.31
Mellon	8.96
Mott	0.65
NED[c]	4.00
Naumann	3.39
PCT	1.15
RBF	1.49
Sasakawa (from 1991)	0.10
Smith Richardson	0.05
SFH*	47.49
Thyssen (from 1990)[d]	2.35
Trust for Mutual Understanding	0.04
Volkswagen	1.11
Westminster (from 1992)	0.21
Total	95.31

a) Figures listed for the cooperating Dutch foundations are taken from the Institute for EastWest Studies survey, *Assistance to Transition 1995*.

b) Figures for Humboldt are estimated based on the number of foreign scholars and research awards each year and the amount of stipends or awards.

c) Figures for NED include grants made to their sister organizations, CIPE, FTUI, IRI, and NDI, as well as to other intermediaries.

d) Figures for Thyssen represent its investment in Collegium Budapest only.

* Figures for Soros Foundations in 1994 may include grants made by the Open Society Institute in the respective country.

TABLE A.5 Foundation Assistance to Poland, 1989–1994
(U.S. dollars, in millions)

Foundation	
Adenauer (from 1990)	3.89
Stefan Batory*	9.77
Bosch (from 1990)[a]	9.95
Bradley	0.28
CKH (1991–93)	0.24
Doen (from 1990)	0.34
Ebert	8.93
ECF	0.03
Fondation de France (from 1990)	1.86
Ford	4.65
Freedom Forum (1992–93)	0.22
GMF	2.32
Getty (from 1994)	0.49
Humboldt[b]	18.10
Fund (from 1990)	1.46
IYF	1.82
MacArthur	0.11
Mellon	11.71
Merck (from 1990)	0.04
Mertz-Gilmore	0.04
Mott	0.93
NED[c]	10.02
Naumann	2.96
PCT	3.46
RBF	1.76
Sasakawa (from 1991)	0.25
Thyssen (from 1990)	0.22
Trust for Mutual Understanding	0.09
Volkswagen	0.20
Westminster (from 1992)	0.28
Total	96.41

a) Figures listed for the Bosch Foundation are taken from the Institute for EastWest Studies survey, *Assistance to Transition 1995*.
b) Figures for Humboldt are estimated based on the number of foreign scholars and research awards each year and the amount of stipends or awards.
c) Figures for NED include grants made to their sister organizations, CIPE, FTUI, IRI, and NDI, as well as to other intermediaries.
* Figures for Soros Foundations in 1994 may include grants made by the Open Society Institute in the respective country.

TABLE A.6 Foundation Assistance to Slovakia, 1993–1994
(U.S. dollars, in millions)

Foundation	
Adenauer	0.28
Carnegie	0.30
CEU Foundation	0.01
CKH	0.04
CSDF - Slovakia (from 1994)	0.37
CDF	0.50
ECF	0.03
Ford	0.13
GMF	0.24
Getty (from 1994)	0.07
Humboldt[a]	1.13
Fund	0.90
MacArthur	0.01
Mellon	1.31
Mott	0.20
NED[b]	0.66
OSF Bratislava (from 1994)*	2.36
PCT	0.32
RBF	0.11
Sasakawa	0.15
Westminster	0.17
Total	9.28

a) Figures for Humboldt are estimated based on the number of foreign scholars and research awards each year and the amount of stipends or awards.

b) Figures for NED include grants made to their sister organizations, CIPE, FTUI, IRI, and NDI, as well as to other intermediaries.

* Figures for Soros Foundations in 1994 may include grants made by the Open Society Institute in the respective country.

TABLE A.7 **Foundation Assistance to Central Europe, Regional Grants, 1989–1994**
(U.S. dollars, in millions)

Foundation	
Stefan Batory	0.12
Bosch (from 1990)[a]	1.93
Bradley	0.20
CEU Foundation (from 1993)	53.89
CKH (1991–93)	0.01
ECF	0.03
Ford	3.46
GMF	0.89
MacArthur	0.06
Mellon	0.20
Mertz-Gilmore (from 1990)	0.15
Mott	1.55
NED[b]	0.36
PCT	4.84
RBF	5.22
Sasakawa (from 1991)	4.35
Thyssen (from 1990)	0.41
Trust for Mutual Understanding	0.15
Westminster (from 1992)	0.04
Total	77.86

a) Figures listed for the Bosch Foundation are taken from the Institute for EastWest Studies survey, *Assistance to Transition 1995*.
b) Figures for NED include grants made to their sister organizations, CIPE, FTUI, IRI, and NDI, as well as to other intermediaries.

TABLE A.8 Foundation Assistance to Central and Eastern Europe, Interregional Grants, 1989–1994

(U.S. dollars, in millions)

Foundation	
Adenauer (from 1990)	3.22
Stefan Batory*	0.71
Bertelsmann	3.48
Boll (from 1993)[a]	1.08
Bradley	2.04
Carnegie	10.68
CEU Foundation (from 1993)	3.00
CKH (1991–93)	0.29
Doen (from 1990)	0.04
Ebert	0.56
ECF	2.05
Ford	10.05
Freedom Forum (1992–93)	0.43
GMF	0.61
Getty (from 1994)[b]	1.40
Gilman	0.59
Fund (from 1990)	1.30
Jones	0.55
MacArthur	2.37
Mellon	6.14
Mertz-Gilmore	0.08
Mott	4.25
NED[c]	5.42
Naumann	3.22
Nuffield (1990–92)	0.35
PCT	19.64
RBF	1.01
Smith Richardson	1.01
Seidel (from 1992)[d]	8.16
SFH*	0.22
Stifterverband (from 1990)	1.11
Thyssen (from 1990)	0.10
Trust for Mutual Understanding	1.24
Volkswagen	21.73
Westminster (from 1992)	0.74
Total	118.87

a) Figures for Bertelsmann, Boll, Seidel, and Volkswagen may include programs in Southeastern Europe and the former Soviet Union.

b) Figures for inter-regional grants by the Getty Grant Program include a total of $900.000 in unspecified grants made between 1990 and 1992 in the region as a whole.

c) Figures for NED include grants made to their sister organizations, CIPE, FTUI, IRI, and NDI, as well as to other intermediaries.

d) Figures for Seidel in 1993 are as estimated in the 1992 Annual Report.

* Figures for Soros Foundations in 1994 may include grants made by the Open Society Institute in the respective country.

TABLE A.9 Foundation Assistance to Central Europe by Modality, 1989–1994

(US dollars, in thousands)

Foundation	Education and Training	Technical assistance	Policy research	Institution building	Funding for intermediaries	Other	Total
Stefan Batory	1,505	209	227	2,106	0	1,527	5,575
Bradley	618	290	178	525	1,211	204	3,026
Calihan (1990–93)	0	0	0	2	0	0	2
Carnegie	200	2,685	2,041	1,625	4,150	300	11,001
CEU Foundation (from 1993)	0	0	0	54,541	3,857	0	58,398
CKH (1991–93)	667	374	0	14	0	0	1,055
Charta 77 Foundation (1989–91)	50	5	3	68	0	1,636	1,762
Charta 77 - Stockholm (1991)	2	3	0	0	0	164	169
CSDF - Slovakia (1994)	56	97	0	0	0	217	370
Doen (from 1990)	445	0	0	0	0	0	445
ECF	470	0	230	446	333	753	2,233
Fondation de France (from 1990)	0	0	0	1,863	0	0	1,863
Ford	4,181	5,181	3,619	2,220	2,835	2,795	20,831
Freedom Forum (1992–93)	471	110	154	75	0	0	809
GMF	2,114	965	84	1,231	24	533	4,953
Getty (from 1994)[a]	503	0	478	0	0	1,403	2,385
Gilman	0	0	396	5	0	190	591
Humboldt[b]	0	0	29,398	0	0	4,158	33,556
IYF	509	81	0	1,235	0	0	1,825
Jones	0	250	297	50	0	0	597
MacArthur	1,138	90	234	4,010	500	0	5,973
Mellon	9,004	15,973	0	5,698	1,065	4,258	35,998
Merck (from 1990)	38	10	0	0	20	0	68
Mertz-Gilmore	53	20	20	100	70	0	263
Mott	1,824	1,985	360	3,167	250	570	8,155
NED[c]	1,090	4,133	144	2,857	13,876	1,223	23,323
Nuffield (1990–92)[d]	130	35	0	48	84	52	349
Olin	0	0	0	9	0	0	9
PCT	16,990	5,490	1,720	3,190	0	3,690	31,080
RBF	1,856	1,902	470	4,753	1,400	673	11,053
Sasakawa (from 1991)	1,322	0	120	450	0	3,159	5,051
Smith Richardson	0	0	0	68	1,010	54	1,132
SFH	8,355	802	1,465	6,940	0	14,193	31,754
Stifterverband (from 1990)	0	0	0	0	0	1,108	1,108
Thyssen (from 1990)[e]	752	0	0	2,402	0	75	3,228
Trust for Mutual Understanding	1,341	100	0	0	0	373	1,814
Volkswagen[f]	9,069	4,242	4,569	4,955	0	197	23,033
Westminster (from 1992)	985	309	76	70	0	126	1,566
Total	65,738	45,340	46,285	104,722	30,685	43,631	336,401

Note: Totals do not equal those in tables A.1 to A.8. and A.17. due to the impossibility of disaggregating certain foundations' grants.

a) Figures for "other" grants made by the Getty Grant Program include $900,000 of unspecified grants made between 1990 and 1992.

b) Figures for Humboldt are estimated based on the number of foreign scholars and research awards each year and the average amount of stipends or awards.

c) Figures for NED include all grants made to its sister organizations (CIPE, FTUI, IRI, and NDI) as well as grants to intermediaries.

d) Figures for the Nuffield Foundation do not include expenditures on fellowships and conferences in 1991, which were unavailable.

e) Figures for Thyssen represent its investment in Collegium Budapest only.

f) Figures for Volkswagen may include programs in Southeastern Europe and the Former Soviet Union; $12,357,782 spent on a program to fund collaborative projects and summer schools has been split evenly between "institution building," "training," and "research."

TABLE A.10 Foundation Assistance to the Czech Republic by Modality, 1993–1994
(US dollars, in thousands)

Foundation	Education and Training	Technical assistance	Policy research	Institution building	Funding for intermediaries	Other	Total
Bradley	0	0	0	50	0	25	75
Calihan (1993)	0	0	0	2	0	0	2
CKH (1993)	97	25	0	0	0	0	123
Doen[a]	44	0	0	0	0	0	44
Ford	0	100	176	118	0	50	444
Freedom Forum (1993)	6	0	0	0	0	0	6
GMF	62	39	0	11	0	81	194
Getty (from 1994)	0	0	50	0	0	213	263
Humboldt[b]	0	0	994	0	0	103	1,097
Jones	0	0	0	50	0	0	50
MacArthur	0	0	0	1,300	0	0	1,300
Mellon	100	673	0	450	0	16	1,239
Mott	0	0	0	226	0	0	226
NED[c]	10	0	0	0	408	0	418
Olin	0	0	0	9	0	0	9
PCT	85	0	0	0	0	0	85
RBF	90	352	50	480	0	24	996
Sasakawa	30	0	0	0	0	40	70
Thyssen	78	0	0	21	0	0	99
Trust for Mutual Understanding	56	5	0	0	0	108	169
Westminster	68	9	0	8	0	33	118
Total	727	1,204	1,270	2,725	408	693	7,027

Note: Totals do not include approximately $8 million in interregional grants provided by Adenauer, CSDF (Czech), CDF, Fund, OSF (Prague) which could not be disaggregated, and may not add due to rounding.

a) Figures listed for the cooperating Dutch foundations are taken from the Institute for EastWest Studies survey, "Assistance to Transition 1995."

b) Figures for the Humboldt Stiftung are estimated based on the number of foreign scholars and research awards each year and the average amount of stipends or awards.

c) Figures for NED include grants made to their sister organizations, CIPE, FTUI, IRI, and NDI, as well as to other intermediaries.

TABLE A.11 **Foundation Assistance to Czechoslovakia and Czech and Slovak, Regional Grants, by Modality, 1989–1994**

(US dollars, in thousands)

Foundation	Education and Training	Technical assistance	Policy research	Institution building	Funding for intermediaries	Other	Total
Bradley	0	0	0	425	0	2	427
CKH (1991–93)	93	47	0	0	0	0	140
Charta 77 Foundation (1989–91)	50	5	3	68	0	1,636	1,762
Charta 77 - Stockholm (1991)	2	3	0	0	0	164	169
ECF	17	0	45	6	0	0	68
Ford	0	1,087	0	75	0	0	1,162
GMF	117	5	0	70	24	130	346
Humboldt[a]	0	0	4,256	0	0	666	4,922
MacArthur	0	25	0	2,100	0	0	2,125
Mellon	1,006	3,065	0	1,070	140	1,155	6,435
Merck (from 1990)	0	10	0	0	20	0	30
Mott	15	52	0	75	200	0	342
NED[b]	27	806	29	307	1,155	118	2,442
PCT	750	850	0	0	0	0	1600
RBF	50	35	35	150	200	0	470
Sasakawa (from 1991)	0	0	0	0	0	132	132
Smith Richardson	0	0	0	68	0	0	68
Thyssen (from 1990)	0	0	0	30	0	9	39
Trust for Mutual Understanding	24	25	0	0	0	86	135
Westminster (from 1992)	0	6	0	0	0	0	6
Total	2,150	6,021	4,368	4,444	1,739	4,098	22,820

Note: Totals do not include approximately $3 million in interregional grants provided by Adenauer, CDF, Ebert and Naumann which could not be disaggregated.

a) Figures for Humboldt are estimated based on the number of foreign scholars and research awards each year and the average amount of stipends or awards.

b) Figures for NED include grants made to their sister organizations, CIPE, FTUI, IRI, and NDI, as well as to other intermediaries.

TABLE A.12 **Foundation Assistance to Hungary by Modality, 1989–1994**
(US dollars, in thousands)

Foundation	Education and Training	Technical assistance	Policy research	Institution building	Funding for intermediaries	Other	Total
Carnegie	0	25	0	0	0	0	25
CEU Foundation (from 1993)	0	0	0	1,500	0	0	1,500
CKH (1991-93)	151	68	0	0	0	0	219
Doen (from 1990)[a]	17	0	0	0	0	0	17
ECF	9	0	0	10	0	9	27
Ford	381	510	0	0	0	46	937
Freedom Forum (1992–93)	154	0	0	0	0	0	154
GMF	332	6	2	0	0	13	353
Getty (from 1994)	0	0	60	0	0	100	160
Humboldt[b]	0	0	6,913	0	0	1,396	8,308
Mellon	2,176	5,019	0	889	0	878	8,962
Mott	40	87	0	520	0	0	647
NED[c]	65	155	0	217	3,490	76	4,003
PCT	345	0	0	65	0	735	1,145
RBF	106	125	55	1,143	0	60	1,489
Sasakawa (from 1991)	0	0	0	0	0	100	100
Smith Richardson	0	0	0	0	0	54	54
SFH[d]	8,341	802	1,403	6,940	0	14,047	47,490
Thyssen (from 1990)[e]	0	0	0	2,351	0	0	2,351
Trust for Mutual Understanding	42	0	0	0	0	0	42
Volkswagen	0	0	0	1,109	0	0	1,109
Westminster (from 1992)	111	67	0	0	0	34	212
Total	12,268	6,865	8,432	14,743	3,490	17,547	79,304

Note: Totals do not include approximately $14 million in interregional grants provided by Adenauer, CDF, Ebert, Fund, Naumann which could not be disaggregated, and may not add due to rounding.

a) Figures listed for the cooperating Dutch foundations are taken from the Institute for EastWest Studies survey, "Assistance to Transition 1995."

b) Figures for Humboldt are estimated based on the number of foreign scholars and research awards each year and the average amount of stipends or awards.

c) Figures for NED include grants made to their sister organizations, CIPE, FTUI, IRI, and NDI, as well as to other intermediaries.

d) Total for Soros Foundation Hungary includes 15,959.000 for 1994 that can not be split by modality. That amount may also include grants made by the Open Society Institute in Hungary in 1994.

e) Figures for Thyssen represent its investment in Collegium Budapest only.

TABLE A.13 Foundation Assistance to Poland by Modality, 1989–1994

(US dollars, in thousands)

Foundation	Education and Training	Technical assistance	Policy research	Institution building	Funding for intermediaries	Other	Total
Stefan Batory[a]	1,408	149	179	1,614	0	1,396	9,768
Bradley	0	10	0	50	190	34	284
CKH (1991–93)	133	90	0	14	0	0	236
Doen (from 1990)	342	0	0	0	0	0	342
ECF	5	0	6	0	0	19	31
Fondation de France (from 1990)	0	0	0	1,863	0	0	1,863
Ford	303	2,244	767	1,305	0	35	4,654
Freedom Forum (1992–93)	223	0	0	0	0	0	223
GMF	654	657	45	713	0	253	2,322
Getty (from 1994)	0	0	348	0	0	140	488
Humboldt[b]	0	0	16,285	0	0	1,811	18,095
IYF	509	81	0	1,235	0	0	1,825
MacArthur	15	0	92	0	0	0	107
Mellon	1,722	6,333	0	2,589	375	694	11,713
Merck (from 1990)	38	0	0	0	0	0	38
Mertz-Gilmore	0	10	0	0	25	0	35
Mott	524	185	70	105	50	0	934
NED[c]	726	2,543	0	1,347	5,335	65	10,016
PCT	350	2,580	0	200	0	325	3,455
RBF	370	390	15	875	0	107	1,757
Sasakawa (from 1991)	0	0	0	0	0	250	250
Thyssen (from 1990)	222	0	0	0	0	0	222
Trust for Mutual Understanding	36	25	0	0	0	25	86
Volkswagen	0	0	0	0	0	197	197
Westminster (from 1992)	210	36	23	0	0	10	279
Total	7,790	15,333	17,829	11,910	5,975	5,361	69,220

Note: Totals do not include approximately $17.5 million in interregional grants provided by Adenauer, Bosch, Ebert, Fund, Naumann which could not be disaggregated, and may not add due to rounding.

a) Total for Batory includes 5,022.000 for 1994 that can not be split by modality and thus is not represented in the six categories. That amount may also include grants made by the Open Society Institute in Poland in 1994.

b) Figures for Humboldt are estimated based on the number of foreign scholars and research awards each year and the average amount of stipends or awards.

c) Figures for NED include grants made to their sister organizations, CIPE, FTUI, IRI, and NDI, as well as to other intermediaries.

TABLE A.14 Foundation Assistance to Slovakia by Modality, 1993–1994
(US dollars, in thousands)

Foundation	Education and Training	Technical assistance	Policy research	Institution building	Funding for intermediaries	Other	Total
Carnegie	0	0	0	300	0	0	300
CEU Foundation	0	0	0	9	0	0	9
CKH (1993)	32	5	0	0	0	0	37
CSDF - Slovakia (1994)	56	97	0	0	0	217	370
ECF	0	0	27	0	0	0	27
Ford	50	75	0	0	0	0	125
GMF	3	153	4	70	0	11	240
Getty (from 1994)	0	0	20	0	0	50	70
Humboldt[a]	0	0	951	0	0	183	1,134
MacArthur	10	0	0	0	0	0	10
Mellon	1,171	110	0	25	0	0	1,306
Mott	98	86	0	15	0	0	200
NED[b]	18	27	50	0	548	17	660
PCT	90	165	0	0	0	60	315
RBF	110	0	0	0	0	0	110
Sasakawa	30	0	120	0	0	0	150
Westminster	53	99	0	0	0	22	174
Total	1,720	818	1,172	419	548	560	5,236

Note: Totals do not include approximately $4 million in interregional grants provided by Adenauer, CDF, Fund, OSF (Bratislava) which could not be disaggregated, and may not add due to rounding.

a) Figures for Humboldt are estimated based on the number of foreign scholars and research awards each year and the average amount of stipends or awards.

b) Figures for NED include grants made to their sister organizations, CIPE, FTUI, IRI, and NDI, as well as to other intermediaries.

TABLE A.15 **Foundation Assistance to Central Europe, Regional Grants, by Modality, 1989–1994**

(US dollars, in thousands)

Foundation	Training	Technical assistance	Policy research	Institution building	Funding for intermediaries	Other	Total
Stefan Batory	25	8	7	65	0	16	122
Bradley	0	0	24	0	95	80	199
CEU Foundation (from 1993)	0	0	0	53,032	857	0	53,889
CKH (1991–93)	5	0	0	0	0	0	5
ECF	20	0	2	0	0	3	25
Ford	653	375	1,987	372	0	75	3,462
GMF	496	10	33	337	0	13	889
MacArthur	0	0	60	0	0	0	60
Mellon	0	0	0	0	150	50	200
Mertz-Gilmore	53	0	0	100	0	0	153
Mott	360	803	115	225	0	50	1,553
NED[a]	119	50	15	0	181	0	365
PCT	2,520	600	625	600	0	495	4,840
RBF	980	700	306	2,105	800	329	5,220
Sasakawa (from 1991)	1,262	0	0	450	0	2,637	4,349
SFH	0	0	0	0	0	4	4
Thyssen (from 1990)	412	0	0	0	0	0	412
Trust for Mutual Understanding	128	0	0	0	0	18	146
Westminster (from 1992)	35	1	0	0	0	4	40
Total	7,068	2,547	3,175	57,286	2,083	3,774	75,933

a) Figures for NED include grants made to their sister organizations, CIPE, FTUI, IRI, and NDI, as well as to other intermediaries.

TABLE A.16 Foundation Assistance to Central and Eastern Europe, Interregional Grants, by Modality, 1989–1994

(US dollars, in thousands)

Foundation	Training	Technical assistance	Policy research	Institution building	Funding for intermediaries	Other	Total
Stefan Batory	72	52	41	428	0	115	707
Bradley	618	280	154	0	926	63	2,041
Carnegie	200	2,660	2,041	1,325	4,150	300	10,676
CEU Foundation (from 1993)	0	0	0	0	3,000	0	3,000
CKH (1991–93)	156	139	0	0	0	0	295
Doen (from 1990)	41	0	0	0	0	0	41
ECF	419	0	151	430	333	722	2,054
Ford	2,794	790	690	350	2,835	2,589	10,048
Freedom Forum (1992–93)	88	110	154	75	0	0	427
GMF	452	96	0	30	0	32	610
Getty (from 1994)[a]	503	0	0	0	0	900	1,403
Gilman	0	0	396	5	0	190	591
Jones	0	250	297	0	0	0	547
MacArthur	1,113	65	83	610	500	0	2,371
Mellon	2,830	773	0	675	400	1,465	6,142
Mertz-Gilmore	0	10	20	0	45	0	75
Mott	787	771	175	2,001	0	520	4,254
NED[b]	125	553	50	985	2,758	948	5,419
Nuffield (1990–92)[c]	130	35	0	48	84	52	349
PCT	12,850	1,295	1,095	2,325	0	2,075	19,640
RBF	150	300	9	0	400	153	1,012
Smith Richardson	0	0	0	0	1,010	0	
SFH	14	0	63	0	0	142	218
Stifterverband (from 1990)	0	0	0	0	0	1,108	1,108
Thyssen (from 1990)	39	0	0	0	0	65	105
Trust for Mutual Understanding	1,055	45	0	0	0	136	1,236
Volkswagen[d]	9,069	4,242	4,569	3,846	0	0	21,727
Westminster (from 1992)	509	89	53	62	0	24	737
Total	34,015	12,554	10,039	13,195	16,441	11,598	97,842

Note: Totals do not include approximately $21 million in interregional grants provided by Adenauer, Bertelsman, Boll, Ebert, Fund, Naumann, and Seitel which could not be disaggregated.

a) Figures for inter-regional grants by the Getty Grant Program include a total of $900.000 in unspecified grants made between 1990 and 1992 in the region as a whole.

b) Figures for NED include grants made to their sister organizations, CIPE, FTUI, IRI, and NDI, as well as to other intermediaries.

c) Figures for Nuffield do not include expenditures on fellowships and conferences in 1991, which were unavailable.

d) Figures for Volkswagen may include programs in Southeastern Europe and the Former Soviet Union; $12,357,782 spent by Volkswagen on a program to fund collaborative projects has been split evenly between "institution building," "training," and "research."

TABLE A.17 Foundation Assistance to Central Europe by Type, 1989–1994

(US dollars, in thousands)

Foundation	Human rights	Non-governmental organizations	Rule of law	Electoral assistance	Democratic institutions	Civic education	Higher education	Free press
Stefan Batory*	534	1,611	58	0	63	33	2,540	346
Bradley	53	0	24	0	112	84	0	505
Calihan (1990–93)	0	0	0	0	0	15	0	0
Carnegie	300	25	0	0	225	0	4,175	25
CEU Foundation (from 1993)	0	1,509	0	0	0	0	53,032	0
CKH (1991–93)	52	485	0	0	0	6	8	7
Charta 77 Foundation (1989–91)	0	27	3	0	7	1	35	84
Charta 77 - Stockholm (1991)	0	0	0	0	0	0	162	3
CSDF - Czech (1993–95)	0	3,052	0	0	0	0	0	0
CSDF - Slovakia (1994)	0	370	0	0	0	0	0	0
Doen (from 1990)	0	247	0	0	0	0	0	0
ECF	44	59	18	0	243	8	78	327
Fondation de France (from 1990)	0	1,863	0	0	0	0	0	0
Ford	2,123	2,565	566	0	2,584	0	2,918	114
Freedom Forum (1992–93)	0	0	0	0	0	0	0	709
GMF	226	370	147	24	448	191	55	849
Getty (from 1994)	0	0	0	0	0	0	0	0
Gilman	0	0	0	0	0	0	0	0
Humboldt[a]	0	0	0	0	0	0	33,556	0
Fund (from 1990)	0	0	0	0	0	0	0	6,571
IYF	0	1,702	0	0	0	0	0	0
Jones	50	0	0	0	0	0	0	0
MacArthur	515	150	5	0	27	0	975	10
Mellon	100	345	93	0	380	0	8,501	0
Merck (from 1990)	10	20	0	0	0	38	0	0
Mertz-Gilmore	45	98	0	0	10	0	0	0
Mott	105	2,918	380	35	174	160	35	0
NED[b]	459	8,876	467	2,039	1,961	1,239	171	1,776
Nuffield (1990-92)	0	84	46	0	0	0	0	0
Olin	0	0	0	0	0	9	0	0
OSF Bratislava (from 1994)*	0	338	0	0	0	0	687	290
OSF Prague (from 1994)*	0	0	0	0	0	0	517	54
PCT	0	300	0	0	4,185	4,460	3,510	0
RBF	450	1,694	0	0	475	0	0	34
Sasakawa (from 1991)	0	210	0	0	0	0	0	0
Smith Richardson	230	0	0	0	0	68	0	480
SFH*	4,406	1,953	149	107	162	125	9,888	5,992
Stifterverband (from 1990)	0	0	0	0	0	0	1,108	0
Thyssen (from 1990)[c]	0	0	0	0	0	0	3,015	0
Trust for Mutual Understanding	0	0	0	0	0	0	00	
Volkswagen[d]	0	0	0	0	0	0	18,790	0
Westminster (from 1992)	99	163	6	235	723	45	0	45
Total	9,800	31,033	1,962	2,440	11,778	6,481	143,755	18,222

a) Figures for Humboldt are estimated based on the number of foreign scholars and research awards each year and the average amount of stipends or awards.

b) Figures for NED include grants made to its sister organizations, CIPE, FTUI, IRI, and NDI, as well as to other intermediaries.

c) Figures for Thyssen represent its investment in Collegium Budapest only.

d) Figures for Volkswagen may include programs in Southeastern Europe and the former Soviet Union.

* Figures for the Soros Foundations in 1994 may include grants made by the Open Society Institute in each respective country.

TABLE A.17 **Foundation Assistance to Central Europe by Type, 1989–1994 (*Continued*)**
(US dollars, in thousands)

Foundation	Public administration/ local government	Public discourse	Economic reform	Elementary/ secondary education	Economic education	Management education
Stefan Batory*	18	212	167	582	192	5
Bradley	0	1,148	10	0	0	0
Calihan (1990–93)	0	0	0	0	0	0
Carnegie	0	0	175	0	0	0
CEU Foundation (from 1993)	0	0	0	0	0	0
CKH (1991–93)	0	0	2	16	4	6
Charta 77 Foundation (1989–91)	0	0	2	0	0	2
Charta 77 - Stockholm (1991)	0	0	0	0	0	0
CSDF - Czech (1993–95)	0	0	0	0	0	0
CSDF - Slovakia (1994)	0	0	0	0	0	0
Doen (from 1990)[a]	0	0	0	0	0	0
ECF	0	341	11	15	0	0
Fondation de France (from 1990)	0	0	0	0	0	0
Ford	50	0	5,182	0	819	112
Freedom Forum (1992–93)	0	0	0	0	0	100
GMF	169	108	748	36	92	21
Getty (from 1994)[b]	0	0	0	0	0	0
Gilman	0	5	0	0	0	0
Humboldt	0	0	0	0	0	0
Fund (from 1990)	0	0	0	0	0	0
IYF	0	0	0	32	0	0
Jones	0	297	0	0	0	0
MacArthur	0	3,275	0	0	0	0
Mellon	964	0	2,231	0	1,567	3,147
Merck (from 1990)	0	0	0	0	0	0
Mertz-Gilmore	0	0	0	0	0	0
Mott	25	0	447	0	0	233
NED[c]	342	927	769	177	0	311
Nuffield (1990–92)[d]	0	0	19	0	0	39
Olin	0	0	0	0	0	0
OSF Bratislava (from 1994)*	0	0	47	0	0	0
OSF Prague (from 1994)*	0	0	3	0	0	0
PCT	540	2,010	9,455	0	300	360
RBF	0	1,025	0	75	0	800
Sasakawa (from 1991)	0	104	116	0	2,557	0
Smith Richardson	0	0	0	0	0	0
SFH*	10	61	556	4,256	188	136
Stifterverband (from 1990)	0	0	0	0	0	0
Thyssen (from 1990)[e]	0	0	0	0	39	0
Trust for Mutual Understanding	0	0	0	0	0	0
Volkswagen[f]	0	0	0	0	0	0
Westminster (from 1992)	0	76	87	0	0	6
Total	2,118	9,589	20,027	5,190	5,758	5,279

Note: Totals do not equal those in tables A.1 to A.8 and A.9 to A.13 due to the impossibility of disaggregating certain foundations' grants.
a) Figures for "other" grants made by the Doen Stichting represent grants unable to be categorized based on the grants list information.
b) Figures for "other" grants made by the Getty Grant Program include $900,000 in unspecified grants made between 1990 and 1992.
c) Figures for Nuffield do not include expenditures on fellowships and conferences in 1991, which were unavailable.
d) Figures for NED include grants made to its sister organizations, CIPE, FTUI, IRI, and NDI, as well as to other intermediaries.
e) Figures for Thyssen represent its investment in Collegium Budapest only.
f) Figures for Volkswagen may include programs in Southeastern Europe and the former Soviet Union.
* Figures for the Soros Foundations in 1994 may include grants made by the Open Society Institute in each respective country.

TABLE A.17 **Foundation Assistance to Central Europe by Type, 1989–1994** *(Continued)*
(US dollars, in thousands)

Business education	Environment	Libraries	Safety net	Arts and culture	Conflict resolution	Security	Other	Total
1	31	36	837	1,201	5	2	2,123	10,597
450	0	0	0	3	0	0	637	3,026
0	0	0	0	0	0	0	0	15
0	0	0	0	0	3,350	1,516	1,210	11,001
0	0	0	0	0	0	0	3,857	58,398
0	89	0	281	42	0	0	57	1,055
0	3	13	603	11	0	0	971	1,762
0	0	0	2	3	0	0	0	169
0	0	0	0	0	0	0	0	3,052
0	0	0	0	0	0	0	0	370
0	149	0	0	0	0	0	49	445
0	8	0	0	305	13	0	763	2,233
0	0	0	0	0	0	0	0	1,863
210	385	0	200	0	48	1,855	1,102	20,831
0	0	0	0	0	0	0	0	809
44	831	0	28	0	86	5	479	4,953
0	0	596	0	807	0	0	982	2,385
0	396	0	0	0	0	0	190	591
0	0	0	0	0	0	0	0	33,556
0	0	0	0	0	0	0	0	6,571
0	91	0	0	0	0	0	0	1,825
0	0	0	0	0	0	250	0	597
0	467	0	0	13	360	33	143	5,973
6,195	250	10,021	0	25	0	25	2,153	35,998
0	0	0	0	0	0	0	0	68
0	110	0	0	0	0	0	0	263
0	1,675	0	0	0	1,370	0	598	8,155
0	0	0	1,996	315	296	0	1,202	23,323
0	0	100	0	0	0	0	61	349
0	0	0	0	0	0	0	0	9
0	0	0	51	210	0	0	739	2,362
0	0	0	21	79	0	0	649	1,323
0	825	0	0	0	1,065	1,900	2,170	31,080
260	5,206	0	0	0	0	0	1,035	11,053
0	492	0	0	0	0	0	1,572	5,051
0	0	0	0	0	0	0	354	1,132
1,105	233	930	5,845	3,245	9	0	8,354	47,713
0	0	0	0	0	0	0	0	1,108
0	0	0	0	30	0	0	144	3,228
0	181	0	0	1,633	0	0	0	1,814
0	0	4,242	0	0	0	0	0	23,033
36	4	0	0	0	0	0	39	1,566
8,302	11,426	15,940	9,863	7,922	6,601	5,585	31,633	370,703

TABLE A.18 Foundation Assistance to the Czech Republic by Type, 1993–1994
(U.S. dollars, in thousands)

Foundation	Human rights	Non-governmental organizations	Rule of law	Electoral assistance	Democratic institutions	Civic education	Higher education	Free press	Public administration/ local govt.	Public discourse	Economic reform
Bradley	0	0	0	0	0	50	0	0	0	0	0
Calihan (1993)	0	0	0	0	0	2	0	0	0	0	0
CKH (1993)	4	46	0	0	0	0	0	0	0	0	0
CSDF - Czech	0	3,052	0	0	0	0	0	0	0	0	0
Doen	0	0	118	0	0	0	0	0	0	0	0
Ford	100	50	0	0	0	0	0	6	0	0	176
Freedom Forum (1993)	0	0	0	0	0	0	0	0	0	0	0
GMF	24	0	0	0	0	0	0	20	0	35	0
Getty (from 1994)	0	0	0	0	0	0	0	0	0	0	0
Humboldt Fund	0	0	0	0	0	0	1,097	0	0	0	0
Jones	0	0	0	0	0	0	0	1,128	0	0	0
MacArthur	50	0	0	0	0	0	0	0	0	1,300	20
Mellon	0	0	0	0	0	0	450	0	609	0	0
Mott	0	132	0	0	0	0	0	0	0	0	0
NED	0	128	0	0	0	207	0	54	0	0	83
Olin	0	0	0	0	0	9	0	0	0	0	0
OSF Prague (from 1994)	0	0	0	0	0	0	517	0	0	0	3
PCT	0	0	0	0	0	0	0	0	0	0	0
RBF	0	120	0	0	0	0	0	0	0	150	0
Sasakawa	0	30	0	0	0	0	0	0	0	0	0
Thyssen	0	0	0	0	0	0	21	0	0	0	0
Trust for Mutual Understanding	0	0	0	0	0	0	0	0	0	0	0
Westminster	0	0	0	33	76	0	0	3	0	2	4
Total	179	3,558	118	33	76	268	2,084	1,211	609	1,487	286

Foundation	Elementary/ secondary education	Economic education	Management education	Business education	Environment	Libraries	Safety net	Arts and culture	Conflict resolution	Security	Other	Total
Bradley	0	0	0	25	0	0	0	0	0	0	0	75
Calihan (1993)	0	0	0	0	0	0	0	0	0	0	0	2
CKH (1993)	0	0	0	0	17	0	47	0	0	0	9	123
CSDF - Czech	0	0	0	0	0	0	0	0	0	0	0	3,052
Doen	0	0	0	0	24	0	0	0	0	0	20	44
Ford	0	0	0	0	0	0	0	0	0	0	0	444
Freedom Forum (1993)	0	0	0	0	0	0	0	0	0	0	0	6
GMF	0	0	0	0	114	0	0	0	0	0	0	194
Getty (from 1994)	0	0	0	0	0	130	0	133	0	0	0	263
Humboldt	0	0	0	0	0	0	0	0	0	0	0	1,097
Fund	0	0	0	0	0	0	0	0	0	0	0	1,128
Jones	0	0	0	0	0	0	0	0	0	0	0	50
MacArthur	0	100	0	0	0	0	0	0	0	0	0	1,300
Mellon	0	0	0	44	0	16	0	0	0	0	0	1,239
Mott	0	0	0	0	94	0	0	0	0	0	0	226
NED	0	0	0	0	0	0	0	0	0	0	0	418
Olin	0	0	0	0	0	0	0	0	0	0	0	9
OSF Prague (from 1994)	0	0	0	0	0	0	21	79	0	0	649	1,323
PCT	0	0	0	0	0	0	0	0	0	0	85	85
RBF	0	0	300	0	411	0	0	0	0	0	15	996
Sasakawa	0	0	0	0	0	0	0	0	0	0	40	70
Thyssen	0	0	0	0	0	0	0	0	0	0	78	99
Trust for Mutual Understanding	0	0	0	0	20	0	0	149	0	0	0	169
Westminster	0	0	0	0	0	0	0	0	0	0	0	118
Total	0	100	300	69	680	146	68	361	0	0	896	12,529

Note: Totals do not include approximately $3 million in grants provided by Adenauer and Doen which could not be disaggregated.

TABLE A.19 Foundation Assistance to Czechoslovakia and Czech and Slovak, Regional Grants, by Type, 1989–1994
(U.S. dollars, in thousands)

Foundation	Human rights	Non-governmental organizations	Rule of law	Electoral assistance	Democratic institutions	Civic education	Higher education	Free press	Public administration/ local govt.	Public discourse	Economic reform
Bradley	0	0	0	0	2	0	0	0	0	0	0
CKH (1991–93)	3	61	0	0	0	0	0	0	0	0	0
Charta 77 Foundation (1989–91)	0	27	3	0	7	1	35	84	0	0	2
Charta 77 - Stockholm (1991)	0	0	0	0	0	0	162	3	0	0	0
ECF	23	6	0	0	2	0	15	0	0	0	0
Ford	0	0	0	0	850	0	75	114	0	0	123
GMF	0	24	44	0	9	0	15	76	0	70	5
Humboldt	0	0	0	0	0	0	4,922	0	0	0	0
MacArthur	150	0	0	0	0	0	0	0	0	1,950	0
Mellon	0	270	0	0	25	0	2,305	0	0	0	0
Merck (from 1990)	10	20	0	0	0	0	0	0	0	0	0
Mott	0	200	0	0	0	0	0	0	0	0	127
NED	0	658	27	891	65	41	171	209	0	0	206
PCT	0	0	0	0	500	0	175	0	0	500	75
RBF	0	235	0	0	0	0	0	0	0	150	0
Sasakawa (from 1991)	0	0	0	0	0	0	0	0	0	0	0
Smith Richardson	0	0	0	0	0	68	0	0	0	0	0
Thyssen (from 1990)	0	0	0	0	0	0	9	0	0	0	0
Trust for Mutual Understanding	0	0	0	0	0	0	0	0	0	0	0
Westminster (from 1992)	0	0	0	0	0	0	0	0	0	0	6
Total	186	1,500	74	891	1,460	110	7,883	486	0	2,670	544

Foundation	Elementary/ secondary education	Economic education	Management education	Business education	Environment	Libraries	Safety net	Arts and culture	Conflict resolution	Security	Other	Total
Bradley	0	0	0	425	0	0	0	0	0	0	0	427
CKH (1991–93)	7	1	1	0	19	0	28	12	0	0	7	140
Charta 77 Foundation (1989–91)	0	0	2	0	3	13	603	11	0	0	971	1,762
Charta 77 - Stockholm (1991)	0	0	0	0	0	0	2	3	0	0	0	169
ECF	0	0	0	0	0	0	0	0	0	0	22	68
Ford	0	0	0	0	0	0	0	0	0	0	0	1,162
GMF	0	0	6	0	0	0	0	0	0	0	97	346
Humboldt	0	0	0	0	0	0	0	0	0	0	0	4,922
MacArthur	0	0	0	0	0	0	0	0	0	0	25	2,125
Mellon	0	180	1,033	907	0	1,470	0	0	0	0	246	6,435
Merck (from 1990)	0	0	0	0	15	0	0	0	0	0	0	30
Mott	0	0	0	0	0	0	0	0	0	0	0	342
NED	0	0	0	0	0	0	0	162	0	0	12	2,442
PCT	0	0	0	0	0	0	0	0	150	0	200	1,600
RBF	0	0	0	0	35	0	0	0	0	0	50	470
Sasakawa (from 1991)	0	0	0	0	32	0	0	0	0	0	100	132
Smith Richardson	0	0	0	0	0	0	0	0	0	0	0	68
Thyssen (from 1990)	0	0	0	0	0	0	0	30	0	0	0	39
Trust for Mutual Understanding	0	0	0	0	13	0	0	122	0	0	0	135
Westminster (from 1992)	0	0	0	0	0	0	0	0	0	0	0	6
Total	7	181	1,043	1,332	117	1,483	633	340	150	0	1,729	22,820

Note: Totals do not include approximately $9 million in grants provided by Adenauer, CDF, Ebert, and Naumann which could not be disaggregated.

TABLE A.20 Foundation Assistance to Hungary by Type, 1989–1994
(U.S. dollars, in thousands)

Foundation	Human rights	Non-governmental organizations	Rule of law	Electoral assistance	Democratic institutions	Civic education	Higher education	Free press	Public administration/ local govt.	Public discourse	Economic reform
Carnegie	0	0	0	0	0	0	25	0	0	0	0
CEU Foundation (from 1993)	0	1,500	0	0	0	0	0	0	0	0	0
CKH (1991–93)	20	134	0	0	0	6	8	0	0	0	1
Doen (from 1990)	0	0	0	0	0	0	0	0	0	0	0
ECF	0	10	0	0	0	0	0	0	0	0	0
Ford	510	0	336	0	0	0	0	0	0	0	0
Freedom Forum (1992–93)	0	0	0	0	0	0	0	53	0	0	0
GMF	9	25	18	15	137	44	0	47	0	0	2
Getty (from 1990)	0	0	0	0	0	0	0	0	0	0	0
Humboldt	0	0	0	0	0	0	8,308	0	0	0	0
Fund (from 1991)	0	0	0	0	0	0	0	1,781	0	0	0
Mellon	0	0	49	0	205	0	1,833	0	0	0	1,199
Mott	105	195	0	0	0	125	0	0	0	0	0
NED	0	1,616	0	1,066	765	95	0	24	0	200	118
PCT	0	0	0	0	50	275	0	0	0	65	295
RBF	450	99	0	0	25	0	0	0	0	200	0
Sasakawa (from 1991)	0	0	0	0	0	0	0	0	0	0	0
Smith Richardson	0	0	0	0	0	0	0	0	0	0	100
SFH	4,406	1,953	149	107	162	125	9,884	5,992	10	61	556
Thyssen (from 1990)	0	0	0	0	0	0	2,351	0	0	0	0
Trust for Mutual Understanding	0	0	0	0	0	0	0	0	0	0	0
Volkswagen	0	0	0	0	0	0	1,109	0	0	0	0
Westminster (from 1992)	0	30	6	63	89	0	0	17	0	0	0
Total	5,500	5,559	557	1,251	1,433	670	23,518	7,915	10	526	2,272

Foundation	Elementary/ secondary education	Economic education	Management education	Business education	Environment	Libraries	Safety net	Arts and culture	Conflict resolution	Security	Other	Total
Carnegie	0	0	0	0	0	0	0	0	0	0	0	25
CEU Foundation (from 1993)	0	0	0	0	0	0	0	0	0	0	0	1,500
CKH (1991–93)	3	1	3	0	3	0	25	11	0	0	5	219
Doen (from 1990)	0	0	0	0	0	0	0	0	0	0	17	17
ECF	9	0	0	0	0	0	0	0	9	0	0	27
Ford	0	45	0	0	0	0	0	0	0	0	46	937
Freedom Forum (1992–93)	0	0	100	0	0	0	0	0	0	0	0	154
GMF	36	0	0	0	21	0	0	0	0	0	0	353
Getty (from 1990)	0	0	0	0	0	100	0	60	0	0	0	160
Humboldt	0	0	0	0	0	0	0	0	0	0	0	8,308
Fund (from 1991)	0	0	0	0	0	0	0	0	0	0	0	1,781
Mellon	0	0	597	2,615	0	2,414	0	0	0	0	50	8,962
Mott	0	0	0	0	185	0	0	0	0	0	37	647
NED	38	0	0	0	0	0	0	0	0	0	80	4,003
PCT	0	100	360	0	0	0	0	0	0	0	0	1,145
RBF	0	0	300	0	415	0	0	0	0	0	0	1,489
Sasakawa (from 1991)	0	0	0	0	0	0	0	0	0	0	0	100
Smith Richardson	0	0	0	0	0	0	0	0	0	0	54	54
SFH	4,254	188	136	1,105	233	927	5,840	3,217	9	0	8,176	47,490
Thyssen (from 1990)	0	0	0	0	0	0	0	0	0	0	0	2,351
Trust for Mutual Understanding	0	0	0	0	12	0	0	30	0	0	0	42
Volkswagen	0	0	0	0	0	0	0	0	0	0	0	1,109
Westminster (from 1992)	0	0	0	0	0	0	0	0	0	0	8	212
Total	4,340	334	1,497	3,720	869	3,441	5,864	3,318	18	0	8,472	81,085

Note: Totals do not include approximately $14 million in grants provided by Adenauer, CDF, Ebert, and Naumann which could not be disaggregated.

TABLE A.21 Foundation Assistance to Poland by Type, 1989–1994
(U.S. dollars, in thousands)

Foundation	Human rights	Non-governmental organizations	Rule of law	Electoral assistance	Democratic institutions	Civic education	Higher education	Free press	Public administration/ local govt.	Public discourse	Economic reform
Stefan Batory	495	1,589	58	0	32	33	2,434	328	7	212	110
Bradley	0	0	0	0	0	34	0	250	0	0	0
CKH (1991–93)	11	94	0	0	0	0	0	0	0	0	0
Doen (from 1990)	0	247	0	0	0	0	0	0	0	0	0
ECF	6	0	0	0	0	0	0	0	0	0	0
Fondation de France (from 1990)	0	1,863	0	0	0	0	0	0	0	0	1,851
Ford	730	615	0	0	207	0	368	0	50	0	0
Freedom Forum (1992–93)	0	0	0	0	0	0	0	223	0	0	0
GMF	64	240	33	9	189	95	35	477	169	3	639
Getty (from 1990)	0	0	0	0	0	0	0	0	0	0	0
Humboldt	0	0	0	0	0	0	18,095	0	0	0	0
Fund (from 1991)	0	0	0	0	0	0	0	1,459	0	0	0
IYF	0	1,702	0	0	0	0	0	0	0	0	0
MacArthur	0	0	5	0	0	0	0	0	0	0	0
Mellon	0	0	0	0	0	0	988	0	355	0	848
Merck (from 1990)	0	0	0	0	0	38	0	0	0	0	0
Mertz-Gilmore (from 1990)	0	25	0	0	10	0	0	0	0	0	0
Mott	0	415	0	0	89	0	35	0	25	0	270
NED	50	5,067	0	35	268	422	0	441	342	169	799
PCT	0	300	0	0	0	1,810	0	0	240	0	555
RBF	0	272	0	0	0	0	0	0	0	225	0
Sasakawa (from 1991)	0	0	0	0	0	0	0	0	0	0	0
Thyssen (from 1990)	0	0	0	0	0	0	222	0	0	0	0
Trust for Mutual Understanding	0	0	0	0	0	0	0	0	0	0	0
Volkswagen	0	0	0	0	0	0	197	0	0	0	0
Westminster (from 1992)	0	40	0	3	148	6	0	10	0	23	13
Total	1,356	12,470	96	47	943	2,437	22,376	3,188	1,188	631	5,086

Foundation	Elementary/ secondary education	Economic education	Management education	Business education	Environment	Libraries	Safety net	Arts and culture	Conflict resolution	Security	Other	Total
Stefan Batory	572	192	5	1	6	36	836	1,106	5	2	1,709	9,768
Bradley	0	0	0	0	0	0	0	0	0	0	0	284
CKH (1991–93)	0	1	1	0	10	0	90	19	0	0	9	236
Doen (from 1990)	0	0	0	0	83	0	0	0	0	0	11	342
ECF	0	0	0	0	0	0	0	25	0	0	0	31
Fondation de France (from 1990)	0	0	0	0	0	0	0	0	0	0	0	1,863
Ford	0	240	0	100	385	0	60	0	48	0	0	4,654
Freedom Forum (1992–93)	0	0	0	0	0	0	0	0	0	0	0	223
GMF	0	87	0	44	126	0	10	0	25	0	78	2,322
Getty (from 1990)	0	0	0	0	0	140	0	348	0	0	0	488
Humboldt	0	0	0	0	0	0	0	0	0	0	0	18,095
Fund (from 1991)	0	0	0	0	0	0	0	0	0	0	0	1,459
IYF	32	0	0	0	91	0	0	0	0	0	0	1,825
MacArthur	0	0	0	0	82	0	0	0	10	0	10	107
Mellon	0	230	914	1,972	0	5,836	0	0	0	0	570	11,713
Merck (from 1990)	0	0	0	0	0	0	0	0	0	0	0	38
Mertz-Gilmore (from 1990)	0	0	0	0	0	0	0	0	0	0	0	35
Mott	0	0	0	0	50	0	0	0	0	0	50	934
NED	24	0	0	0	0	0	1,996	153	0	0	250	10,016
PCT	0	200	0	0	0	0	0	0	0	0	350	3,455
RBF	75	0	175	60	950	0	0	0	0	0	0	1,757
Sasakawa (from 1991)	0	0	0	0	0	0	0	0	0	0	250	250
Thyssen (from 1990)	0	0	0	0	0	0	0	0	0	0	0	222
Trust for Mutual Understanding	0	0	0	0	25	0	0	61	0	0	0	86
Volkswagen	0	0	0	0	0	0	0	0	0	0	0	197
Westminster (from 1992)	0	0	0	36	0	0	0	0	0	0	0	279
Total	703	950	1,096	2,214	1,808	6,012	2,992	1,712	88	2	3,288	70,679

Note: Totals do not include approximately $26 million in grants provided by Adenauer, Bosch, Ebert and Naumann which could not be disaggregated.

TABLE A.22 Foundation Assistance to Slovakia by Type, 1993–1994
(U.S. dollars, in thousands)

Foundation	Human rights	Non-governmental organizations	Rule of law	Electoral assistance	Democratic institutions	Civic education	Higher education	Free press	Public administration/ local govt.	Public discourse	Economic reform
Carnegie	300	0	0	0	0	0	0	0	0	0	0
CEU Foundation	0	9	0	0	0	0	0	0	0	0	0
CKH	9	9	0	0	0	0	0	3	0	0	0
CSDF - Slovakia (from 1994)	0	370	0	0	0	0	0	0	0	0	0
ECF	0	0	0	0	15	0	0	0	0	0	11
Ford	75	50	0	0	0	0	0	0	0	0	0
GMF	34	36	0	0	3	23	0	58	0	0	0
Getty	0	0	0	0	0	0	0	0	0	0	0
Humboldt	0	0	0	0	0	0	1,134	0	0	0	0
Fund	0	0	0	0	0	0	0	903	0	0	0
MacArthur	0	0	0	0	0	0	0	0	0	0	0
Mellon	0	75	0	0	0	0	60	0	0	0	14
Mott	0	185	0	0	0	0	0	0	0	0	0
NED	0	151	0	0	132	350	0	0	0	0	0
OSF Bratislava (from 1994)	0	338	0	0	0	0	687	290	0	0	47
PCT	0	0	0	0	0	0	90	0	0	0	60
RBF	0	100	0	0	0	0	0	0	0	0	0
Sasakawa	0	30	0	0	0	0	0	0	0	104	16
Westminster	0	4	0	81	60	0	0	10	0	13	0
Total	417	1,356	0	81	210	373	1,971	1,264	0	117	149

Foundation	Elementary/ secondary education	Economic education	Management education	Business education	Environment	Libraries	Safety net	Arts and culture	Conflict resolution	Security	Other	Total
Carnegie	0	0	0	0	0	0	0	0	0	0	0	300
CEU Foundation	0	0	0	0	0	0	0	0	0	0	0	9
CKH	6	0	0	0	5	0	4	0	0	0	1	37
CSDF - Slovakia (from 1994)	0	0	0	0	0	0	0	0	0	0	0	370
ECF	0	0	0	0	0	0	0	0	0	0	0	27
Ford	0	0	0	0	0	0	0	0	0	0	0	125
GMF	0	0	0	0	15	0	0	0	0	0	73	240
Getty	0	0	0	0	0	50	0	20	0	0	0	70
Humboldt	0	0	0	0	0	0	0	0	0	0	0	1,134
Fund	0	0	0	0	0	0	0	0	0	0	0	903
MacArthur	0	0	0	0	10	0	0	0	0	0	0	10
Mellon	0	1,057	100	0	15	0	0	0	0	0	0	1,306
Mott	0	0	0	0	0	0	0	0	0	0	0	200
NED	27	0	0	0	0	0	0	0	0	0	0	660
OSF Bratislava (from 1994)	0	0	0	0	0	0	51	210	0	0	739	2,362
PCT	0	0	0	0	0	0	0	0	165	0	0	315
RBF	0	0	0	0	10	0	0	0	0	0	0	110
Sasakawa	0	0	0	0	0	0	0	0	0	0	0	150
Westminster	0	0	6	0	0	0	0	0	0	0	0	174
Total	33	1,057	106	0	55	50	55	230	165	0	812	8,501

Note: Totals do not include approximately $700,000 in grants provided by Adenauer and CDF which could not be disaggregated.

TABLE A.23 Foundation Assistance to Central Europe, Regional Grants, by Type, 1989–1994
(U.S. dollars, in thousands)

Foundation	Human rights	Non-governmental organizations	Rule of law	Electoral assistance	Democratic institutions	Civic education	Higher education	Free press	Public administration/ local govt.	Public discourse	Economic reform
Stefan Batory	19	0	0	0	0	0	65	5	11	0	0
Bradley	0	0	24	0	0	0	0	0	0	95	0
CEU Foundation (from 1993)	0	0	0	0	0	0	53,032	0	0	0	0
CKH (1991–93)	0	5	0	0	0	0	0	0	0	0	0
ECF	0	0	0	0	0	5	6	0	0	0	0
Ford	0	0	0	0	248	0	697	0	0	0	1,828
GMF	0	0	0	0	52	30	5	123	0	0	69
MacArthur	0	0	0	0	0	0	60	0	0	0	0
Mellon	0	0	0	0	0	0	200	0	0	0	0
Mertz-Gilmore (from 1990)	0	53	0	35	0	0	0	0	0	0	0
Mott	0	235	50	0	0	0	0	0	0	0	50
NED	15	124	0	0	57	0	0	69	0	0	0
PCT	0	0	0	0	300	1,875	845	0	0	250	600
RBF	0	769	0	0	0	0	0	25	0	300	0
SFH	0	150	0	0	0	0	0	0	0	0	0
Sasakawa (from 1991)	0	0	0	0	0	0	0	0	0	0	0
Thyssen (from 1990)	0	0	0	0	0	0	412	0	0	0	0
Trust for Mutual Understanding	0	0	0	0	0	0	0	0	0	0	0
Westminster (from 1992)	0	8	0	0	21	0	0	0	0	1	0
Total	34	1,343	74	35	677	1,910	55,321	222	11	646	2,546

Foundation	Elementary/ secondary education	Economic education	Management education	Business education	Environment	Libraries	Safety net	Arts and culture	Conflict resolution	Security	Other	Total
Stefan Batory	0	0	0	0	4	0	0	18	0	0	0	122
Bradley	0	0	0	0	0	0	0	0	0	0	80	199
CEU Foundation (from 1993)	0	0	0	0	0	0	0	0	0	0	857	53,889
CKH (1991–93)	0	0	0	0	0	0	0	0	0	0	0	5
ECF	0	0	0	0	0	0	0	14	0	0	0	25
Ford	0	234	112	110	0	0	0	0	0	210	24	3,462
GMF	0	0	15	0	536	0	18	0	14	5	23	889
MacArthur	0	0	0	0	0	0	0	0	0	0	0	60
Mellon	0	0	0	0	0	0	0	0	0	0	0	200
Mertz-Gilmore (from 1990)	0	0	0	0	100	0	0	0	0	0	0	153
Mott	0	0	0	0	743	0	0	0	225	0	215	1,553
NED	0	0	0	0	0	0	0	0	0	0	100	365
PCT	0	0	0	0	600	0	0	0	0	0	370	4,840
RBF	0	2,557	25	200	3,052	0	0	0	0	0	850	5,220
SFH	0	0	0	0	460	0	0	0	0	0	1,182	4,349
Sasakawa (from 1991)	0	0	0	0	0	0	0	4	0	0	0	4
Thyssen (from 1990)	0	0	0	0	0	0	0	0	0	0	0	412
Trust for Mutual Understanding	0	0	0	0	50	0	0	96	0	0	0	146
Westminster (from 1992)	0	0	0	0	0	0	0	0	0	0	10	40
Total	0	2,791	152	310	5,544	0	18	132	239	215	3,711	75,933

Note: Totals do not include approximately $1.9 million in grants provided by Bosch which could not be disaggregated.

TABLE A.24 Foundation Assistance to Central and Eastern Europe, Interregional Grants, by Type, 1989–1994
(U.S. dollars, in thousands)

Foundation	Human rights	Non-governmental organizations	Rule of law	Electoral assistance	Democratic institutions	Civic education	Higher education	Free press	Public administration/local govt.	Public discourse	Economic reform
Stefan Batory	19	22	0	0	32	0	40	13	0	0	57
Bradley	53	0	0	0	110	0	0	255	0	1,053	10
Carnegie	0	25	0	0	225	0	4,150	25	0	0	175
CEU Foundation (from 1993)	0	0	0	0	0	0	0	0	0	0	0
CKH (1991–93)	4	137	0	0	0	0	0	4	0	0	0
Doen (from 1990)	0	0	0	0	0	0	0	0	0	0	0
ECF	14	43	18	0	225	3	57	327	0	341	0
Ford	708	1,850	113	0	1,279	0	1,778	0	0	0	1,204
Freedom Forum (1992–93)	0	0	0	0	0	0	0	427	0	0	0
GMF	95	45	52	0	57	0	0	49	0	0	33
Getty (from 1994)	0	0	0	0	0	0	0	0	0	0	0
Gilman	0	0	0	0	0	0	0	0	0	5	0
Fund (from 1990)	0	0	0	0	0	0	0	1,300	0	0	0
Jones	0	0	0	0	0	0	0	0	0	297	0
MacArthur	365	150	0	0	27	0	915	10	0	25	0
Mellon	100	0	44	0	150	0	2,665	0	0	0	150
Mertz-Gilmore	45	20	0	0	0	35	0	0	0	0	0
Mott	0	1,556	330	0	85	123	0	0	0	0	0
NED	394	1,132	440	47	675	0	0	1,033	0	0	120
Nuffield (1990–92)	0	84	46	0	0	0	0	0	0	0	19
PCT	0	0	0	0	3,335	500	2,400	0	300	1,195	7,870
RBF	0	100	0	0	450	0	0	9	0	0	0
Smith Richardson	230	0	0	0	0	0	0	480	0	0	0
SFH	0	0	0	0	0	0	4	0	0	0	0
Stifterverband (from 1990)	0	0	0	0	0	0	1,108	0	0	0	0
Thyssen (from 1990)	0	0	0	0	0	0	0	0	0	0	0
Trust for Mutual Understanding	0	0	0	0	0	0	0	0	0	0	0
Volkswagen	0	0	0	0	0	0	17,484	0	0	0	0
Westminster (from 1992)	99	82	0	55	329	39	0	5	0	38	64
Total	2,126	5,246	1,043	102	6,978	700	30,602	3,937	300	2,954	9,702

Foundation	Elementary/ secondary education	Economic education	Management education	Business education	Environment	Libraries	Safety net	Arts and culture	Conflict resolution	Security	Other	Total
Stefan Batory	10	0	0	0	22	0	1	77	0	0	414	707
Bradley	0	0	0	0	0	0	0	3	0	0	557	2,041
Carnegie	0	0	0	0	0	0	0	0	3,350	1,516	1,210	10,676
CEU Foundation (from 1993)	0	0	0	0	0	0	0	0	0	0	3,000	3,000
CKH (1991–93)	0	0	0	0	35	0	87	0	0	0	27	295
Doen (from 1990)	0	0	0	0	41	0	0	0	0	0	0	41
ECF	6	0	0	0	8	0	0	266	4	0	742	2,054
Ford	0	300	0	0	0	0	140	0	0	1,645	1,032	10,048
Freedom Forum (1992–93)	0	0	0	0	0	0	0	0	0	0	0	427
GMF	0	5	0	0	19	0	0	0	47	0	208	610
Getty (from 1994)	0	0	0	0	0	176	0	245	0	0	982	1,403
Gilman	0	0	0	0	396	0	0	0	0	0	190	591
Fund (from 1990)	0	0	0	0	0	0	0	0	0	0	0	1,300
Jones	0	0	0	0	0	0	0	0	0	250	0	547
MacArthur	0	0	0	0	375	0	0	13	350	33	108	2,371
Mellon	0	0	503	658	250	286	0	25	0	25	1,287	6,142
Mertz-Gilmore	0	0	0	0	10	0	0	0	0	0	0	75
Mott	0	0	233	0	574	0	0	0	1,145	0	296	4,254
NED	88	0	311	0	0	0	0	0	296	0	761	5,419
Nuffield (1990–92)	0	0	39	0	0	100	0	0	0	0	61	349
PCT	0	0	0	0	225	0	0	0	750	1,900	1,165	19,640
RBF	0	0	0	0	333	0	0	0	0	0	120	1,012
Smith Richardson	3	0	0	0	0	0	0	24	0	0	300	1,010
SFH	0	0	0	0	0	3	6	0	0	0	178	218
Stifterverband (from 1990)	0	0	0	0	0	0	0	0	0	0	0	1,108
Thyssen (from 1990)	0	39	0	0	61	0	0	0	0	0	65	105
Trust for Mutual Understanding	0	0	0	0	0	4,242	0	1,175	0	0	0	1,236
Volkswagen	0	0	0	0	0	0	0	0	0	0	0	21,727
Westminster (from 1992)	0	0	0	0	4	0	0	0	0	0	21	737
Total	107	344	1,086	658	2,353	4,808	233	1,828	5,942	5,369	12,724	99,142

Note: Totals do not include approximately $19 million in grants provided by Adenauer, Bertelsmann, Boll, Ebert, Naumann and Seidel which could not be disaggregated.

Notes

1

Introduction: A New World

1. AID, *Scoreboard of Assistance Commitments to the CEEC* (Washington, D.C.: AID, 1994).

2. There is a rich literature on the mediating role of civil society. Alexis de Tocqueville's *Democracy in America* (1840) is a classic in this regard. For a more recent discussion regarding mediating institutions, see Robert Wuthnow, *Between States and Market: The Voluntary Sector in Comparative Perspective* (Princeton, N.J.: Princeton University Press, 1991).

3. Examples of these German political foundations include Adenauer, Ebert, Naumann, and the Seidel Stiftungen. Sometimes called *party foundations* because of their ties with the largest German political parties, all of their funding is from government appropriations. Despite this, they act autonomously.

4. These NED-related organizations are Center for International Private Enterprise (CIPE), Free Trade Union Institute (FTUI), International Republican Institute (IRI), and National Democratic Institute (NDI). These organizations receive their core budgets from the United States Information Agency (USIA) and project-related support from AID. Similar to the German party foundations, despite receiving public funds these organizations act autonomously.

5. There is a burgeoning literature on links between markets and democracy. Although this literature is far from conclusive, the international community acted as if there were a positive link between the two and that free markets generally precede democracy. See, for example, Gabriel A. Almond "Capitalism and Democracy," *PS: Political Science and Politics* 24 (September 1991): 13–20; Robert

Bartley, ed., *Democracy and Capitalism: Asian and American Perspectives* (Singapore: Institute for Southeast Asian Studies, 1993); John R. Freeman, *Democracy and Markets: The Politics of Mixed Economies* (Ithaca: Cornell University Press, 1989); Charles E. Lindblom, *Politics and Markets: The World's Political Economic System* (New York: Basic Books, 1977); Seymour Martin Lipset, *Political Man: The Social Bases of Conflict* 2nd ed. (Baltimore: Johns Hopkins University Press, 1981); Adam Przeworski, *Democracy and the Market: Political and Economic Reform in Eastern Europe and Latin America* (New York: Cambridge University Press, 1991); and Joseph A. Schumpeter, *Capitalism, Socialism, and Democracy* (New York: Harper and Row, 1950).

6. Reflecting this, President Clinton stated in a speech outlining the goals of his foreign policy: "If we could make a garden of democracy and prosperity . . . the world would be a safer and better and a more prosperous place." ("American Leadership and Global Change," speech at Centennial Celebration, American University, Washington, D.C., 26 February 1993; printed in *U.S. Department of State Dispatch,* 1 March 1993, 115.)

7. Thomas Carothers, "Democracy Promotion under Clinton," *Washington Quarterly* 18 (Autumn 1995): 13–25.

8. For example, these countries are among those involved in underwriting the Institute for Democracy and Electoral Assistance, which seeks to advance sustainable democracy worldwide.

9. See Larry Diamond, *Promoting Democracy in the 1990s: Actors and Instruments, Issues and Imperatives* (New York: Carnegie Commission on Preventing Deadly Conflict, 1995).

10. This is a conservative estimate based primarily on information compiled for this study by the author and Nancy Popson from foundations, especially those in the United States and Germany. This also draws on information in Krzysztof J. Ners and Ingrid T. Buxell, *Assistance to Transition Survey 1995,* Annex 3, (Warsaw: IEWS Policy Education Center on Assistance to Transition, 1995) 109–10, and AID, *Scoreboard of Assistance Commitments to the CEEC.*

11. This general lack of a well-defined programming strategy seems to contrast with the approach taken by a number of public donors, such as AID, which also has its shortcomings. See Thomas Carothers's discussion of AID's "check-list approach" in *Assessing Democracy Assistance: The Case of Romania* (Washington, D.C.: Carnegie Endowment for International Peace, 1996).

12. Carl Gershman (president, NED), interview by author, Washington, D.C., 6 December 1995.

13. For a discussion of foundation programs in Eastern Europe, see Kevin F. F. Quigley, "Philanthropy's Role in East Europe," *Orbis* 37 (fall 1993): 581–98, and "For Democracy's Sake: How Funders Fail—and Succeed," *World Policy Journal* 13 (spring 1996): 109–19. This latter article provided a preview of this study.

14. János Kovács (fellow, IWM), interview by author, Vienna, Austria, 18 July 1995.

15. See, for example, Thomas Carothers, *Assessing Democracy Assis-*

tance, and Janine R. Wedel, "U.S. Aid to Central and Eastern Europe: Results and Recommendations," *Problems of Post-Communism* 42 (May–June 1995): 45–50.

16. An earlier version of this discussion of the phases of assistance appeared in Kevin F. F. Quigley, "For Democracy's Sake: How Funders Fail— and Succeed," 109–18. Michael Dauderstädt from Ebert sees comparable phases but with slightly different emphases. He describes phase I as understanding how markets and democracy work, phase II as developing relevant political cultures, and phase III as learning how to make institutions compatible with European institutions. (Interview by author, Bonn, Germany, 30 January 1996.)

17. Jane Wales (former program chair, Carnegie), interview by author, Washington, D.C., 5 October 1995.

18. Lecture at the Woodrow Wilson Center, Zora Bútorová (FOCUS) Washington, D.C., 5 April 1995.

19. Interview by author, Washington, D.C., 8 February 1996.

20. For example, Joyce Mertz-Gilmore Foundation, Mellon, and Pew Charitable Trusts have announced plans to phase out their operations in Central Europe over the next one to two years. The boards of other foundations, such as Charles Stewart Mott Foundation and John D. and Catherine T. MacArthur Foundation, have debated their continued involvement.

21. Notable examples include the European Union's Poland and Hungary Assistance for Restructuring of the Economy (Phare) Democracy Programme and AID's Democracy Network Program (DemNet), both of which provide small grants to indigenous NGOs and were modeled to some extent on programs begun by foundations.

22. Lorne Craner (president, IRI), remarks made at a For Democracy's Sake (FDS) workshop, Woodrow Wilson Center, Washington, D.C., 5 June 1996.

23. The need to focus on sustainability, broadly defined, was the major finding from the FDS workshop, Bratislava, Slovakia, 2–3 November 1995, conducted as part of this study. This was also echoed in numerous interviews by the author, including an interview with Dan Siegel and Jenny Yancey, directors of Civil Society Development Program (CSDP), Budapest, Hungary, 17 July 1995.

24. This definition is based on Robert Dahl, *Polyarchy: Participation and Opposition* (New Haven, Conn.: Yale University Press, 1971). Although Dahl's definition of democracy is a useful starting point, it needs to be augmented, since it addresses only processes. It does not address the issue of the institutions that comprise a democracy. Democracy entails both institutions and processes; the institutions of a democracy should promote democratic ends by democratic means. For this study, essential democratic institutions constitute not only the formal institutions of legislatures and independent judiciaries operating at national and local levels, but also a complex network of informal, self-governed institutions—such as NGOs—that are sometimes overlooked by democratic theorists.

25. These democratizing assets are discussed in, among many others, Seymour Martin Lipset, "Some Social Requisites of Democracy: Economic Development and Political Legitimacy," *American Political Science Review* 53 (March 1959): 69–105. Lipset provides his current views on democratizing assets in "The Social Requisites of Democracy Revisited," *American Sociological Review* 59 (February 1994): 3.

26. The NGO sector is sometimes referred to as the *third sector,* the *nonprofit sector,* or the *independent sector,* each phrase indicating a subtle distinction, but as these distinctions are not especially relevant here, this study will simply refer to this as the *NGO sector.*

27. These workshops are discussed in greater detail in Kevin F. F. Quigley, *Conversations on Democracy Assistance* (Washington, D. C.: East European Studies, Woodrow Wilson Center, 1996).

28. See Ralf Dahrendorf, *Reflections on the Revolution in Europe* (New York: Random House, 1990), 99–100.

2

Czech Republic: Standing Apart

1. This profile of the Czech Republic's current political and economic circumstances relies on Vladimir Handl and Cestmir Konecny, "Czech Republic," in *Central and Eastern Europe and the European Union,* ed. Bertelsmann Foundation (Gütersloh, Ger.: Bertelsmann Foundation Publishers, 1995); Freedom House, *Nations in Transit: Civil Society, Democracy, and Markets in East Central Europe and the Newly Independent States* (New York: Freedom House, 1995); as well as reporting from Open Media Research Institute (OMRI) following the June 1996 election.

2. Speech at Heritage Foundation, Washington, D.C., 15 October 1993, cited in *Vital Speeches of the Day* 60 (15 December 1993): 130–32.

3. Ibid.

4. See, for example, his comments on reform in Václav Klaus, Václav Havel, and Petr Pithart, "Rival Visions," *Journal of Democracy* 7 (January 1996): 11–23.

5. "Normal Politics Arrives in the Czech Republic," *Washington Post,* 6 June 1996, sec. A, 22.

6. Marian Calfa, a former Communist, served as prime minister before and after the June 1990 elections.

7. For an extensive discussion of efforts throughout Eastern Europe to reform the police, see *Transition* 2 (8 March 1996).

8. This data is based on reporting by the International Center for Foundations and Other Not-for-Profit Organizations (ICN). Also see *Basic Information about the Non-Profit Sector in the Czech Republic* (Prague: CSDF, 1994).

9. Stanley N. Katz, "Philanthropy and Democracy: Which Comes First?" *Advancing Philanthropy* 2 (summer 1994): 35.

10. Petr Pajas (chairman, ICN), remarks made at FDS workshop, Bratislava, Slovakia, 25–26 April 1996.

11. See, for example, Václav Havel's classic, *The Power of the Powerless* (Armonk, N.Y.: M. E. Sharpe, 1985).

12. Normandy Madden, "In the Czech Republic, All Eyes Are on TV Nova," *Transition* 2 (19 April 1996): 14–15.

13. OMRI, *OMRI Economic Digest* 5 (30 November 1995).

14. World Bank, *World Bank Group Brief: Europe and Central Asia* (Washington, D.C.: World Bank, 1995), and World Bank, *World Development Report: Workers in an Integrating World* (Oxford: Oxford University Press, 1995), 225, table 32.

15. Usenet FAQ International, www.nsrc.org/EUROPE/europe.html; data compiled by Olivier M. J. Crepin-Leblond.

16. James Fallows, "Economic and Market Reform in the Czech Republic, and the Past and Future Role of Charitable Efforts There," a report prepared for PCT, 22 December 1994, 8.

17. AID, *Scoreboard of Assistance Commitments to the CEEC* (Washington, D.C.: AID, 1994), table 5.

18. AID, *SEED Act Implementation Report* (Washington, D.C.: AID, 1995), 1–30.

19. "Tourism Fuels Growth," *Newsweek*, 29 April 1996 (special section on the Czech Republic).

20. Klaus, Havel, and Pithart, "Rival Visions," 17.

21. Fallows, 3.

22. Petr Pajas (ICN), remarks made concerning an environmental project that relied on technical assistance, FDS workshop, Bratislava, Slovakia, 25–26 April 1995.

23. High-ranking Czech official, interview by author, Washington, D.C., 8 February 1996.

24. This section is based on a 1990 proposal prepared by Jan Svenjar and submitted to PCT, as well as numerous conversations between then and now with Svenjar and with Mellon's Richard Quandt.

25. In the author's experience of reviewing hundreds of proposals, no more than a handful provided a strategic plan with the initial proposal.

26. This section is based on ICN's *1993 Annual Report* and interviews with its chairman of the board of directors, Petr Pajas, its founding director, Jana Ryšlinková, as well as staff from some of its principal funders.

27. Although *Phare* initially described an effort to promote economic reform in Poland and Hungary, the name became applied more generally to an initiative of the EU that "supports the development of a larger democratic family of nations within a prosperous and stable Europe. Its aim is to help the countries of Central and Eastern Europe rejoin the mainstream of European development through future members of the EU." European Commission, *Phare: Indicative Programmes*, no. 1, 1995 (Brussels: Directorate General External Relations, European Commission, 1995), 4.

28. These include Ford, Mott, Trust for Mutual Understanding (Trust), Eurasia Foundation (EF), German Marshall Fund of the United States (GMF), John Merck Fund (Merck), Joyce Mertz-Gilmore Foundation (Mertz), NED, Open Society Fund (OSF), Open Society Institute (OSI), PCT, RBF, Sasakawa, and the Whitehead Foundation. In addition, FCS has received considerable support from AID.

29. Wendy Luers (president, FCS), interview by author, Washington, D.C., 5 October 1995.

30. For example, of its twenty-two living board members identified in its *1993–1994 Report* (New York: FCS, 1995), only four are Czech and only one is Slovak.

31. For example, Raymond Barre, William H. Luers, Anthony Solomon, and Krzysztof J. Ners, *Moving Beyond Assistance: Final Report of the IEWS Task Force on Western Assistance to Transition in the Czech and Slovak Federal Republic, Hungary, and Poland* (New York: IEWS, 1992), and Krzysztof J. Ners and Ingrid T. Buxwell, *Assistance to Transition Survey 1995.*

32. Czech embassy official, comments made during the discussion period following a lecture "Foundation and Democracy Assistance in Central Europe" by the author at the Woodrow Wilson Center, Washington, D.C., 21 May 1996.

33. This project is discussed in Richard E. Quandt, "Library Support in Eastern Europe by the Andrew W. Mellon Foundation," (report, Andrew W. Mellon Foundation, New York, October 1995 [revised February 1996]), 13–14.

34. Ibid., and Richard Quandt (Mellon), conversation with author, Washington, D.C., 24 June 1995.

35. Alexander von Humboldt Stiftung, *Annual Report* (: Alexander von Humboldt Stiftung, 1989–1994).

36. This grant-making logic was suggested in an interview by Susan Berresford (president, Ford) New York, 20 March 1996.

37. Workshop participants, FDS workshop, Bratislava, Slovakia, 2–3 November 1995.

38. Ibid.

3

Hungary: The Long Road

1. This profile of Hungary's current political and economic circumstances relies on András Inotai, "Hungary," in *Central and Eastern Europe and the European Union;* and Freedom House, *Nations in Transit: Civil Society, Democracy and Markets in East Central Europe and the Newly Independent States,* ed. Bertelsmann Foundation (Gütersloh, Ger.: Bertelsmann Foundation Publishers, 1995) (New York: Freedom House, 1995).

2. For elaboration regarding disappointment with change, see Kristof

Zoltan Varga, "Just How Much Has Been Changed? The Relationship between Civil Society and the State during the Democratic Political Transition in Hungary" (Institute for Policy Studies, Johns Hopkins University, Baltimore, Md., 1995, photocopy).

3. See EBRD, *Transition Report 1995* (London: EBRD, 1995), 44–45.

4. For a discussion of Hungary's more recent economic performance see Zsofia Szilagyi, "A Year of Economic Controversy," *Transition* 1 (17 November 1995): 62–67.

5. Joseph Schull, letter to author, 23 August 1996.

6. Kristof Varga conversation with the author, Washington, D.C., 7 July 1996.

7. See Eva Kuti, "Defining the Nonprofit Sector: Hungary," working paper no. 13 Institute for Policy Studies, the Johns Hopkins University, Baltimore, Md., May 1993, and "Changing Size, Structure and Role of the Nonprofit Sector in a Changing Economy and Society: The Case of Hungary" (paper presented at the World Launch Conference of the Johns Hopkins Comparative Nonprofit Sector Project, Brussels, Belgium, 23–24 June 1994). Also see Robert M. Jenkins, "Politics and the Development of the Hungarian Non-profit Sector," *Voluntas* 6 (1995): 183–201.

8. See Zsofia Szilagyi, "Hungary Has a Broadcast Media Law, at Last," *Transition* 2 (10 April 1996): 22–25.

9. This flaw in the law was mentioned by the European Media Institute and the International Press Institute in February 1996. Szilagyi, "Broadcast Media Law," 25.

10. For example, Dr. Martin Tardos (chairman, Economic Committee, Hungarian Parliament), Symposium for Public Policy Institutes, Budapest, Hungary, 17 May 1996.

11. AID, *Scoreboard of Assistance Commitments to the CEEC* (Washington, D.C.: AID, 1994). table 5.

12. AID, *SEED Act Implementation Report* (Washington, D.C.: AID, 1995), app., iii.

13. This discussion is based on Nancy Popson, "How to Develop a Sustainable Institution Involved in an Unpopular Issue: Autonómia Alapitaveny—A 'Success Story,'" Institute for the Study of Diplomacy, Georgetown University (forthcoming).

14. Miklós Marschall, FDS workshop, Bratislava, Slovakia, 2–3 November 1995.

15. András Biró, *Supporting Roma Communities in the Development of Small Ventures* (Budapest: Autonómia, 1995), 1.

16. Ibid.

17. Reports of discrimination and hazing abound in the human rights yearbooks. Incidents include police persecution, denial of fair trial, and various acts of violence against members of the community. Amnesty International, *Amnesty International Annual Report* (New York: Amnesty International, 1993,

1994); U.S. Department of State, *Country Reports on Human Rights Practices* (Washington, D.C.: U.S. Government Printing Office, 1992, 1993, 1994); OMRI, *OMRI Daily Bulletin* 7 March 1996.

18. Autonómia, "Information Sheet on Roma Projects," 5 May 1995, 1.

19. András Biró, FDS workshop, Bratislava, Slovakia, 25–26 April 1996.

20. Biró, "Supporting Roma Communities," 2.

21. Biró, FDS workshop, Bratislava, Slovakia, 25–26 April 1996.

22. Autonómia, *Financial Report 1994* (Budapest: Autonómia, 1994), and Biró, "Supporting Roma Communities," 2.

23. Attila Kiss, "Training Roma Entrepreneurs," *Link '95* (autumn/winter 1995): 2.

24. Consensus of the participants, FDS workshop, Bratislava, Slovakia, 25–26 April 1996.

25. Biró, FDS workshop, Bratislava, Slovakia, 25–26 April 1996.

26. For a discussion of this interest in strengthening civil society, see Daniel Siegel and Jenny Yancey, *The Rebirth of Civil Society* (New York: RBF, 1992).

27. Autonómia, *Financial Report 1994.* Total income from these eight donors in 1994 was $832,539.

28. Autonómia, *Narrative Report 1994* (Budapest: Autonómia, 1994), 7.

29. Autonómia staff, information provided to author, Budapest, Hungary, January 1996.

30. Rudolf Andorka (rector, Budapest University of Economic Sciences) interview by author, Budapest, Hungary, 23 April 1996.

31. Fred Girod (secretary, Collegium) interview by author, Budapest, Hungary, 24 April 1996.

32. Richard Quandt, "Library Support in Eastern Europe by the Andrew W. Mellon Foundation," (Andrew W. Mellon Foundation, New York, N.Y., October 1995 [revised February 1996]), photocopy. 7.

33. This information derives from numerous conversations about business education with Bill Moody and Richard Quandt, foundation staff from RBF and Mellon, respectively. In addition, conversations and correspondence with Dan Fogel, acting dean of the Katz School of Business, University of Pittsburgh, who was instrumental in establishing IMC and a parallel institution in Prague, also contributed.

34. This view is based on the author's experiences beginning in 1990 with participants in both these programs.

35. András Biró, conversation with author, Budapest, Hungary, 14 July 1995; Katalin Koncz (OSI), conversation with author, Budapest, Hungary, 15 July 1995; Sue Chudleigh (Westminster), conversation with author, London, England, 14 February 1996.

4

Poland: First among Equals

1. This profile on Poland relies on Wojtek Lamentowicsz, "Poland," in *Central and Eastern Europe and the European Union,* ed. Bertelsmann Foundation (Gütersloh, Ger.: Bertelsmann Foundation Publishers, 1995) 95–107. For a discussion on recent changes in Poland from an astute observer, see Timothy Garton Ash, "Neo-Pagan Poland," *New York Review of Books,* 11 January 1996, 10–14.

2. "A Wobbly Giant," *Economist,* 18 November 1995, 11–12.

3. Jakub Karpinski, "The Constitutional Mosaic," *Transition* 1 (11 August 1995): 4–9.

4. Conversation with Senator Jerzy Madej (member, Constitutional Committee of the Polish Parliament) Budapest, Hungary, 16 May 1996.

5. For further information about the NGO sector in Poland see KLON, "Basic Statistics Concerning the Scope of Activities of Nongovernmental Organizations in Poland," (KLON, Warsaw, photocopy).

6. Karpinski, "Constitutional Mosaic," 4–9.

7. Open Media Research Institute, *Daily Digest,* 19 December 1995.

8. Jakub Karpinski, "Politicians Endanger Independence of Polish Public TV," *Transition* 2 (19 April 1996): 28–30.

9. For example, both Freedom House, *Comparative Survey of Freedom* (New York: Freedom House, 1996) and State Department, *Country Report on Human Rights Practices* (Washington, D.C., 1990–1995) indicate that there is freedom of the press in Poland.

10. Karpinski, "Politicians Endanger Independence," 30.

11. Aleksander Smolar, interview by author, Washington, D.C., 8 October 1995.

12. For a vivid analysis of attempts to come to grips with this legacy, see Tina Rosenberg, *The Haunted Land: Facing Europe's Ghosts after Communism* (New York: Random House, 1995).

13. See, for example, Robert D. Putnam, *Making Democracy Work: Civic Traditions in Modern Italy* (Princeton, N.J.: Princeton University Press, 1993), and Francis Fuyukama, *Trust: The Social Virtues and the Creation of Prosperity* (New York: The Free Press, 1995).

14. AID, *Scoreboard of Assistance Commitments to the CEEC* (Washington, D.C.: AID, 1994), Appendix, table 5.

15. Ibid.

16. European Community, *PHARE 1994 Annual Report* (Brussels: European Community, 1994), 3–4.

17. AID, *Seed Act Implementation Report* (Washington, D.C.: AID, 1995), Appendices.

18. Among all the other foundations, only Mellon played a larger role than Bosch. Mellon's role, however, was considerably smaller than Humboldt's. See table A.1, pp. 122–23.

19. Paul Samogyi (executive director, FTUI) interview by author, Washington, D.C., 5 March 1996. FTUI is sometimes criticized for being zealously anti-Communist and supporting unions overseas to raise wages and diminish the chances that U.S. jobs would move overseas. These criticisms do not apply in the case of FTUI's work in Poland. For a discussion of some of these criticisms, see Thomas Carothers, "The NED at 10," *Foreign Policy* 95 (Summer 1994): 123–39.

20. This profile is based on conversations with key FSLD officials, during the period 1990–1996, as well as documentation prepared by the Foundation, such as FSLD, *The Annual Report on the Activity of FSLD in 1994* (Warsaw: FSLD, 1995).

21. Joanna Regulska, interview by author, Washington, D.C., 4 January 1996.

22. Jacek Kozlowski (executive director, FSLD), remarks made at FDS workshop, Bratislava, Slovakia, 25–26 April 1996.

23. In a 23 August 1996 letter to the author Joseph Schull (Ford) emphasized the point that this absence of independent institutions resulted in foundations' having few choices other than to build their projects on these bridging individuals. Zdeněk Drábek also remarked about the importance of these "bridging individuals" at the first FDS workshop, Bratislava, Slovakia, 2–3 November 1995.

24. Joanna Regulska, "Building Local Democracy: The Role of Western Assistance," (paper presented at Western Aid to Central and Eastern Europe Conference, Woodrow Wilson Center, Washington, D.C., 18–19 April 1995).

25. Humboldt, *Annual Report* (Bonn, Germany: Humboldt, 1989–1994).

26. This information was drawn from the Mellon Central European grants list provided to the author by Richard Quandt and Richard Quandt, "Library Support in Eastern Europe by the Andrew W. Mellon Foundation" (Andrew W. Mellon Foundation, New York, N.Y., October 1995 [revised February 1996], photocopy).

27. Foundation de France, *Rapport Annuel 1993* (Paris, France: Fondation de France, 1994).

28. See Wojtek Lamentowicz, "Nongovernmental Think Tanks in Poland," in *Beyond Government: Extending Public Debate in Emerging Democracies* ed. Craufurd D. Goodwin and Michael Nacht (Boulder, Colo.: Westview Press, 1995), 389–400, and Kevin F. F. Quigley, "Think Tanks in Newly Democratic Eastern Europe," in *Think Tanks in a Democratic Society: An Alternative Voice*, ed. Jeffrey Telgarsky and Makiko Ueno (Washington, D.C.: Urban Institute, 1996), 83–92.

29. Gdańsk Institute for Market Economics, *Newsletter* (January–March 1996): 1.

30. This discussion draws on an unpublished case study of WSF developed by its executive director, Piotr Szczepański, and grant-related material prepared by Ford staff.

31. International Media Fund, *International Media Fund Five Year Report: A Free Press: Hope for Eastern Europe* (Washington, D.C.: International Media Fund, give year) 5.

32. See, for example, Goodwin and Nacht, *Beyond Government.*

33. `FTUI played a very important role in supporting Solidarity during the martial law period. One executive even suggested that FTUI "kicked out the Communists." Paul Somogyi, (executive director, FTUI), interview by author, Washington, D.C., 5 March 1996; Randy Garton (deputy director, FTUI), interview by author, Washington, D.C., 5 March 1996; and Richard Wilson (regional director, (FTUI), interview by author, 5 March 1996.

34. This view was influenced by Aleksander Smolar, interview by author, Washington, D.C., 8 October 1995.

5

Slovakia: Slipping Behind

1. This profile of Solvakia's current political and economic circumstances relies on Pavel Ondrcka, "Slovakia," in *Central and Eastern Europe and the European Union,* ed. Bertelsmann Foundation (Gütersloh, Ger.: Bertelsmann Foundation Publishers, 1995), 135–50; Freedom House, *Nations in Transit: Civil Society, Democracy and Markets in East Central Europe and the Newly Independent States* (New York: Freedom House, 1995). Soňa Szomolányi and Grigorij Mesežnikov, eds., *The Slovak Path of Transition to Democracy?* (Bratislava: Slovak Political Science Association, 1994); as well as reporting from Open Media Research Institute (OMRI), including OMRI reporter Sharon Fisher, "Slovakia: An Overview of Developments since Independence," (paper presented at "Two Transitions: The New Practice of Governance in Western and Eastern Europe, Woodrow Wilson Center, Washington, D.C., 15 August 1995).

2. For more discussion about Slovakia's difficulties in democratic development, see Peter M. Benda and Kevin F. F. Quigley, "Dark Stirrings in Slovakia," *Christian Science Monitor,* 12 April 1993, 18.

3. *PlanEcon Reports* 9 (10 December 1993).

4. Sharon Fisher, "Turning Away from Slovakia," *Transition* 2 (9 February 1996): 38–41.

5. *CED Slovak Economic Sheet* (December 1995).

6. These results were obtained in a December 1994 opinion poll conducted by FOCUS and presented by Zora Bútorová, "Slovakia: The Year after Elections," (lecture presented at Woodrow Wilson Center, Washington, D.C., 5 April 1995).

7. Sharon Fisher, "Ethnic Hungarians Back Themselves into a Corner," *Transition* 1 (29 December 1995): 58–63.

8. Martin Bútora and Zuzana Fialová, *Nonprofit Sector and Volunteering in Slovakia* (Bratislava: SAIA and FOCUS, 1995), 17.

9. "Lexa Speaks Out on the President, the Media, and the Rash Radicalization of Political Life," *Transition* 2 (28 June 1996): 47.

10. For example, UN High Commissioner for Human Rights Jose Ayal Lasso expressed reservations about this law. *OMRI Daily Digest* (20 August 1996).

11. Pavol Demeš and Katarína Koštálová, (FDS workshop, Bratislava, Slovakia, 25–26 April 1996); Pavol Demeš, FDS workshop, Washington, D.C., 5 June 1996.

12. Andrej Skolkay, "Slovak Government Tightens Its Grip on the Airwaves," *Transition* 2 (19 April 1996): 18–21.

13. Although it has received relatively little attention from the international community there are exceptions and these have evolved over time. For example, AID has provided more resources per capita to Slovakia than to the other three Central European nations. See AID, *Scoreboard of Assistance Commitments to CEEC.*

14. AID, *Scoreboard of Assistance Commitments to the CEEC* (Washington, D.C.: AID, 1994), table 5; Ners and Buxell, *Assistance to Transition 1995*; and data collected for this project from the grants lists of various foundations such as Ford, Mellon, PCT, RBF, and Soros, among others.

15. AID, *SEED Act Implementation Report* (Washington, D.C.: AID, 1995), 1–30.

16. SAIA-SCTS, "Service Center for the Third Sector" (brochure, Brahslava: SAIA-SCTS, 1995).

17. This information on SAIA is based on numerous conversations with Pavol Demeš and David Daniel, in Brahslava and Washington, D.C., over the past six years and materials produced by SAIA-SCTS.

18. Demeš conversations; Daniel, conversations.

19. Annetta Zubeková (head, program management unit) conversations with author, Bratislava, Slovakia, 2 November 1995; CSDF, "CSDF" (brochure, CSDF, Bratislava, Slovakia, 1995).

20. Alena Brunovska, letter to author, 7 February 1996.

21. These include Ford, Mott, Trust, EF, GMF, NED, OSF, OSI, PCT, RBF, Sasakawa, and the Whitehead Foundation. In addition, FCS has received considerable support from AID.

22. IEWS, *Annual Report 1995* (New York: Institute for EastWest Studies, 1996) 41–42.

23. Humboldt, *Annual Report* (Bonn, Germany: Alexander von Humboldt Stiftung, 1989–1994).

24. See Bútora and Fialová, *Nonprofit Sector,* 20.

6

Regional Projects: Going against the Grain

1. See table A.7, p. 129.

2. Comments made by Dorel Sandor (director, Center for Political

Studies and Comparative Analysis, Bucharest, Romania) at a workshop on public policy institutes organized by CIPE, Budapest, Hungary, 17 May 1996.

3. The discussion of EPCE draws on a case study by Michael Strübin, who worked as an intern on this research project, and numerous conversations the author had with EPCE staff in the region and in Washington, D.C. The author also benefitted from attending the Fifth Funders Meeting, Banska Bystrica Slovakia, 21–25 July 1995.

4. EPCE, *Environmental Partnership for Central Europe Report 1994/95*, (Washington, D.C.: EPCE, 1995) 10.

5. Bill Moody (RBF), FDS workshop, Woodrow Wilson Center, Washington, D.C., 5 June 1996.

6. The EPCE Hungarian office was organized differently than were the offices in the other countries, which retained their full independence. In Hungary, EPCE joined Autonómia, which hired a program officer, aided by a three-person advisory board (compared to five in the other countries), to administer the EPCE program. Although the EPCE office in Hungary was as effective in its activities as the other country offices, concerns over the autonomy of EPCE led to a reform in July 1994: EPCE became the independent foundation Oekotars; the advisory board expanded its role and size and became a board of trustees; a bookkeeper and an assistant joined the staff to support the director.

7. Juraj Mesík (director, EPCE—Slovakia), FDS workshop, Bratislava, Slovakia, 25–26 April 1996.

8. Robert C. Wilkinson, "The Environmental Partnership for Central Europe" (Independent Review, GMF, 1993, photocopy).

9. There is, however, evidence that local giving is growing dramatically. In Hungary, United Way International raised $7 million from local groups in 1995. This is a substantial sum. What is especially remarkable is that just a few years ago no local money was raised at all. Leon Irish, (president, United Way International), FDS workshop, Woodrow Wilson Center, Washington, D.C., 5 June 1996.

10. See table A.15, p. 137.

11. The origins of this program are discussed in a 5 April 1996 final narrative report prepared by the Hoover Institution for PCT.

12. See pp. 4–5 of the report mentioned in note 11.

13. 1989–1995 Grants list provided by Mellon and PCT; further information derived from conversations with participants in these seminars and fellowships, 1992–1995.

14. Projects funded by AID and others often overstate project goals. Given this propensity to overstate, that the projects do not achieve the desired goals is nearly inevitable.

15. The MBA Enterprise Corps is now building on its experience in Eastern Europe and the Newly Independent States to expand to Latin America. Dr. Jack Behrman (founding director, MBA Enterprise Corps), telephone conversation with author, 19 August 1996.

16. Janos Kovacs, FDS workshop, Bratislava, Slovakia, 2–3 November 1995.

17. David Siegel and Jenny Yancey, *The Rebirth of Civil Society* (New York: RBF, 1992).

18. Dan Siegel and Jenny Yancey, interview by author, Budapest, Hungary, 17 July 1995, and facsimile to the author, 2 December 1996.

19. Zorá Bútorová, "Slovakia: The Year after Elections," (Woodrow Wilson Center, Washington, D.C., 5 April 1995).

7

George Soros: Leader of the Band

1. Interview by author, Washington, D.C., 13 April 1995.

2. A number of candidates might qualify for this honor, including David Packard, who donated more than $4 billion to a foundation that bears his name, and Charles Getty, who provided more than $6 billion—primarily in art works—to his foundation.

3. George Soros, *Underwriting Democracy* (New York: Free Press, 1990), 175–217.

4. George Soros, "Toward Open Societies," *Foreign Policy* 98 (spring 1995): 65.

5. Soros Foundations, *Building Open Societies* (New York: Soros Foundations, 1994), 8.

6. George Soros, "George Soros's Address to the CEU Budapest Graduation Ceremony," *CEU Gazette,* no. 2 (spring/summer 1995): 8.

7. Soros, *Underwriting Democracy,* 5.

8. *Building Open Societies.*

9. This statement is based on the views of numerous people interviewed for this project, a number of whom did not wish to be identified out of concern that their comments would jeopardize their funding from the Soros Foundations.

10. Andras Biró (founder, Autonómia), FDS workshop, Bratislava, Slovakia, 2–3 November 1995.

11. Soros, "Toward Open Societies," 66.

12. For example, Aryeh Neier, president of the Soros Foundation, mentioned in an interview by the author in New York (28 February 1996) that the need for local structures and staff were probably the most important lessons learned from their grant making. This view was echoed by Kennette Benedict of MacArthur in an interview by the author in Chicago, Ill., on 1 September 1995.

13. This discussion draws on Batory, *Annual Report 1993* (Warsaw: Stefan Batory Foundation, 1994), Batory, *Annual Report 1994* (Warsaw: Stefan Batory Foundation, 1995) and an interview by the author with Aleksander Smolar Washington, D.C., on 8 October 1995, as well as numerous conversations with Jacek Wojnarowski (executive director), Anna Rozicka (media program coordinator), and Krzysztof Michalski (member, Foundation Council) over the spring of 1996.

14. Batory, *Annual Report 1994*, 4.

15. Aleksander Smolar, interview by author, Washington, D.C., 8 October 1995.

16. Irena Lasota, president, Institute for Democracy in Eastern Europe.

17. Anna Rozicka, facsimile to the author, 8 August 1996.

18. Batory, *Annual Report 1995*, 122–24.

19. Joseph Schull (then deputy director, International Affairs, Ford), telephone conversation with author, 3 June 1996, and Jacek Wojnarowski, interview by author, Warsaw, Poland, 18 July 1996.

20. Soros Foundations, *Building Open Societies*, 142.

21. Richard Quandt (professor emeritus at Princeton University and director of Mellon's work in Central Europe), conversation with author, Washington, D.C., 24 June 1995.

22. Miroslav Pospíšil, executive director of the Jan Hus Education Foundation, which promotes educational reform in the Czech Republic and Slovakia, made a comment suggesting this at FDS workshop, Bratislava, Slovakia, 25–26 April 1996.

23. See, for example, Seymour Martin Lipset, "The Social Requisites of Democracy Revisited," *American Sociological Review* 59 (February 1994): 1–22.

24. Andrew Lass (director, CASLIN), telephone conversations with the author during the spring and fall of 1992.

25. Michael Vachon (director of public affairs, OSI), letter to author, n.d.

26. Soros Foundations, *Building Open Societies*, 158–59.

27. This draws on a case study prepared by Nancy Popson done under the auspices of this project. This case served as the basis for a discussion at FDS workshop, Bratislava, Slovakia, 25–26 April 1996, regarding whether foundations and other funders working in societies in transition should seek to innovate, start new institutions, or renovate existing institutions.

28. Soros, *Underwriting Democracy*, 129.

29. Soros (comments delivered as part of a panel, "Leadership and International Experience: The Private Sector and Cultural Diplomacy," at the International Cultural Forum, Washington, D.C., 13 December 1991.) in Malcolm Richardson, ed., *Shaping the New World Order: International Cultural Opportunities and the Private Sector* (New York: Institute for International Education, 1992), 32–3.

30. Paul Flather, "Opening Up the Centre," in *Continental Responsibility*, ed. Mary E. Kirk and Aaron A. Rhodes (New York: Institute of International Education, 1994), 18.

31. CEU, *1996–1997 Prospectus* (Budapest: CEU, 1995), 50–51.

32. Flather, "Opening Up the Centre," 19.

33. Jay Branegan, Sally B. Donnelly, and Sribala Subramanian, "Master Giver," *Time International* 146 (10 July 1995): 38.

34. Data provided by Professor Ernó Zalai (chairman, Department of

Mathematical Economics and Econometrics), Budapest University of Economic Sciences, Budapest, Hungary, 24 April 1996.

35. Petr Pajas (board member, CEU—Prague) FDS workshop, Bratislava, Slovakia, 25–26 April 1996.

36. This view was reflected time and time again in interviews and conversations with Central European scholars and the author in Bratislava, Budapest, Prague, and Washington, D.C., August 1995–May 1996.

37. Miroslav Pospíšil, FDS workshop, Bratislava, Slovakia, 25–26 April 1996.

38. Ralf Dahrendorf, "Main Problems of the Reform of Higher Education and Research in Former Eastern Europe," in *Changes in Central Europe: Challenges and Perspectives for Higher Education and Research*, ed. Colin G. Campbell and Ralf Dahrendorf, vol. 6, *TERC Reports* (Vienna: IWM, 1994), 15.

39. SFH's average staff salaries are approximately $400 per month. This is less than 10 percent of the average salary of a U.S. expatriate working on a project funded by either AID or the Bank. Thomas Carothers, author of *Assessing Democracy Assistance: The Case of Romania* (Washington, D.C.: Carnegie Endowment for International Peace, 1996), suggested in a phone conversation to the author that it was less expensive for Soros to fund his five offices and staff of fifty-five in Romania than it was for AID to place three U.S. employees in Bucharest.

40. SFH, *Név Soros: Soros Alapítvány 1984–1994* (Budapest: Soros Alapítvány, 1994).

41. Tereza Grellová (executive director, Milan Šimečka Foundation) FDS workshop, Bratislava, Slovakia, 25–26 April 1996.

42. Aleksander Smolar, interview by author, 8 October 1995.

43. Despite repeated efforts through various channels, including a promise of support from Aryeh Neier, president of the SFH, this researcher was only able to obtain the sketchiest data prior to 1993.

44. Katalin Koncz (executive director, OSI), conversation with author, Budapest, Hungary, 24 April 1996.

8

Conclusions and Recommendations

1. Earlier versions of this discussion appear in Kevin F. F. Quigley, *Conversations on Democracy Assistance* (Washington, D.C.: East European Studies, Woodrow Wilson International Center for Scholars, 1996) and "For Democracy's Sake: Where Funders Fail—and Succeed" *World Policy Journal* 13 (spring 1996): 109–18.

Select Bibliography

Agopsowicz, Monika, and James Landon. "Promoting Pluralism in Eastern Europe." *Journal of Democracy* 6 (October 1995): 155–64.

Albright, Madeleine. "The Role of the United States in Central Europe." *In The New Europe: Revolution in East-West Relations. Proceedings of the Academy of Political Science* 38, no. 1 (1991): 71–84.

Allison, Graham T., and Robert P. Beschel. "Can the United States Promote Democracy?" *Political Science Quarterly* 107 (spring 1992): 81–98.

Almond, Gabriel A., and Sidney Verba. *The Civic Culture: Political Attitudes and Democracy in Five Nations.* Princeton, N.J.: Princeton University Press, 1963.

Amnesty International. *Amnesty International Annual Reports.* New York: Amnesty International, 1984–1994.

Andrew W. Mellon Foundation. "Democratic Institution Building in East and Central Europe." Study prepared by the Twenty-first Century Foundation for the Andrew W. Mellon Foundation, March 1993.

Ash, Timothy Garton. *The Magic Lantern.* New York: Vintage Books, 1993.

Banac, Ivo, ed. *Eastern Europe in Revolution.* Ithaca, N.Y.: Cornell University Press, 1992.

Barany, Zoltan. "Visegrad Four Contemplate Separate Paths." *Transition* 1 (11 August 1995), 56–59.

Barre Raymond, et al. *Moving Beyond Assistance: Final Report of the IEWS Task Force on Western Assistance to Transition in the Czech and Slovak Federal Republic, Hungary, and Poland.* New York: Institute for EastWest Studies, 1992.

Basora, Adrian A. "Central and Eastern Europe: Imperative for Active U.S. Engagement." *Washington Quarterly* 16 (winter 1993): 67–78.

Berger, Peter, and Richard Neuhaus. *To Empower People: The Role of Mediating Structures in Public Policy.* Washington, D.C.: American Enterprise Institute for Public Policy Research, 1977.

Bermeo, Nancy G. *Liberalization and Democratization: Change in the Soviet Union and Eastern Europe.* Baltimore: Johns Hopkins University Press, 1992.

Bernhard, Michael. "Civil Society and Democratic Transition in East Central Europe." *Political Science Quarterly* 108, no. 2 (1993): 307–26.

Bertelsmann Foundation. *Central and Eastern Europe and the European Union.* Gütersloh, Ger.: Bertelsmann Foundation, 1995.

Beschel, Robert P. "The Role of U.S. Foundations in East/Central Europe." Report from a conference sponsored by the Ford Foundation, the Pew Charitable Trusts, and Rockefeller Brothers Fund, New York, N.Y., 11 January 1991.

Blair, Harry. "Civil Society and Building Democracy: Lessons from International Donor Experience." Paper presented at the Ninety-first Annual Conference of the American Political Science Association, Chicago, Ill., 31 August–3 September 1995.

Blanchard, Olivier Jean, Kenneth A. Froot, and Jeffrey D. Sachs, eds. *The Transition in Eastern Europe.* Chicago: University of Chicago Press, 1994.

Bobbio, Norberto. *Democracy and Dictatorship: The Nature and Limits of State Power.* Minneapolis: University of Minnesota Press, 1989.

Bresser Periera, Luiz Carlos, Jose Maria Maravall, and Adam Przeworski. *Economic Reform in New Democracies: A Social Democratic Approach.* New York: Cambridge University Press, 1993.

Brown, James F. "Helping Eastern Europe: Thoughts, Suggestions, and Some Mild Obsessions." In *Promoting Democracy and Free Markets in Eastern Europe,* ed. Charles Wolf, Jr., 119–27. San Francisco: Institute for Contemporary Studies, 1992.

Bruck, Connie. "The World According to Soros." *New Yorker,* 23 January 1995, 54–78.

Business–Higher Education Forum. "Making Change Last: Lessons Learned in Providing Management Training and Economics Education to Central and Eastern Europe." Highlights of a conference sponsored by Business–Higher Education Forum, Washington, D.C., 1–2 December 1992.

Bútora, Martin, and Zora Bútorová. "Slovakia after the Split." *Journal of Democracy* 4 (April 1993): 71–83.

Bútora, Martin, and Zuzana Fialová. *Nonprofit Sector and Volunteering in Slovakia.* Bratislava: Slovak Academic Information Agency—Service Center for the Third Sector and Center for Social and Market Analysis, 1995.

Campbell, Colin G., and Ralf Dahrendorf. "Changes in Central Europe: Challenges and Perspectives for Higher Education and Research." Proceedings of a symposium with the same title, the Ford Foundation, New York, N.Y. 28 January 1994.

Carothers, Thomas. *Assessing Democracy Assistance: The Case of Romania.* Washington, D.C.: Carnegie Endowment for International Peace, 1996.

———. "Democracy Promotion under Clinton." *Washington Quarterly* 18 (Autumn 1995): 13–25.

Civic Education Project. *Assessing the Impact of Book and Journal Donations to Central and Eastern Europe.* Prague: Trevor Top, 1994.

Civil Society Development Foundation. *Basic Information about the Non-Profit Sector in the Czech Republic.* Prague: Civil Society Development Foundation, 1994.

Cohen, Jean L., and Andrew Arato. *Civil Society and Political Theory.* Cambridge, Mass.: MIT Press, 1992.

Commission on Security and Cooperation in Europe. *Briefing on U.S. Assistance to Central and Eastern Europe and the NIS: An Assessment.* Washington, D.C.: Commission on Security and Cooperation in Europe, 1995.

"Comparative Survey of Freedom," *Freedom at Issue* (January–February, 1985–1990).

"Comparative Survey of Freedom," *Freedom Review* (January–February 1991, 1994–1995).

Connolly, Barbara, Tamar Gutner, and Hildegard Bedarff. "Organizational Inertia and Environmental Assistance to Eastern Europe." Paper presented at the Ninety-first Annual Conference of the American Political Science Association, Chicago, Ill., 31 August–3 September 1995.

Council of Europe. *Assistance with the Development and Consolidation of Democratic Security: Annual Report 1995.* Strasbourg: Council of Europe Press, 1996.

Council of Europe. *From Assistance to Democracy to Democratic Security.* Strasbourg: Council of Europe Press, 1990.

Council of Europe. *Human Rights: A Continuing Challenge for the Council of Europe.* Strasbourg: Council of Europe Press, 1996.

Dahl, Robert A. *Democracy and its Critics.* New Haven, Conn.: Yale University Press, 1989.

———. *Polyarchy: Participation and Opposition.* New Haven, Conn.: Yale University Press, 1971.

Dahrendorf, Ralf. *Reflections on the Revolution in Europe.* New York: Random House, 1990.

Dauderstädt, Michael. "A Comparison of the Assistance Strategies of the Western Donors." Bonn: Friedrich Ebert Stiftung, 1995, photocopy.

Dawisha, Karen. *Eastern Europe, Gorbachev and Reform.* 2d ed. New York: Cambridge University Press, 1993.

Dervis, Kemal, Marcelo Selowsky, and Christine Wallich. *The Transition in Central and Eastern Europe and the Former Soviet Union.* Washington, D.C.: World Bank, 1995.

Diamond, Larry. *Promoting Democracy in the 1990s: Actors and Instruments, Issues and Imperatives.* New York: Carnegie Commission on Preventing Deadly Conflict, 1995.

Diamond, Larry, and Marc F. Plattner, eds. *The Global Resurgence of Democracy.* Baltimore: Johns Hopkins University Press, 1993.

Downs, Anthony. *An Economic Theory of Democracy.* New York: Harper Collins, 1957.

Eberstadt, Nicholas. "A Skeptic's View of Aid." In *Promoting Democracy and Free Markets in Eastern Europe,* ed. Charles Wolf, Jr., 39–70. San Francisco: Institute for Contemporary Studies, 1992.

"Emerging Market Indicators." *Economist,* multiple issues.

"Environmentally Sustainable Development." *The World Bank Participation Sourcebook.* Washington, D.C.: World Bank, 1996.

European Bank for Reconstruction and Development. *Transition Report 1995.* London: European Bank for Reconstruction and Development, 1995.

European Foundation Centre. *International Guide to Funders Interested in Central and Eastern Europe*. Brussels: European Foundation Centre, 1993.

Fallows, James. "Economic and Market Reform in the Czech Republic, and the Past and Future Roles of Charitable Efforts There." Report prepared for the Pew Charitable Trusts, 1994, photocopy.

Fisher, Sharon. "Slovakia: An Overview of Developments since Independence." Paper presented at Two Transitions: The New Practice of Governance in Western and Eastern Europe conference, Woodrow Wilson International Center for Scholars, Washington, D.C., 29 August 1995.

Flickner, Charles. "The Russian Aid Mess." *National Interest* no. 38 (winter 1994–1995): 13–18.

Ford Foundation. "Report of the Soviet and East European Study Group." Ford Foundation, New York, N.Y., September 1989, photocopy.

Freedom House and United States Agency for International Development. *Nations in Transit: Civil Society, Democracy and Markets in East Central Europe and the Newly Independent States*. New York: Freedom House, 1995.

Gastil, Raymond D. *Freedom in the World: Political Rights and Civil Liberties*. Freedom House: New York, 1973–78, 1980, 1988–92; Boston: G. K. Hall, 1979; Westport, Conn.: Greenwood Press, 1981–87.

Geremek, Bronislaw. "Civil Society Then and Now." *Journal of Democracy* 3 (April 1992): 3–12.

German Federal Ministry of Economics. *Transform: Technical Assistance for Central and Eastern Europe in Rebuilding Democracy and Social Market Economies*. Report No. 371, Bonn, Germany, April 1995.

German Marshall Fund of the United States. "Political Development in Central and Eastern Europe." *TransAtlantic Perspectives* 30 (autumn 1994): 2–51.

Goodwin, Craufurd D. "Understanding Markets: A Report on Economics Education in Central and Eastern Europe." Prepared for Pew Charitable Trusts, Philadelphia, Pa., December 1994, photocopy.

Goodwin, Craufurd D., and Michael Nacht, eds. *Beyond Government: Extending the Public Policy Debate in Emerging Democracies*. Boulder, Colo.: Westview Press, 1995.

Gray, John. "From Post-Communism to Civil Society: The Reemergence of History and the Decline of the Western Model." In *Liberalism and the Economic Order*, ed. Ellen Frankel Paul et al., 26–50. Cambridge: Cambridge University Press, 1993.

Gross, Jan. "Poland: From Civil Society to Political Nation." In *Eastern Europe in Revolution*, ed. Ivo Banac, 56–71. Ithaca, N.Y.: Cornell University Press, 1992.

Grudzińska-Gross, Irena, ed. *Constitutionalism in East Central Europe*. Bratislava: Czecho-Slovak Committee of the European Cultural Foundation, 1994.

Habermas, Jurgen. *The Structural Transformation of the Public Sphere: An Inquiry into a Category of Bourgeois Society*. Cambridge, Mass.: MIT Press, 1991.

Hague Club. *Foundation Profiles*. Hague: Hague Club, 1991.

Hardi, Peter. *Environmental Protection in East-Central Europe: A Market-Oriented Approach*. Gütersloh, Germany: Bertelsmann Foundation, 1994.

Hardt, John P. *Poland's Renewal and US Options: A Policy Reconnaissance, Update*. Washington, D.C.: Congressional Research Service, July 1987.

Harper, John, and Janine R. Wedel. "Western Aid to Eastern and Central Europe: What We Are Doing Right, What We Are Doing Wrong, and How We Can Do It Better?" Report from a conference with the same name, Woodrow Wilson International Center for Scholars, Washington, D.C., 18–20 April 1995.

Havel, Václav. *Summer Meditations.* New York: Vintage Books, 1993.

Havel, Václav, et al. *The Power of the Powerless.* Armonk, N.Y.: M. E. Sharpe, 1985.

Howard, A. E. Dick. *Democracy's Dawn.* Washington, D.C.: Endowment of United States Institute of Peace, 1991.

Huntington, Samuel P. *The Third Wave: Democratization in the Late Twentieth Century.* Norman, Okla.: University of Oklahoma Press, 1991.

Jenkins, Robert M. "Hungarian Nonprofit Organizations and the Politics of the Post-Communist State." Unpublished paper, December 1995, photocopy.

Jurzyca, Eugen. "The Experience of the Center for Economic Development with American Sponsorship." Paper presented at the United States and Central and Eastern Europe: The Emerging Relationship conference, Budapest, 17–19 November 1995.

Karpinski, Jakub. "The Constitutional Mosaic." *Transition* 1, (11 August 1995) 4–9.

———. "Roads from Communism." *Uncaptive Minds* 7 (summer 1994): 5–16.

Katz, Stanley N. "Philanthropy and Democracy: Which Comes First?" *Advancing Philanthropy* 2 (summer 1994): 34–39.

Keane, John. *Civil Society and the State: New European Perspectives.* New York: Verso, 1988.

Kirk, Mary E. *Where Walls Once Stood: U.S. Responses to New Opportunities for Academic Cooperation with East Central Europe.* New York: Institute of International Education, 1992.

Klaus, Václav, Václav Havel, and Petr Pithart. "Rival Visions." *Journal of Democracy* 7, (January 1996): 11–23.

Kornai, Janos. *Vision and Reality, Market and State.* New York: Routledge, 1986.

Kuti, Éva. "Changing Size, Structure, and Role of the Nonprofit Sector in a Changing Economy and Society: The Case of Hungary." Paper presented at the World Launch conference of the Johns Hopkins Comparative Nonprofit Sector Project, Brussels, Belgium, 23–24 June 1994.

Laurenti, Jeffrey, ed. *Searching for Moorings: East Central Europe in the International System.* New York: United Nations Association of the United States of America, 1994.

Leś, Ewa. *The Voluntary Sector in Post-Communist East Central Europe.* Washington, D.C.: Civicus, 1994.

Lewis, Paul, ed. *Democracy and Civil Society in Eastern Europe.* New York: St. Martin's Press, 1992.

Lindblom, Charles E. "Market and Democracy—Obliquely." *PS: Political Science and Politics* 28 (December 1995): 684–88.

———. *Politics and Markets: The World's Political Economic System.* New York: Basic Books, 1977.

Linz, Juan. *The Breakdown of Democratic Regimes: Crisis, Breakdown, and Reequilibration.* Baltimore: Johns Hopkins University Press, 1978.

Lipset, Seymour Martin. *Political Man: The Social Bases of Conflict*, 2d ed. Baltimore: Johns Hopkins University Press, 1981.

———. "The Social Requisites of Democracy Revisited." *American Sociological Review* 59 (February 1994): 1–22.

Lubin, Nancy, and Monica Ware. "Aid to the Former Soviet Union: When Less is More." Paper presented at the Conference on U.S. Assistance to the NIS: Policies, Priorities and Partnerships, Washington, D.C., 19 March 1996.

Manser, Roger. *Failed Transitions: The Eastern European Economy and Environment since the Fall of Communism*. New York: New Press, 1993.

Michnik, Adam. *Letters from Prison*. Berkeley: University of California Press, 1985.

Michta, Andrew A., and Ilya Prizel, eds. *Postcommunist Eastern Europe: Crisis and Reform*. New York: St. Martin's Press, 1992.

Micou, Ann McKinstry, and Birgit Lindsnaes, eds. *The Role of Voluntary Organizations in Emerging Democracies*. New York: Institute of International Education and the Danish Centre for Human Rights, 1993.

Nagorski, Andrew. *The Birth of Freedom*. New York: Simon and Schuster, 1993.

National Democratic Institute for International Affairs. *NDI Handbook: How Domestic Organizations Monitor Elections*. Washington, D.C.: National Democratic Institute for International Affairs, 1995.

Ners, Krzysztof J., and Ingrid T. Buxell. *Assistance to Transition Survey 1995*. Warsaw: Institute for EastWest Studies Policy Education Center on Assistance to Transition, 1995.

O'Donnell, Guillermo, Philippe C. Schmitter, and Lawrence Whitehead, eds. *Transitions from Authoritarian Rule: Tentative Conclusions about Uncertain Democracies*. Baltimore: Johns Hopkins University Press, 1986.

Oujezdská, Dana. "The Activity of Foundations and Civil Associations Working in Health and Social Services." *ICN Bulletin* (1995): 6–7.

Palmer, Tom G. *Philanthropy in Central and Eastern Europe: A Resource Book for Foundations, Corporations, and Individuals*. Fairfax, Va.: Institute for Humane Studies at George Mason University, 1991.

Payne, Julian H. "Economic Assistance to Support Democratization in Developing Countries: A Canadian Perspective." *Development—Journal of the Society for International Development* no. 3 (1992): 12–16.

Perez-Diaz, Victor M. *The Return of Civil Society: The Emergence of Democratic Spain*. Cambridge, Mass.: Harvard University Press, 1993.

PlanEcon. *Review and Outlook for Eastern Europe, June 1995*. Washington, D.C.: PlanEcon, 1995.

Pogany, Istvan. "Constitutional Reform in Central and Eastern Europe: Hungary's Transition to Democracy." *International and Comparative Law Quarterly* 42 (April 1993): 332–55.

Pridham, Geoffrey, Eric Herring, and George Sanford, eds. *Building Democracy: The International Dimension of Democratization in Eastern Europe*. New York: St. Martin's Press, 1994.

Prins, Gwyn, ed. *Spring in Winter*. Cambridge: Cambridge University Press, 1990.

Przeworksi, Adam. *Democracy and the Market: Political and Economic Reform in*

Eastern Europe and Latin America. New York: Cambridge University Press, 1991.

Putnam, Robert D. *Making Democracy Work: Civic Traditions in Modern Italy.* Princeton, N.J.: Princeton University Press, 1993.

Quandt, Richard E. "Library Support in Eastern Europe by the Andrew Mellon Foundation." Andrew W. Mellon Foundation, New York, N.Y., October 1995 (revised February 1996), photocopy.

———. "Report on the Baltics." Unpublished report, 17 April 1995.

Quigley, Kevin F. F. *Conversations on Democracy Assistance.* Washington, D.C.: East European Studies, Woodrow Wilson International Center for Scholars, 1996.

———. "For Democracy's Sake: How Funders Fail—and Succeed." *World Policy Journal* 13 (spring 1996): 109–18.

———. "Philanthropy's Role in East Europe." *Orbis* 37 (fall 1993): 581–98.

Ramet, Sabrina. *Social Currents in Eastern Europe.* Durham, N.C.: Duke University Press, 1991.

Rau, Zbigniew, ed. *The Reemergence of Civil Society in Eastern Europe and the Soviet Union.* Boulder, Colo.: Westview Press, 1991.

Regulska, Joanna. "Building Local Democracy: The Role of Western Assistance." Paper presented at Western Aid to Central and Eastern Europe conference, Woodrow Wilson International Center for Scholars, Washington, D.C., 18–20 April 1995.

"Return of the Hapsburgs: A Survey of Central Europe." *Economist,* 18 November 1995,

Rollo, J. M. C. *The New Eastern Europe: Western Responses.* Cahtam House Papers. London: Royal Institute of International Affairs, 1990.

Rosenberg, Tina. *The Haunted Land: Facing Europe's Ghosts after Communism.* New York: Random House, 1995.

Salamon, Lester M. "The Rise of the Nonprofit Sector." *Foreign Affairs* 73 (July–August 1994): 109–22.

Samuels, David. "At Play in the Fields of Oppression." *Harper's,* May 1995, 47–54.

Schelling, Thomas C. "The Marshall Plan: A Model for Eastern Europe?" In *Promoting Democracy and Free Markets in Eastern Europe,* ed., Charles Wolf, Jr., 21–28. San Francisco: Institute for Contemporary Studies, 1992.

Schimpp, Michele Wozniak. "AID and Democratic Development: A Synthesis of Literature and Experience." In AID Documents [on-line gopher site], May 1992 [cited November 1995].

Schmitter, Phillipe C. "Interest Systems and the Consolidation of Democracy." In *Reexamining Democracy: Essays in Honor of Seymour Martin Lipset,* ed. Gary Marks and Larry Diamond, 156–81. Newbury Park, Calif.: Sage Publications, 1992.

Schopflin, George. "Post-Communism: Constructing New Democracies in Central Europe." *International Affairs* 67, no. 2 (1991): 235–50.

Seligman, Adam B. *The Idea of Civil Society.* Glencoe, N.Y.: Free Press, 1992.

Shils, Edward. "The Virtue of Civil Society." *Government and Opposition* 26 (winter 1991): 3–20.

Siegel, Daniel, and Jenny Yancey. *The Rebirth of Civil Society.* New York: Rockefeller Brothers Fund, 1992.

Silberman, James M. "The History of the Technical Assistance Programs of the Marshall Plan and Successor Agencies, 1948–1961," draft report. World Bank: Industry Development Division, 1992.

Smith, Tony. *America's Mission: The United States and the Worldwide Struggle for Democracy in the Twentieth Century.* Princeton, N.J.: Princeton University Press, 1994.

Smolar, Aleksander. "Kwasniewski's Legitimacy Deficit." *Transition* 2 (22 March 1996) 17–21.

Soros, George. "Toward Open Societies." *Foreign Policy* no. 98 (spring 1995): 65–75.

———. *Underwriting Democracy.* New York: Free Press, 1990.

Stokes, Gail. *The Walls Came Tumbling Down: The Collapse of Communism in Eastern Europe.* New York: Oxford University Press, 1993.

Struyk, Raymond J. "Lessons on Delivering Technical Assistance." Paper presented at Western Aid to Central and Eastern Europe conference, Woodrow Wilson International Center for Scholars, Washington, D.C., 18–20 April 1995.

Szalai, Alexander. "Some Thoughts about the Difficulties and Complexities Encountered by the Ford Foundation in its Dealings with East European Countries." Report for the Ford Foundation, Cambridge, Mass., 1964, photocopy.

Szilagyi, Zsofia. "A Year of Economic Controversy." *Transition* 1 (17 November 1995): 62–66.

Szomolányi, Soňa, and Grigorij Mesežnikov, eds. *The Slovak Path of Transition— to Democracy?* Bratislava: Slovak Political Science Association, 1994.

Tester, Keith. *Civil Society.* New York: Routledge, 1992.

Thomas, Scott. "Granting U.S. Aid to Central and Eastern Europe (Using the Example of Privatization)." Paper presented at Western Aid to Central and Eastern Europe conference, Woodrow Wilson International Center for Scholars, Washington, D.C., 18–20 April 1995.

Tismaneanu, Vladimir, ed. *In Search of Civil Society.* New York: Routledge, 1990.

———. *Reinventing Politics: Eastern Europe from Stalin to Havel.* New York: Free Press, 1992.

Tocqueville, Alexis de. *Democracy in America.* New York: Vintage Books, 1945.

United States Agency for International Development. "Building Democracy: AID's Strategy." In AID Documents [on-line gopher site], started May 1992, [cited November 1995].

———. "Fiscal Year 1996 Assistance to Central and Eastern Europe Request." Czech Republic, Hungary, Poland, and Slovak Republic. In AID Documents [on-line gopher site], [cited November 1995].

———. "Rule of Law Programs." Compendium of Evaluation Findings. In AID Documents [on-line gopher site], March 1994 [cited November 1995].

———. *SEED Act Implementation Report.* Washington, D.C.: AID, 1995, 1996.

———. "Weighing in on the Scales of Justice: Strategic Approaches for Donor-Supported Rule of Law Programs." *AID Programs and Operations Assessment Report No. 7,* February 1994.

U.S. Congress Joint Economic Committee. *East European Economies in Transition.* 103d Cong., 2d sess., 1994. S. Prt. 103–540.

————. *Eastern Europe: Reforms Spur Recovery: Hearings of the Subcommittee on Technology and National Security.* 103d Congress, 2nd session, 15 July 1994.

U.S. Senate Committee on Foreign Relations. *Country Reports on Human Rights Practices.* 101–104 Congress.

Volten, Peter M. E., ed. *Bound to Change: Consolidating Democracy in East Central Europe.* New York: Institute for EastWest Studies, 1992.

Walzer, Michael, ed. *Toward a Global Civil Society.* Providence, R.I.: Berghahn Books, 1995.

Wedel, Janine R. "U.S. Aid to Central and Eastern Europe: Results and Recommendations." *Problems of Post-Communism* 42 (May–June 1995): 45–50.

Weidenfeld, Werner, and Manfred Huterer. *Eastern Europe: Challenges—Problems—Strategies.* Vol. 8., *Strategies and Options for the Future of Europe* Gütersloh, Germany: Bertelsmann Foundation, 1993.

World Bank. *Eastern Europe and Central Asia.* Vol. 1, *Trends in Developing Economies.* Washington, D.C.: World Bank, 1995.

————. *The World Bank Group Regional Brief: Europe and Central Asia.* Washington, D.C.: World Bank, 1995.

————. *World Development Report 1995.* Washington, D.C.: World Bank, 1995.

World without War Council. *Raising the Curtain: A Guide to Independent Organizations and Contacts in Eastern Europe.* Seattle: World without War Council, 1990.

Wuthnow, Robert, ed. *Between States and Markets: The Voluntary Sector in Comparative Perspective.* Princeton, N.J.: Princeton University Press, 1991.

Index

DATE DUE

MAY 2 3 2000			
DEC 2 0 2000			
			Printed in USA